KU-825-512

NML/AR

THE SUNDAY TIMES

SMALL GARDENS
FOR MODERN LIVING

First published in Great Britain in 2001 by
Hamlyn, a division of Octopus Publishing Group Ltd
2–4 Heron Quays, London E14 4JP

First published in paperback in 2003

Copyright © Octopus Publishing Group Ltd 2001, 2003

All rights reserved. No part of this work may be reproduced or utilized
in any form or by any means, electronic or mechanical, including
photocopying, recording or by any information storage and retrieval
system, without the prior written permission of the publisher.

ISBN 0 600 60952 9

A CIP catalogue record for this book is available from the British Library

Printed and bound in China

10 9 8 7 6 5 4 3 2 1

Some of the material in this book has been previously been published
by Hamlyn

NOTE
In describing all the projects in this book, every care has been taken
to recommend the safest methods of working. Before starting any
task, you should be confident that you know what you are doing, and
that you know how to use all tools and equipment safely. The
Publishers cannot accept any legal responsibility or liability for
accidents or damage arising from the use of any items mentioned, or
in the carrying out of any of the projects.

THE SUNDAY TIMES
SMALL GARDENS
FOR MODERN LIVING

making the most of your outdoor space

hamlyn

NORFOLK LIBRARY AND
INFORMATION SERVICE

SUPP	FARR
INV. NO.	C715891
ORD DATE	19/09/03

712.6

contents

How small is a small garden? The simple answer is that a garden can be as small as you wish: it is possible to create gardens on roofs and balconies. You could also, of course, divide a large garden into several small, discrete 'rooms', each with its own character. Most modern gardens, however, are small, generally 10 x 10m (about 33 x 33ft) or less. The equivalent houses built half a century or so ago would have had much larger gardens, often 30m (100ft) long.

The fact that the gardening sections of bookshops are overflowing with books on small gardens suggests that authors and editors have at last realized that most gardening books are written by and for people with large gardens. The features described in these books range from summerhouses and arbours to elegant pergolas, swathed in wisteria and climbing roses, and from large, informal pools to fountains and waterfalls. Recommended plants include potentially large shrubs and trees and climbers that will not only quickly cover boring walls but will also take over the entire garden before you have time to put away your spade and take out your secateurs.

This book is written specifically with small gardens in mind. The ideas can be

scaled up or down to fit the space that is available, although obviously the number of different ideas that can be successfully incorporated into any one plot will vary. In a long, narrow garden, for instance, several different types of area can be included, perhaps separated from each other by screens. In a small, compact garden, on the other hand, it will be necessary to concentrate on creating a cohesive plot, with just one or two integrated ideas.

If your garden is small or awkwardly shaped you can disguise the fact by using various design devices. Most people want to increase the apparent size of their plot and make the existing space feel less confined. If the plot is broad but shallow, you may want to make it appear longer than it is, and if it is long but narrow you may want to make it appear less like a tunnel.

There are many ways of increasing the sense of depth in a garden. Vistas can be emphasized and 'lengthened' by stressing a distant perspective. Eye-catching features can be used to draw the eye away into the distance, but there is no need to rely solely on the features within your own boundaries to do this. Make use of the landscape beyond. Let the outside world become the focus of your garden vista. If you are fortunate

introduction

enough to have a garden with an extensive view, make the most of it and use trees or shrubs to frame a glimpse of the scene beyond the garden.

Creating false perspective is another useful approach. Placing large plants in the foreground and small ones of the same general shape some distance away has the effect of making them appear to be the same size, although they recede into the distance. It is possible to do the same with foliage, by planting plants with thin, airy leaves near to the house and plants with denser foliage further away. Lawnmower stripes in a lawn can be used to give direction to a view or to draw the eye in a particular direction, lengthening or shortening the perspective as desired.

Arches, trellises and fences have a strong linear impact, which can be useful when you are trying to create sight lines. Trellis can also be used for *trompe l'oeil* effects, giving the impression of three dimensions when only two exist. Even mirrors can be used in garden doorways and against walls to double the length of a vista, and water can be used to reflect the garden and enhance the impression of space.

Before you can begin to think about the 'cosmetic' changes that you can

use to give the impression of more space, however, you should consider the underlying layout of your garden. Getting the basic structure right is the most time-consuming but most important stage of changing your garden. There are three distinct phases to creating or making over a garden or outside space, each necessary no matter how large or small the area available and each pleasurable in a different way. The first stage is the planning: the process of deciding what you want and how you are going to achieve it. The second stage is carrying out the plans and adding the features that bring that design to life. Even if you do not do all the work yourself, there is still the excitement of anticipation and of watching the new garden begin to take shape. The third and, for most people, the most important aspects are the enjoyment and satisfaction that come from being in and using the garden.

This last aspect, the enjoyment of your garden, is entirely up to you, and no one can help you, but we can help with the other two elements of the process, which establish the framework for that pleasure and create the environment in which that enjoyment can be achieved. On the pages that

follow we set out to give you some ideas about what you can do with your space and some practical advice about how to adapt that space to suit your tastes and your lifestyle.

To be successful, any garden should be a personal one. It should reflect the interests, aspirations and character of the owner. A naturally untidy person is likely to have an informal space, while a stickler for neatness is more likely to have a formal one or at least one with a clear design.

By impressing your personality on

the garden you will make it into a personal space: it will be unique. You will not be copying someone else or using someone else's ideas. You will be making a garden that you will be able to enjoy, but when others visit it the unique character will stand out and visitors will be more interested and impressed with it than they would be if it were nothing more than a copy of many other gardens. While it is a good thing to plan and design a garden, let it evolve about you so that you get the end result that you really want.

1

For many people, planning a garden is the most difficult part of the whole process. In this chapter we look at how you can get started on transforming your garden and at the factors you need to consider when you are making your initial decisions about the type of garden you want.

The first step, even before you begin to think about the style of garden you would like, is to carry out a thorough assessment of the plot. If you are new to the garden, it is worth spending some time on this stage – getting to know the micro-climate, the areas of sun and shade, the soil type and so on – before you think about the new features you want to introduce. Even if you are transforming the garden of the house in which you have lived for several years – perhaps to make it less hard work to maintain as you approach retirement or because your children no longer need space to play – and you think you are already familiar with the plot's good and bad points, it is still sensible to look at the garden with a fresh eye to make sure you have not overlooked factors that might affect your new plans.

Whether your garden is brand new or is an old, established plot, therefore, the same principles apply to the planning and designing stages.

making plans

assessing the plot

above: The use of brick, gravel and chipped bark make this narrow town plot easy to maintain, while privacy is ensured by the addition of trellis to the top of the boundaries. Willow panels disguise the utility area at the far end of the garden.

The most important task in deciding how to make a new garden or to change an existing one is to get to know your garden. This is more than simply looking at its shape and size, although these are important, of course. The character of the garden is also influenced by climatic conditions, the soil, the aspect, the views (or a lack of them), the buildings around you and so on. Even if the combination of conditions seems unpromising, remember that no site is incapable of being improved by careful design and a thoughtful choice of plants, hard landscaping and built features.

The mood of your garden is always an important consideration. Even when you are working on a bare site the potential of the space needs to be assessed and compared with the atmosphere you want to achieve. Walk around the area, taking measurements as you go, and observe the natural features. The emphasis of the planning stage should be making use of the natural resources and converting the apparently insignificant areas into eye-catching features.

SIZE AND SHAPE

In order to get the most from the available space, you must familiarize yourself with the dimensions. Size matters, of course, and in a small garden it is particularly important because it will limit the number of different areas you can create and the size and number of plants and features within those areas. There are several ways in which the available space can

be used efficiently and effectively. Vertical surfaces, for example, offer scope for climbers, wall shrubs and hanging baskets. Raised beds and terraces extend the growing areas, and containers make maximum use of paved areas and patios.

The shape of the plot will also have a bearing on the design. Few plots are perfectly symmetrical, but that does not really matter – in fact, a triangle or an L-shape can offer even more design potential than a rectangle. Sometimes, the most difficult shape of all is a square, particularly when it is too small to subdivide, as is the case with many front gardens.

A design for an awkward shape needs to be carefully thought out. A long, narrow plot, for example, can be divided into contrasting sections with barriers across the width but leaving a view running through them from one end to the other to create an additional sight line. Placing an ornamental feature, such as a statue or seat, at the far end of a garden will allow you to gain the full benefit from the length of the site while the screens will minimize the disadvantages of the shape.

EXISTING FEATURES

In some ways it is easiest to begin with a bare site, when you can do more or less what you want with it. It is far more difficult to rework an established garden. Before you demolish everything in sight, however, you should wait for at least one season. Even an apparently hideous layout is likely to have some redeeming feature that will be worth

above: Mounds of evergreen grass *Festuca glauca* (blue fescue) soften the stark edges of the gravelled surface, while the white-painted walls reflect all the available light.

saving, even though it may not be immediately obvious.

Advice to newcomers to a garden always includes the suggestion that they should wait a year before making any changes to see what comes up, and that is a sound principle. Spring bulbs, shrubs for winter colour, attractive autumn seedheads, boggy, waterlogged areas or especially dry, hot summer beds will not be identifiable during a single assessment of the garden, but you might find that you want to include one or more of these aspects in your new scheme.

INCORPORATING FEATURES

Obvious features, such as large trees or an established pool, can cause problems when you are trying to decide if they can be incorporated into a new layout. It is impossible to suggest general solutions, but you should consider whether the existing feature is a rare or an exceptionally fine example or is special in some other way. Would it be possible to reshape your design to work around the feature? Maturity is always lacking in new gardens, and you will invariably want to achieve an established look fairly quickly. Can you adjust your proposed design so that the feature can be retained for the medium term until the new garden has mellowed and matured and then think about replacing it with your ideal specimen tree or statue?

Hard landscaping and architectural or ornamental features often present less of a problem than plants because they can, in most cases, be dismantled and reused in new positions. The advantage of recycling materials – stone walls and troughs, paving slabs, millstones and so on – is that they will already be weathered and worn, compared with the rather sterile appearance of new materials. You will also, of course, save money.

left: Even a small garden provides opportunity for growing a wide range of plants. The structure here is provided by carefully positioned evergreens.

climate and micro-climate

Climate is all-important to the success of your garden because it dictates the kinds of plants you can grow, and this, in turn, will influence the design. If you have moved to a new area it is easy enough to discover the average temperature and rainfall, although you should always allow for extremes of temperature and weather conditions. Regional climate is influenced by fundamental geographical factors, such as latitude and altitude, the proximity of large land masses and the sea, the influence of major sea currents and wind patterns. Some districts also have their own weather patterns, such as rainfall or wind direction.

THE MICRO-CLIMATE

In addition to the regional climate, gardens are influenced by all micro-climates, both natural and artificial. Gardens in large cities, for example, are nearly always frost-free because of the heat that is trapped by the built environment during the day and released at night. As a result, it is often possible to grow outdoors many tender or borderline hardy plants that would have to be protected or taken under cover in winter if they were grown outdoors in an open, country area. In cold areas, frost and snow will do no harm provided you grow reliably hardy plants and do not leave tender perennials unprotected.

Although it is necessary to find out about your local climate, it is just as important to learn how you can create a micro-climate. You cannot do much about the weather, but there is a lot

that can be done to minimize its effects, such as erecting a windbreak to protect your garden from cold, drying winds, which will allow you to grow a wider range of more delicate and more interesting plants. Gardens near the sea often benefit from comparatively mild weather, but strong, salt-laden winds can be a particular problem. Planting a hedge of salt-tolerant shrubs to form a windbreak will provide shelter for the rest of the garden and also create an attractive barrier.

SUN, SHADE AND SHELTER

The quality of light will have a major influence on the design of your garden. Shade is often a problem in towns, where neighbouring buildings and walls and fences cast shadows for at least part of the day. If only a corner of your garden receives sun, it will make sense to site a bench, patio or greenhouse there so that you do not waste what sun you do get. Discovering when and where sunlight falls in a new garden can be a problem because, ideally, you need to observe the way that shadows are cast in both summer, when the sun is high, and winter, when the sun is low. If you have time, develop your design over several months so that you can see how different light levels affect the site at various times.

Shelter is something else to consider. Plants need a sheltered position if they are to give the best possible results. Ideally, the garden should provide an enclosed haven in which they can thrive. Wind can be a major problem, not just because it can

left: Despite being a few degrees warmer than larger gardens, the small garden is still prone to frost. Tender plants should be kept in containers for moving to a frost-free area in the winter.

cause branches to break off but also because it dehydrates soil and inhibits the growth of plants. If the site is badly exposed, the first thing you should plan to do is build a windbreak of some kind. The worst thing you can do is build a solid wall, however, because the wind will simply eddy over the top and swirl downwards, creating a whirlpool effect. Much more effective is a windbreak that filters the wind. A hedge or openwork fence will achieve the best results.

Frost protection is as important as wind protection. Frost in winter need

not be a problem, given that there are more than 60,000 hardy plants to choose from. Even the coldest areas can be planted up to suit most tastes. Frost at the wrong time of year, on the other hand, will kill plant growth. In valleys or ground hollows you may well get what is known as a 'frost pocket'. This occurs when cold, frosty air sinks at the lowest point of the landscape and collects beneath walls and solid fences. If you thin or remove trees and shrubs, or remove walls and replace them with trellis fences or a hedge, you

plant list:

SMALL CONIFERS

- *Abies lasiocarpa* '**Arizonica Compacta**'
  A compact, slow-growing, conical tree, to 5m (15ft) tall, with bluish-grey leaves.

- *Calocedrus decurrens* (incense cedar)
  A narrow, upright, graceful tree, to 5m (15ft) tall after 20 years (although ultimately larger), with bright green foliage.

- *Cedrus deodara* '**Aurea**' (deodar)
  A slow-growing, conical tree, to 5m (15ft) tall, with golden-yellow foliage that darkens to greenish-yellow as the tree ages.

- *Chamaecyparis lawsoniana* '**Pygmaea Argentea**'
  A slow-growing, rounded plant, ultimately to 2m (6ft) tall and ideal for a container, with white-tipped, bluish-green foliage.

- *Chamaecyparis obtusa* '**Nana Gracilis**'
  A very slow-growing, pyramidal tree, eventually to 6m (20ft) tall but only to 1m (3ft) across, with golden foliage; not reliably hardy.

- *Cupressus sempervirens* '**Swane's Gold**'
  A narrow, upright tree, eventually to 6m (20ft) tall but only to 1m (3ft) across, with golden foliage; not reliably hardy.

- *Juniperus chinensis* '**Obelisk**'
  A slender shrub, to 2.5m (8ft) tall, with attractive blue-green to grey-green foliage.

- *Juniperus communis* '**Compressa**'
  A slow-growing, dwarf plant, ultimately to 1m (3ft) tall, with greyish foliage; ideal for rock gardens and containers.

- *Picea glauca* var. *albertiana* '**Alberta Globe**'
  A slow-growing, rounded shrub, to 2m (6ft) tall, with grey-green foliage.

- *Pinus mugo* '**Mops**' (Dwarf Mountain Pine)
  A dense, rounded bush, to 1m (3ft) tall, with bright green foliage.

above: A well-planted, shady garden creates a peaceful haven in an overlooked town garden. Woodland plants and ferns enjoy the protected environment as long as the soil is enriched with well-rotted compost.

will allow the cold air to flow through the boundaries in and out of the garden rather than being trapped inside it.

RAIN SHADOW

A problem that is more likely to arise in urban than in more open gardens in the countryside is the rain shadow effect, which is caused by walls and other buildings. The ground in the lee of a solid barrier receives less rainfall than the ground on the windward side of the wall or fence, and in a garden entirely enclosed by walls this can limit

the scope for planting climbers and shrubs against the walls. The planting hole for climbers and shrubs intended to grow and cover a wall should always be about 45cm (18in) away from the wall. Until the plant is established, a cane should be used to guide the climber towards the wall-mounted wires or trellis against which it will eventually be trained. Planting away from the wall or fence in this way should ensure that the plant receives sufficient rainfall and will not need continual watering.

topography and soil

Although it is unlikely that there will be significant changes in level in a small garden, think twice before levelling any slopes that do exist. A level site offers less exciting design potential than one with interesting, gradual changes. Slopes, banks and changes of level offer the opportunity for building steps, terraces, retaining walls or stepped beds or for introducing features such as rock gardens or even tiered water features.

CHANGES OF LEVEL

There is no doubt, however, that a level plot makes gardening easier and that changes of level pose problems both with planting and with access. Your decision will depend partly on the relationship of the slope to the house. A garden that slopes up from the house will appear far more dominant than one that slopes away. If the view is good and can be relied on to remain so, make the most of it. If, on the other hand, you want to keep the focus within the garden, try introducing a formal arrangement of large pots or upright conifers. These may not entirely mask a poor view, but they will give details of some substance to draw the eye.

Irregular changes of level within a garden can make it more interesting and offer the chance to create surprise views and features. The move from one level to another does not necessarily have to be negotiated in one go: a flight of steps can be divided into two or more shallow levels, with intermediate areas of planting or hard surfacing between them. If the garden contains large mounds or deep

above: Using the same hard surfacing material for the patio and shallow steps creates a unified, calm atmosphere in a 'busy' garden.

hollows, consider enlarging them to create a major feature, such as a pond or rock garden.

Steep slopes can be used for streams, but to maximize on planting space you could terrace the slope, using either retaining walls or turf banks. Groups of Mediterranean-type plants, such as lavender and santolina, will thrive in sunny, well-drained conditions. These are also the ideal conditions for a scree or gravel garden, which will be more interesting to look at than a single planting. Cold, shady slopes can be used to create a

woodland effect, but they are equally suitable for a terraced alpine garden, because they are naturally well-drained but do not have the drying heat found on a sunny slope.

SOIL TYPES

The better the quality of soil in your garden, the better the plants will grow. If your soil is poor and infertile you will have to take steps to improve it, but,

gardening tip:

PH LEVELS

Soil-testing kits will show the acidity or alkalinity of your soil by indicating the pH of the sample, which is measured on a scale of 1 to 14. Neutral soil has a pH of 7; alkaline soil will give a higher reading and acid soil will be lower. Most plants will tolerate soil that has a pH of between 6.5 and 7.5, but if your soil has a pH of around 5 you will have to grow plenty of rhododendrons, heathers and camellias, and if it is about 8 you will have to grow plants such as clematis and philadelphus that will enjoy those conditions. Altering the pH of an entire garden is never going to be a practicable undertaking, and it is far better (and easier) to choose plants that will thrive in the existing conditions rather than adapt the soil conditions.

left: Acid soil, with a pH of about 5, will allow you to grow pieris, camellias and azaleas. Plants that prefer more alkaline conditions can be grown in containers.

plant list:

PLANTS FOR MOIST, ACID SOIL

- **Cornus canadensis** (dwarf cornel)
  A low, spreading perennial with mid-green leaves and small, green flowers surrounded by white bracts in spring to early summer.

- **Gaultheria procumbens** (checkerberry, wintergreen)
  A creeping evergreen shrub with glossy foliage and, in summer, white or pink flowers.

- **Gentiana sino-ornata**
  Semi-evergreen rosettes of dark green leaves surmounted by blue flowers in autumn.

- **Kirengeshoma palmata**
  A clump-forming perennial with light green foliage and pale yellow flowers in late summer to early autumn.

- **Lewisia cotyledon**
  In spring and summer clusters of pink-purple flowers are borne above rosettes of dark green, evergreen leaves.

- **Liriope muscari** (lilyturf)
  A clump-forming perennial with strappy, evergreen foliage and spikes of bright purple flowers in early autumn.

- **Lithodora diffusa 'Heavenly Blue'**
  A prostrate evergreen shrub with bright blue flowers in spring and summer.

- **Meconopsis betonicifolia** (Himalayan blue poppy)
  Blue-green leaves form loose rosettes above which the yellow-centred, bright blue flowers are borne in early summer.

- **Smilacina racemosa** (false Solomon's seal)
  A clump-forming perennial with mid-green leaves and panicles of creamy-white flowers in spring.

- **Trillium grandiflorum** (wake robin)
  A clump-forming perennial with dark green leaves and white flowers in spring and summer.

before you do that, work out what type of soil there is in your garden in terms of texture, structure and quality.

Most gardeners need know only if their soil is clay-like or sandy, acid or alkaline, because this will influence their choice of plants. Clay retains moisture, is difficult to work and extremely sticky when wet but sets very hard with cracks on the surface in a dry summer. It needs regular breaking up during winter by the addition of a soil conditioner, but it is often fertile in its own right.

Sandy soil, on the other hand, is easy to work and dries out quickly, but it needs plenty of well-rotted manure or compost to improve its moisture retention. Alluvial silt, the type of soil that is found in a flood plain, is an exception to the rule for sandy soil: it is easy to work, fertile and, although free-draining, has excellent moisture-retaining properties.

ACIDITY AND ALKALINITY

In addition to knowing the type of soil in your garden, you must also know if it is acidic (lime-free) or alkaline (containing lime). If it is alkaline you will not be able to grow calc fuge (lime-hating) plants such as rhododendrons and camellias. In very acid soils plants that naturally occur on limestone ground, such as philadelphus, clematis and dianthus (pinks), will not thrive.

It is worth buying one of the inexpensive soil-testing kits that are available in garden centres and DIY stores so that you can test the pH in your garden. Test the soil in different parts of the garden because conditions can vary within even small areas. To confirm your readings, look at the plants growing in your neighbours' gardens and ask other gardeners who live nearby for their recommendations. If your neighbours grow healthy-looking camellias and pieris your own garden is likely to have acid soil.

If you want to increase the alkalinity of your soil you can add lime, but think carefully before you do this because it is long-lasting. It is not so easy to increase the acidity of soil, and the best solution to growing ericaceous plants is to create raised beds or special enclosures, which you can line with a permeable membrane and fill with acid soil.

preparing a plan

Once you have carried out the 'audit' of your garden you can begin to draw up a plan. There is little point in aimlessly doodling on a piece of paper, however. The first task is to try to define exactly what you want from your garden. The essence of good garden design lies in creating an area or areas that are not only visually pleasing but that also meet your needs. You should also design a garden that you will have the time and energy to maintain.

IDENTIFYING YOUR NEEDS

The easiest way to determine what you want from your garden is to write down a list of everything you would like to be able to do in the garden. You might, for example, want to grow plants because you are a keen gardener; you might, on the other hand; want a lawn for the children to play on; you might want flowerbeds to provide cut flowers for the house; you might want somewhere to grow your own fruit and vegetables; you might want a barbecue area and patio so that you can entertain your friends; you might want nothing more than a peaceful, quiet place where you can relax at weekends and on warm summer evenings. You might want a combination of these things. Jot down everything you can think of at this stage – do not miss anything out, no matter how fanciful it might seem: there might be a way to make it work.

It is quite likely that this list will be far too long for a small garden or you may simply have to scale down your plans because they are too time-consuming or too costly. These three

factors – space, time and money – must be reconciled with your list of what you would like to do in the garden. Some things on your 'list' will have to go: having a large, natural pool to attract wildlife, for instance, might be desirable but might have to be crossed off your list from the start because of lack of space or of funds or both. Other features, even with a great deal of thought, may be irreconcilable. Children playing ball games and borders filled with plants to provide cut flowers are unlikely to share the same small garden for long, and football and a greenhouse is another apparently incompatible combination. Stop and think for a minute before you cross one or other

above: A simple arbour with space for a single seat provides a shady, fragrant hideaway on a summer's day.

above: A garden that is overlooked from upstairs windows will often look better if it has a formal layout, here emphasized by the geometric paving stones and the elegant trellis arches.

feature off your list: you might, for example, be able to erect a trellis or screen in front of the greenhouse to protect it from errant footballs.

Think of the future as well as the present. Your children will not be children for ever. Plant a tree by the side of the lawn on which they tear around playing their games, and by the time they move on to other pursuits it will be large enough for you to relax in its shade, as you use the lawn for far

less strenuous pursuits. What is now a child's sandpit may, one day, be converted into a raised bed or pond. A sandpit should be positioned so that you can keep an eye on the children from the patio or from the kitchen window. Later, the pond will be a focal point in the garden. Both features require the same kind of position, although for different reasons, and, with a little thought and preplanning, the same basic construction.

DRAWING UP A PLAN

Once you have narrowed down your ideas to practical proportions, draw up a plan. Measure the garden accurately and draw a plan showing the existing features and their position relative to each other. Remember to include the route of any mains services if you know them. It will be easier to follow if the plan is on squared paper. Once this is done, make several copies of the basic plan and then draw in, roughly at first, the positions of the various areas and items that you want.

Keep trying different ideas and combinations of various features until you arrive at the best solution. It may be that you can get more features in than you originally thought. You might suddenly find a niche for the barbecue that you thought you would have to sacrifice, but you might have to forgo a shed or a border to get it to fit.

BORDERS AND PATHS

The shapes of the borders and patio and the lie of the paths can be anything that takes your fancy. Curved beds look more appealing than those with straight edges, but it is best to avoid curves that are too extreme and angles that are too awkward, not only because they are difficult to plant successfully, but also because they are hard to edge or mow up to. When you are laying out designs for borders and patios to assess their position on the ground, use a garden hose to work out the curves. Leave the hose on the ground for about 24 hours to see how the shadows fall across the area at different times of the day.

When you are satisfied that everything is in the right place, draw out the definitive copy to scale. A scale plan of the patio will allow you to work out exactly how many paving slabs or edging tiles you will need, which will make ordering easier.

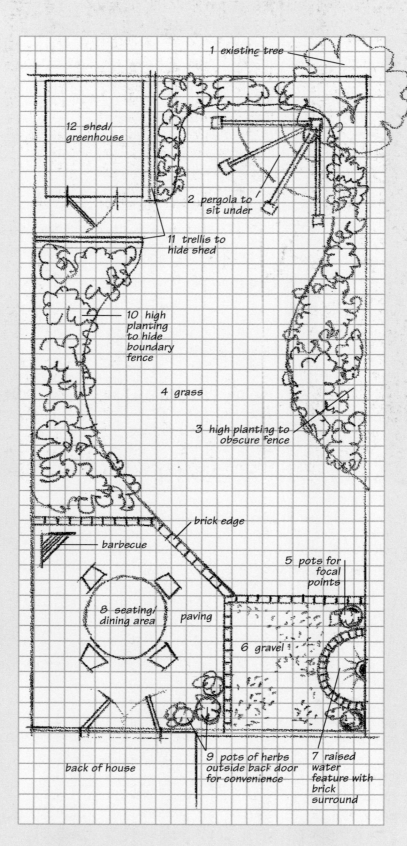

1 existing tree
12 shed/greenhouse
2 pergola to sit under
11 trellis to hide shed
10 high planting to hide boundary fence
4 grass
3 high planting to obscure fence
brick edge
barbecue
5 pots for focal points
8 seating/dining area
paving
6 gravel
9 pots of herbs outside back door for convenience
7 raised water feature with brick surround
back of house

1 An existing tree will provide a focal point, height and shade.

2 A simple pergola over wooden decking creates a shady, private space in an otherwise overlooked garden.

3 The curved border softens the rectangular lines of the garden and offers planting space for tall shrubs to disguise the plain panel fence.

4 The sweeping lines of the lawn carry the eye from side to side, emphasizing the width of the plot.

5 Containers are used to provide seasonal colour.

6 The small raised area is covered with gravel over a semi-permeable membrane to minimize weeding.

7 A small raised water feature is edged with bricks to match the materials used elsewhere.

8 The paved patio, accessible from the back door of the house, has plenty of space for the purpose-built barbecue and for a table and chairs.

9 Culinary herbs are grown in pots near the back door.

10 The wide border offers scope for dense planting to hide the boundary fence.

11 Trellis covered with climbers in front of the shed stops it being viewed from the patio and the pergola.

12 The small shed, used for storing the patio furniture in winter as well as garden tools and the lawnmower, is tucked into the furthest corner.

2

You do not have to be a garden designer to choose the way your garden looks. After all, most of us manage to decorate the inside of our homes to our own satisfaction, so why should we not be capable of doing the same outdoors? Anyway, it can be fun.

The first thing to do when you are laying out a garden is to decide what style you want. There are styles that will suit everybody and that will reflect your tastes and your lifestyle. There are no hard-and-fast rules about what you should like: choosing a garden style is an entirely personal matter. If you have a busy, demanding working life, an informal, relaxed style of garden may be just what you want to provide a contrast. You might, on the other hand, prefer to be formal both on and off duty and like to have everything neat and tidy; in this case, the clear-cut lines of a formal garden may be your choice.

Remember that you have to live with the garden, so do not choose a style that you will be unable to keep up, nor one that conflicts with your lifestyle. Children and precise, formal gardens do not mix, for example, so wait until the children have left home before laying out symmetrical beds and neat box hedges. There are also plenty of variations within each style from which you can choose. Each formal garden, for example, follows roughly the same principles, but each has a different scale, shape, pattern and colour scheme.

If all this sounds daunting, there is no need to worry: some of the best gardeners have had no training in aesthetics or design; instead, they work entirely by eye.

styling space

formal garden

Many people like to have total control over their lives, and the use of formal designs within and outside the house is one way of achieving this ideal. The clean-cut, almost severe lines of such designs are not just symbols of control, however, for there is also enormous pleasure to be derived from the elegance of such designs.

One of the keys to a formal design is simplicity. All fussiness is removed, and restraint is imposed. The lines and shapes are usually simple, consisting of straight lines and regular curves. Out go the tortuously curved borders filled to overflowing with flowers; in come squares, rectangles, circles and ellipses. Shapes such as triangles and stars, unless they are within other features of the design, should be avoided because the points of such geometric features are likely to be too sharp for planting and awkward for mowing.

Symmetry is another key to a formal design. Patterns should be regular and plantings balanced from one side of the bed to another. The regular planting of trees or shrubs or the positioning of containers along a path or around a bed will create a pleasing rhythm that adds to the formality of the garden.

Not everything has to be balanced, of course. Often a single large, plant or container as a focal point works to great effect. These do not have to be symmetrical to the design. A clump of grass or a group of rocks, for example, could be placed to one side of a space rather than being positioned in the very centre of the design.

above: Closely clipped box hedging defines the symmetrical layout, which is softened by the exuberant roses and dense planting around the dining area.

DESIGN ELEMENTS

The basis of the design is provided by gravel or regularly paved areas. Within this framework are various structures and beds, ideally all with regular outlines. If there is a pond, it is not a wild, natural one but instead is regularly shaped, possibly lined with concrete and adorned with a fountain or elegant water spout. Containers with a single specimen, often a clipped or topiarized tree or shrub, are a popular way of displaying plants.

Plants are also often contained within a formal parterre or knot garden. These consist of low, clipped hedges of *Buxus* spp. (*see* plant list, opposite), and, instead of being filled with plants, the areas contained by the hedges can be left bare or filled with plain or coloured gravel. What planting there is should be restrained and simple. Use

A formal water garden

The underlying structure of this densely planted formal garden is provided by two small, square, reflecting pools and the cream-coloured paving, which has been used over the entire plot. The planting is concentrated at the far end of the garden, so that the area nearest the house is lighter and more open. The boundary walls are disguised behind shrubs, and climbing plants, trained on trellises, are used at the sides to increase the apparent width of the area.

single plants, perhaps in large containers or pots stood at strategic positions. Avoid mixing too many colours and planting anything that needs a great deal of maintenance. Many formal gardens rely almost entirely on foliage for effect, and some people like to grow only trees and shrubs, partly because of the foliage and partly because their shapes can be controlled by clipping and pruning.

Ornaments should be limited, but can provide a good focal point as long as they are positioned correctly – formal gardens lend themselves to leading the eye towards an object. Water features can be extremely effective, particularly bubble or millstone fountains.

Lavandula angustifolia

An evergreen shrub, to 1m (3ft) tall, lavender has a bushy but compact habit. The small, grey-green leaves cover the unbranched stems, and in summer pale purple, fragrant flower spikes appear. A versatile plant, lavender can be used for edging, for growing in a container or at the front of a border.

plant profile

plant list:

PLANTS FOR BALANCE AND SYMMETRY

- *Allium giganteum*
  Large round heads of rich pink flowers are borne on erect stems to 1.5m (5ft) tall.

- *Buxus microphylla* (small-leaved box)
  A dense, slow-growing, small-leaved shrub with dark green leaves, it can be clipped to shape and is ideal for edging.

- *Carex conica* 'Snowline'
  A tuft-forming evergreen grass with dark green, white-edged leaves.

- *Cordyline australis* (New Zealand cabbage palm)
  A small to medium-sized palm, perfect as a specimen plant or focal point.

- *Dierama pulcherrimum* (angel's fishing rod)
  An architectural perennial, forming a clump of grassy foliage with tall spikes of bell-shaped pink or purple flowers.

- *Hosta* 'Halcyon'
  A clump-forming perennial with blue-green, heart-shaped leaves and lavender-grey flowers in summer.

- *Juniperus scopulorum* 'Skyrocket'
  A medium-sized to tall conifer forming an erect column.

- *Laurus nobilis* (bay)
  An evergreen tree or shrub, perfect for topiary and hedges.

- *Santolina pinnata* subsp. *neapolitana*
  A low-growing, evergreen shrub, with aromatic foliage. Perfect for shaping and edging.

- *Taxus baccata* (yew)
  An evergreen tree or shrub that is good for hedges or topiary.

- *Yucca gloriosa*
  A medium-sized perennial with a large rosette of stiff, sword-shaped leaves.

informal garden

Although they may admire and even hanker after a neat, formal garden, most gardeners feel more comfortable with an informal style – a garden where a football, watering can or wheelbarrow left lying around will not look out of place or where a weed or two might just be acceptable.

The informal style has its origins in the cottage garden, where vegetables and flowers were often mixed and where plants were placed not according to some overarching, complex design but simply because there was a gap to fill. Colours were often jumbled up, with little thought given to the overall effect: the end result was usually a riot of colour. Bright colours, especially annuals, often play a leading role in this type of garden, but there is no reason why softer, more restrained colours should not be used in the same way. This style of gardening still exists, and it has much to recommend it: there is no need to worry about what plant to place next to another – you just put them where there is space and create a cheerful mixture of a variety of plants.

BORDER PLANNING

Not everyone feels comfortable with such anarchy. Many people prefer to take a much more controlled approach, although still free of the straitjacket imposed by a formal garden. Colours in borders can be grouped so that there is some form of harmony. Borders of single colours can be used – white or pastel shades for a peaceful setting, and red or the hot colours for more excitement, for example – and planting

can be precise rather than random. Flowering plants need not predominate, and the informality may come from foliage plants, including mounds of shrubs. Nevertheless, the overall effect is one of relaxed control.

An informal style can sometimes mean that every detail – down to the last blade of grass – is planned, but this is not the method adopted by most gardeners. They usually take a much more flexible approach to designing. It is, for example, much easier to accommodate plants that are already established in the garden. You do not

have to grub everything out and start from scratch. Shrubs and trees and even existing lawns and paths can be re-used and do not have be moved or removed to fit into the new scheme.

An informal garden is not the same as a low-maintenance scheme: indeed, achieving the effect of relaxed but profuse planting requires careful planning and regular attention. Plant selection is aimed at providing interest over a long period, including structure and form in winter, flowers from spring to autumn and a range of foliage shape, texture and colour. The often dense

above: The relaxed planting creates a green haven in a small town garden, where every available surface has been covered with plants.

planting means that the soil must be regularly mulched with well-rotted compost to keep the plants proviced with the nutrients they need, and vigorous plants have to be clipped and pruned so that they do not outgrow their allotted space and swamp their neighbours.

MIXING IT

An informal garden makes it possible to blend various activities together. The garden is likely to have a lived-in feeling about it and to be something that is not so much for show as to be used and enjoyed. A barbecue or child's play area will, for example, sit happily alongside decorative borders. Vegetable plots will mix with flowers and not need to be restrained in their own well-defined area. Although such a layout may, at first glance, seem completely casual, it does actually require careful preliminary planning to make sure that the garden does not end up looking as if it was just thrown together.

An informal garden is a much more suitable environment for young children than one with a formal scheme. A tangle of shrubs makes an ideal 'camp' and hiding place. Children will always leave playthings lying around and send balls crashing through the undergrowth, leaving gaps in borders. If the garden is likely to be used for ball games, beds and borders with straight sides may be a more suitable choice than ones with curved edges. A well-manicured, bowling-green style lawn and active children cannot coexist. One solution is to select a hard-wearing, tough grass, which will look less formal but will stand up much better to running and cycling.

plant list:

PLANTS FOR WILDFLOWER GARDENS

- **Achillea millefolium** (yarrow)
  A mat-forming perennial with white flowers in spring; the cultivars are less invasive.

- **Ajuga reptans** (bugle)
  A spreading perennial with blue spring flowers.

- **Campanula rotundifolia** (harebell)
  A variable perennial with blue to white bell-shaped flowers in summer.

- **Cardamine pratensis** (lady's smock)
  A small perennial with lilac flowers in spring.

- **Centaurea scabiosa** (knapweed)
  A medium-sized perennial with purple, pincushion-like flowers in summer.

- **Geranium pratense** (meadow cranesbill)
  A medium-sized perennial with blue flowers in summer.

- **Linaria purpurea** (purple toadflax)
  An erect, slender, self-seeding perennial with spikes of light purple flowers in summer and early autumn.

- **Monarda didyma** (bee balm, sweet bergamot)
  Dense heads of bright pink flowers, surrounded by reddish-purple bracts, are borne on erect stems from midsummer to early autumn.

- **Primula veris** (cowslip)
  A low-growing perennial with yellow spring flowers.

- **Prunella vulgaris** (self-heal)
  A low-growing, spreading perennial with blue flowers in summer.

- **Scabiosa atropurpurea** (sweet scabious, pincushion flower)
  An annual, this has dark purple, fragrant flowerheads from midsummer to autumn above the compact leaf rosettes.

Ranunculus acris 'Flore Pleno' (bachelor's buttons)

The relative of the humble meadow buttercup bears bright yellow, double flowers from late spring to midsummer. The flowers, each to 2.5cm (1in) across, are borne on wiry stems above bright green foliage.

Fritillaria meleagris (Snake's head fritillary)

Beautiful bell-shaped, pendent flowers, usually purple or pink-purple but sometimes white, are borne in spring. The narrow leaves are grey-green. This bulb, growing to 30cm (12in) tall, can thrive in sun or shade.

plant profile

oriental-style garden

left: In oriental-style gardens moss can be used to represent water, and it is often planted to grow around and over boulders, which signify islands.

As in all aspects of our lives, the opportunity to travel to other countries has influenced our gardens, and of all countries Japan has probably had the greatest effect on garden design. The simplicity and tranquillity of the gardens there have been widely copied in the West, often to great effect.

The essence of the Japanese garden is simplicity, which creates a sense of calm and peace and which is particularly appropriate in a small garden. In today's hectic world any garden provides a respite from the pressures and hurly-burly of day-to-day life, but a Japanese garden is the archetypal haven. It is an area of total calm set around the house. One aspect of the simplicity is the use of a limited range of materials and plants, and another is the way in which the available space is used. In the past every element in the garden was imbued with its own significance, and to some extent this is still true, but now the symbolism tends to be retained for largely historical reasons rather than because it has any philosophical or religious meaning.

Nature plays a dominant role in Japanese garden design. Everything seems to flow from it, especially the natural landscape. Instead of making miniature copies of the surrounding countryside, as gardeners in the West might do, Japanese design depends on the power of suggestion. Where we might build a rock garden, a Japanese gardener would use rocks and boulders to represent mountains or islands, and areas of carefully raked sand or gravel are used to signify water. Closely clipped shrubs may be used to represent boulders, while small, carefully pruned trees are floating clouds. In nature there are rarely any straight lines, and so it is in the Japanese garden.

WATER

Streams and waterfalls are important landscape elements that are constantly used in Japanese gardens. They are usually imitations of natural streams, representing mountain torrents. Water is also present in the form of small pools or dishes of water, or water can be introduced into the garden as it gently trickles through an artificial course, such as along split-bamboo pipes. Sometimes the system is ingenious, with one pipe slowly filling before it tips and fills the next one, and so on. Everything is done with great simplicity. The water is calm or only just moving: there are no fountains to disturb the tranquillity.

In addition to real water, Japanese gardens contain representations of water. An area of raked gravel, for example, will symbolize swirling water, while rounded rocks positioned on the gravel represent islands set in the sea. Often, a ribbon of moss will pass among the rocks and boulders and give the impression of a stream.

FLOWERS AND FOLIAGE

Although several flowers are used in Japanese garden design, they never play a dominant role as they do in Western gardens. The main flowering plants are chrysanthemums, irises and peonies, and these are used sparingly together with a few other plants, such as grasses. Trees and shrubs are widely used, especially around the perimeter of the garden to create a backdrop and to reinforce the idea of the 'borrowed landscape' beyond the confines of the garden itself. Within the garden certain trees are valued, especially ancient ones. Pines, junipers and acers are particular favourites.

ORNAMENTS

A few ornaments are used within the oriental garden, the best known of which is the Japanese lantern. These stone or metal articles, often resembling miniature buildings, are carefully positioned to illuminate key places along paths or water. They will often be placed next to water so that they produce reflections.

Paths are of gravel or carefully sized paving stones. Stepping stones are another popular feature, made from either slabs of stone or sections of tree trunks. Bridges are often incorporated to cross real or imaginary streams. If there is space there may be a pavilion or tea house, and a loggia may be built near to the house from which the garden can be viewed.

An oriental-style garden

In this tranquil garden the use of timber slats for bridges, stepping stones and steps provides a unifying element in the three main areas of the garden. The geometrical arrangement of the bricks, laid in the patio near to the house and in the small area next to the boundary fence, provides a sympathetic backdrop for container-grown plants, and it extends naturally into the gravelled area at the far end of the garden. The L-shaped water feature is an effective and unusual way of defining the edge of the patio as well as reinforcing the strong, geometric lines of the slats and bricks. Restrained planting is used to soften the linear effect and disguise the boundaries.

plant list:

PLANTS FOR AN ORIENTAL-STYLE GARDEN

- ● *Camellia japonica* 'Lovelight'
  A hardy, evergreen shrub for acid soil, with glossy, dark green leaves and semi-double, yellow-centred, white flowers in early spring.

- ● *Dendranthema grandiflorum*
  (florists' chrysanthemum)
  Perennials in a wide range of colours, shapes and sizes.

- ● *Imperata cylindrica* 'Rubra'
  A rhizomatous perennial with upright, grass-like, blood-red leaves.

- ● *Iris ensata*
  A rhizomatous, beardless iris with red-purple flowers in midsummer.

- ● *Juniperus communis* 'Compressa'
  A dwarf, narrow, slow-growing, evergreen shrub.

- ● *Paeonia suffruticosa* (moutan)
  An upright, deciduous shrub with white, pink, red or purple flowers in late spring.

- ● *Pinus sylvestris* 'Fastigiata' (Scots pine)
  A narrow, upright evergreen.

- ● *Prunus mume* (Japanese apricot)
  A spreading, deciduous tree with fragrant blossom in late winter to early spring.

- ● *Rhododendron* 'Kure-no-yuki'
  A compact, evergreen azalea for acid soil with lovely white flowers in mid-spring.

- ● *Selaginella kraussiana* (Krauss's spikemoss)
  A mat-forming perennial with bright green leaves that will spread indefinitely.

Wisteria sinensis (Chinese wisteria)

Grown for its racemes of lovely, fragrant, mauve-blue flowers, wisteria is a potentially large, vigorous climber, which looks best when it is trained over a pergola, so that the beautiful flowers can hang down.

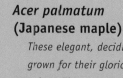

Acer palmatum (Japanese maple)

These elegant, deciduous trees are grown for their glorious autumn leaf colour. There are many named cultivars, providing a range of leaf shape and colour. Some forms have finely divided leaves and are suitable for container cultivation.

plant profile

foliage garden

It is easy to think of gardens in terms of flowers alone rather than of plants, but flowers can be time-consuming to tend, so why not choose to have a foliage garden, created from the huge range of plants with handsome leaves?

A garden with no flowers, or with only a few flowers, need never be dull. Foliage will provide all the interest you need. Although you might think that a garden of green will be monotonous, you will quickly come to realize what a tremendous range of greens there is once you start to assemble the plants, ranging from the light, yellowish-green of *Choisya* 'Sundance' to the dark, almost black-green of *Taxus baccata* (yew). In addition to the colours, there are the textures. Glossy leaves, for example, will illuminate dull corners by reflecting light, while thick, velvety ones will invite you to caress them. Then there is the variation in shapes, from tall, rustling bamboos, low hummocks of moss and rounded clumps of hostas to fountains of cordylines, as well as grass paths, yew hedges ... the possibilities are almost endless.

LOW-MAINTENANCE FOLIAGE

Foliage plants generally need far less attention than flowering ones – there are no dead flowers to remove for a start – and trees and shrubs also need far less maintenance than, say, herbaceous perennials.

Many people would like to have a low-maintenance garden but they do not necessarily want one that is covered in concrete. There is, however, one plant in particular that provides the

last word in low-maintenance gardening: *Hedera helix* (ivy) makes the perfect ground cover. It will cover the soil – and anything else that gets in the way – with a dense blanket of creeping stems and leaves. It works well in both shade and open sunlight, and it is particularly useful in gardens that are

shaded for part or all of the day by adjacent buildings or trees.

For the ultimate low-maintenance garden, first design the area, sculpting the ground with mounds and hollows, perhaps incorporating a low earth wall or shallow ditch. Place a few objects around, such as tree stumps or even a

low fence, and then plant as many ivies as you can afford – the cheapest way is to produce hundreds of plants from cuttings – and let them cover the whole area. Ivy will climb over the humps and hollows and form a sculptural blanket. Variations can be introduced by using variegated ivies and ones with leaves of different shapes and colours at strategic places or over particular features. The result will be truly spectacular and individual and, of course, low-maintenance because all that is required is to clip over the ivy once a year in early spring.

THEME AND VARIATIONS

Not all foliage is green by any means. There are plants with dark, smoky purple leaves and those with dusky, blue-grey leaves; there are plants with golden foliage and a large range with variegated leaves. An entire garden devoted to any of these groups could easily become rather boring, because too many purples or blues tend to appear leaden and heavy, while a lot of variegated plants in one place will clash and look 'busy', with nowhere for the eye to rest: this is the last effect you want to achieve in a small area. Used as a contrast to, or an occasional

left: The bamboo screen is an ideal background for the delicately intricate foliage of shade-loving ferns. In cold winters protect the growing point of *Dicksonia antarctica* (tree fern) with old fronds.

above: Foliage is never just green. Variegated grasses combine happily with glaucous leaves of herbaceous perennials and the hot red of annuals.

change from, plain green foliage, however, variegated plants come into their own, adding interest and distinction to otherwise drab areas.

Plants with variegated foliage are the most numerous of the non-green types. From a distance they may seem the same, but if you look closely at the leaves the variation in leaf patterns and colour will become apparent. It may be in the colour of the variegation, with a wide range of yellows, creams and silver as well as reds, purple and browns providing the contrasting colour to the basic green, but it may also be in the shape of the variegation, which may be fine and regular or bold and irregular, or it may be in the position, sometimes along the margins, sometimes towards the centre and sometimes apparently at random.

plant profile

Cotinus coggygria 'Royal Purple' (smoke bush)

The dark, reddish-purple leaves of this compact shrub turn vivid orange-red before they fall in autumn. In late summer airy plumes of purple flowers are borne at the ends of the branches. It will grow in semi-shade, but the leaf colour is at its best in full sun.

plant list:

PLANTS WITH COLOURFUL FOLIAGE

- *Acer palmatum* f. *atropurpureum* (Japanese maple) A small tree or large shrub with handsome, reddish-purple, divided foliage.

- *Ajuga reptans* 'Atropurpurea' A ground-hugging perennial with glossy purple leaves.

- *Berberis thunbergii* f. *atropurpurea* A striking shrub with tiny leaves and a spreading habit.

- *Cordyline australis* 'Torbay Dazzler' (New Zealand cabbage palm) A palm-like tree with bright green, sword-shaped leaves, boldly striped with white and edged with cream.

- *Dahlia* 'Bishop of Llandaff' A large tuberous plant with purple-black foliage and vivid red flowers in late summer.

- *Foeniculum vulgare* 'Purpureum' (bronze fennel) A tall, upright perennial with feathery purple foliage.

- *Phormium tenax* Purpureum Group A medium to tall perennial with leathery, evergreen, sword-shaped leaves in shades of red-purple.

- *Ricinus communis* 'Gibsonii' (castor oil plant) An impressive annual with huge, glossy leaves.

- *Salvia officinalis* Purpurascens Group (purple sage) A low-growing evergreen shrub.

- *Sedum* 'Vera Jameson' A low-growing perennial with fleshy purple-pink foliage and late-summer flowers.

urban garden

Urban gardens have much to offer to the gardener, providing an exciting, if challenging, opportunity to produce interesting and original garden designs. A little forward planning and careful thought can go a long way towards overcoming any immediate problems, such as lack of sunlight, the shadows cast by neighbouring buildings, poor soil and atmospheric pollution.

In general, an urban garden is easier and cheaper to maintain than most country gardens, simply because they are usually smaller and a regular shape. Urban sites also have the advantage that they tend to be more sheltered than rural ones and may even be entirely frost-free, so that it is possible to grow a wide range of tender plants without having to protect them or take them under cover in winter.

WORKING WITHIN WALLS

Formal and semi-formal designs are usually more popular and successful in town gardens because it is easier to incorporate surrounding party walls and boundaries into a methodical, precise layout. When you are choosing a design, remember that often the garden will be seen as much from the upper windows of your house as from the ground-floor ones, and most formal schemes look better from above than informal ones.

Rather than being regarded as a drawback or a limitation, the small size of a town garden should be seen as a positive opportunity to use the design options that will make the plot seem more spacious. Small areas can be made to seem larger by the use of

different levels linked by shallow steps, for example. When it comes to floor treatments, diagonal or circular paving will enhance the space. Creating one or two separate sections within the overall framework of the garden is another way of disguising the limited size of the area, and a series of small, partially hidden areas linked by a winding path will foster the illusion of space.

Lack of light is another constraint often encountered in town gardens. In an area that is entirely surrounded by walls, simply painting one or all of the surfaces white will immediately increase light levels by reflecting whatever light the garden receives. The inclusion of carefully sited mirrors, which will also help to make a garden appear larger, will have the effect of enhancing the available light, and a reflective pool,

with a still, smooth surface at ground level, will have the same effect.

PLANTS FOR URBAN GARDENS

Shade cast by surrounding buildings is another common problem in town gardens, and the only option here is to select shade-tolerant plants. There is a huge range to choose from, however, and a careful combination of foliage and flowering plants will bring year-round colour and interest. Wall plants and climbers are invaluable because they increase the surface area of the garden vertically rather than horizontally. As an added attraction, a plant-clad wall or fence will provide a degree of privacy, and a trellis or fence covered in climbers can also help to minimize traffic noise. Containers and hanging baskets can be used to add to the number of plants that

above: Stainless-steel containers are the ideal material for a small, minimalist garden, where anything more substantial would overpower the wall-mounted water feature and low-key decking.

can be grown in the limited amount of soil available in the rest of the garden.

Associated with the problem of shade cast by walls is the fact that the soil there is often drier than in a more open garden. Plant selection and soil preparation should reflect this. Again, containers can provide the solution. This active decision to select plants that relish the prevailing situation and make the most of the available light, water and space are the key characteristics of town gardening.

An urban garden

The design for this square garden is based on a diagonal axis, to create a semi-formal arrangement that detracts from the 'boxiness' of the underlying shape. Although regular, square paving has been used for the flooring, the pale colour reflects light and introduces an open, welcoming feel. Every available vertical surface has been used for planting, with trellises used not only on boundary walls but also against the house wall to provide additional greenery.

plant list:

PERENNIALS FOR DRY SHADE

- **Acanthus mollis** (bear's breeches)
  Tall spires of white and mauve flowers are borne in late summer.

- **Aconitum carmichaelii** (monkshood)
  Violet or deep blue flowers are borne in early autumn.

- **Anemone x hybrida** (Japanese anemone)
  Pale pink flowers appear in late summer and last into autumn.

- **Epimedium alpinum**
  Sprays of long-spurred flowers are borne in late spring or early summer.

- **Euphorbia amygdaloides** (wood spurge)
  This evergreen plant has yellowish-green flowers in spring to early summer.

- **Geranium phaeum** (dusky cranesbill)
  In late spring and summer white-eyed, deep purplish-black to mauve flowers are borne above the mounds of foliage.

- **Luzula sylvatica** 'Marginata' (woodrush)
  The deep green, white-margined leaves are evergreen.

- **Saxifraga x urbium** (London pride)
  Rosettes of leathery leaves are topped by dainty sprays of little pink flowers in summer.

- **Vinca minor** (lesser periwinkle)
  A mat-forming evergreen plant with blue to white flowers from spring to late summer.

- **Viola riviniana** Purpurea Group (wood violet)
  Pale violet-blue flowers appear above the pretty heart-shaped leaves in late spring and early summer.

left: Tall boundary walls are a common feature in courtyard gardens. Climbers against trellis growing from a raised bed lend a lush, evergreen feel to a small urban garden.

front garden

Even houses with comparatively large back gardens may have small front gardens, spaces that are often further reduced in size by the need to provide hardstanding for a car and access to the house itself, both for your family and for visitors.

The front garden, no matter how small, will be the first sight that visitors to your house will have, and first impressions count. The area may be thoughtfully laid out and colourful, or it may be bare and unwelcoming. Often, the overwhelming need in a front garden is to have a layout that requires the least possible maintenance, for there is little pleasure to be gained from working in a garden when neighbours and passers-by can watch you at work. However, stop and think before you decide on the ultimate low-maintenance solution and lay concrete over the whole area. There are plenty of shrubs and small trees that will require little attention once established, and these can be brightened with spring- and summer-flowering bulbs to personalize your space.

SPACE FOR THE CAR

If you need an area to park your car, you must make sure that the drive is sufficiently well built to take the weight. A driveway that sags or has a broken surface is not only an eyesore but is potentially dangerous, especially if the pipes for mains services run beneath it. If you have any doubts at all about your capabilities, have it built professionally. A surface that is going to take the weight of a car must have a

right: Neatly clipped spheres of box emphasize the formal nature of the front door, while more relaxed summer annuals are used in the raised beds.

above: A tight space for a front garden may give no room for clever displays or architectural topiaries, but a broad row of maize can mimic a field, giving an illusion of depth.

solid foundation of rammed hardcore, topped with a layer of concrete and then finished with the material of your choice. Although concrete can be left as the final surface, it will look raw for some time until it fades to a less unpleasant tone. If you are planning further building work in the house or in the back garden and it is likely that you

are going to have sand, ballast and cement dumped on it, leave the concrete as it is until you have finished all the additional building work because any other type of surface will be completely spoiled.

Tarmac has the look of a public thoroughfare about it, although it will eventually weather to look less harsh and less uninviting. Normally black, tarmac gradually turns grey, but you can have other colours, and sometimes white chippings are rolled into it to give more interest.

Gravel drives look attractive, and they have much to recommend them, partly because they produce a satisfying crunch under the wheels of a car or even when trodden on, which can be a safety factor if it alerts you to a potential visitor. When gravel is used for drives, it must be laid on a solid foundation and not simply laid on compacted soil. Concrete is the best type of foundation. It should then be sprayed with tar and have a layer of gravel rolled into it. A thin, loose layer can be laid on top so that you have the noise and typical wheel marks. As with gravel paths in the back garden, make sure that areas of gravel are properly edged so that the gravel does not travel mysteriously into the beds and borders that abut the drive.

Bricks and pavers are increasingly popular for drives, providing attractive textures and decorative surfaces. These must be laid on sound foundations, and the work is often best tackled by professionals so that a slight camber is created to allow water to drain safely away. Paving slabs can also be used. They should be laid on a concrete base to prevent uneven subsidence and consequent cracking. The slabs are available in a wide range of colours, shapes and sizes.

An old-fashioned way of creating a drive that is not as overpowering as the all-over paving slabs or pavers is to lay two strips of concrete where the car wheels will run. This leaves a rather awkward, narrow strip of earth down the centre, which can be allowed to grass over or which can, more imaginatively, be used for flowering plants. There are a number of attractive, low-growing plants that are far too thuggish to be allowed into a bed or border but that are ideally contained between the concrete strips. These include acaena, pratia, variegated ground elder and thyme.

WELCOMING SCENTS

It is difficult to disguise a large paved or concreted area. It can be edged with shrubs so that it is not entirely visible from the house, although this might not be ideal from the point of view of security. Herbaceous plants can be used as an attractive alternative. If possible, grow a fragrant plant or shrub near where you stop the car: this will be a delightful 'welcome home' after a day's work and should help to dissipate some of the tensions of the outside world.

FRONT LAWNS

Many gardeners will consider that an area of grass at the front of the house is neither use nor ornament. If there is space for a lawn at the back of the house, it is likely that the more secluded area will be used for relaxation and recreation. Parents will prefer their children to play in safety and isolation at the back of the house, out of sight of passers-by and visitors but in view from indoor windows. People who enjoy entertaining family and friends will choose to have barbecues and dinner parties at the back of the house, partly because of the privacy that is afforded there and partly for the simple reason that kitchen doors usually open on to the back garden, and carrying food, plates and utensils around or through the house is just not practicable even if it were desirable. People who like to sunbathe in the garden on summer afternoons will prefer to do so away from the gaze of casual passers-by.

Even a small lawn needs regular cutting, feeding and weeding if it is to look tidy all year round. In households where there are other pressures on time than regular grass cutting, the front patch is often neglected, to the detriment of the overall appearance of the property. Unless you like grass for its own sake, therefore, think seriously about getting rid of the front lawn and using the space for something more interesting and rewarding.

plant list:

FRAGRANT FLOWERS

- ***Choisya 'Aztec Pearl'***
  (Mexican orange blossom)
  A compact, evergreen shrub with white flowers in late spring with a second flush in late summer.

- ***Convallaria majalis*** (lily-of-the-valley)
  A spreading perennial with white flowers in late spring to early summer.

- ***Daphne tangutica***
  An evergreen shrub with pink-flushed, white flowers in late spring to early summer.

- ***Dianthus 'Mrs Sinkins'***
  An old-fashioned pink with double, white pink flowers in early summer.

- ***Erysimum cheiri*** (wallflower)
  A short-lived, evergreen perennial with bright yellow-orange flowers in spring.

- ***Nicotiana sylvestris***
  Panicles of sweetly fragrant, long-tubed white flowers, which close in full sun, are borne in late summer.

- ***Philadelphus 'Sybille'***
  A deciduous shrub with purple-marked white flowers in early to midsummer.

- ***Sarcococca hookeriana* var. *humilis***
  (Christmas box)
  A dwarf, evergreen shrub with pink-tinged white flowers in winter.

Magnolia stellata

A spreading, hardy, deciduous shrub or small tree, eventually growing to 3m (10ft) tall, this magnolia bears slightly fragrant, star-shaped white flowers in early and mid-spring. The beautiful flowers, which appear before the leaves, are sometimes slightly tinged with pink.

Cosmos atrosanguineus (chocolate cosmos)

The shallowly cup-shaped, dark reddish-brown, velvety flowers, each to 4cm (1½in) across, are deliciously scented of chocolate. They are borne singly on lax stems from midsummer to early autumn above the dark green leaves. Not reliably hardy.

plant profile

contemporary garden

Some people are more conscious of trends and fashions than others, and, just as the inside of the house reflects this, so the garden follows suit. Changing the design of a garden is generally regarded as a longer-term undertaking than simply changing the decor of the sitting room, however, if only because plants need time to grow. It is, nevertheless, possible to regard the garden as a space that can be 'decorated' and 'redecorated' as fashions change.

There have always been gardeners who have followed the trend of the day. In the past it was necessary to employ a fashionable designer to lay out the garden, but now modern styles and materials, still often designer-led, are illustrated in a wide range of magazines and shown on television for anyone to copy. A glance through the gardening periodicals, especially some of the more trendy ones, the weekend supplements and style magazines will provide a wealth of ideas, which can be adapted to meet your own tastes and the demands imposed by your plot.

MATERIAL CONSIDERATIONS

The materials you use in the garden, especially the hard landscaping, will set the tone and largely determine the style of the design. It is not long since walls built of geometrically patterned screen wall blocks were used for both boundary walls and internal screens. More recently, fences have been painted in shades of blue and green, vast swathes of urban gardens have disappeared beneath wooden decking,

above: The bright red flowers of the rose complement the colourful glass squares, which have been set in shingle beside a curved steel rill.

and patios have been re-laid with glass flooring tiles.

The materials used for walls, paths and patios are likely to be among the more expensive components of any garden makeover, and choosing materials that are both stylish and durable deserves careful thought. Bricks and pavers in traditional styles and colours may seem a bit dull compared with brightly coloured Mediterranean-style tiles and pink-painted walls. Although startling shades of red, blue and green look wonderful in sunny weather, think about the way your garden will look in autumn and winter, when light levels are low and plant cover is minimal, before committing yourself to something that catches your eye in a magazine or on display in a builder's merchant.

FASHIONABLE PLANTS

As with materials, so with plants: some are more fashionable than others. Plants, however, are far easier to replace than a patio or terrace wall. Recently there has been a resurgence of interest in grasses, which are ideal for small gardens because they can be used in so many different ways and are available in such a wide range of heights. They can look elegant and smart or tousled and unkempt; they can be grown as specimen plants and in containers or allowed to form a tangled mass. Bamboos can be used in similar ways. Strongly coloured plants, especially exotic ones such as cannas, are becoming more popular, and bright annuals are gradually becoming more widely seen.

PLANTING IN STYLE

The design and style of planting can also be dictated by trends and fashions. The Victorians loved elaborate bedding schemes, which involved planting out large numbers of specially raised plants in intricate schemes, but one of the more fashionable styles of the moment involves natural planting. This is the growing together of plants that would naturally associate and prosper together in the wild, and doing so in a way that emulates their appearance in the wild, so there are plenty of grasses as well as more colourful plants all mixed together as you would find them in a meadow or on a roadside verge. No doubt there will soon be a reaction against this, and the art of formal bedding will return.

A contemporary garden

The rather awkward L-shape of this basement garden has been given a strong, unifying look by the use of bold paving, although the distinction between the two areas has been emphasized by the different arrangement of the paving slabs. The natural change in level between the two areas has been underlined by the grey steps, which echo the colour of the steps leading down from the house. The planting has been kept against the boundaries to make the most of the available space while providing shade and privacy from above.

plant list:

GRASSES

- *Alopecurus pratensis* 'Aureovariegatus' (variegated foxtail grass)
  A medium-sized grass with yellow-variegated foliage.

- *Briza media* (trembling grass)
  A low-growing grass with green leaves and purplish-brown flowerheads.

- *Elymus magellanicus* (blue wheatgrass)
  A low-growing, spreading grass with vivid blue leaves.

- *Festuca glauca* (blue fescue)
  A small grass with blue-grey leaves.

- *Hordeum jubatum* (fox-tail barley)
  In summer the pale green leaves are topped by dense panicles of pink-tinged spikelets, composed of long, silky bristles.

- *Imperata cylindrica* 'Rubra'
  A medium-sized grass with striking, red-tipped, green foliage.

- *Milium effusum* 'Aureum' (Bowles' golden grass)
  A medium-sized, spreading grass with yellow-green leaves.

- *Molinia caerulea* (purple moor grass)
  A medium-sized to tall grass with green leaves and purplish flowerheads.

- *Pennisetum villosum* (feathertop)
  A medium-sized grass with green foliage and fluffy white flowerheads.

- *Phalaris arundinacea* var. *picta* 'Feesey'
  A restrained form of the vigorous gardener's garters, this medium-sized grass has white-variegated leaves.

ARTEFACTS

Another trend in modern gardens is to treat the space as an outside room and to reduce the amount of actual garden. The space is paved in stone or brick, and visual interest is generated by objects of one sort or another rather than by high-maintenance, time-consuming plants. Climbers and vegetation on walls and fences are replaced by mosaics or *trompes l'oeil*. Shrubs and trees are displaced by sculptures and *objets trouvés*, and no lawn maintenance is needed because the grass has been dug up and the space covered with hard surfacing.

These modifications represent a major change in garden maintenance: it is no longer needed. The garden is reduced to bare essentials. It has been turned into a minimal, low-maintenance space. It has become a garden for those who dislike or who have little time for gardening but who still want a stylish space in which to relax.

Hakonechloa macra 'Alboaurea'

The arching leaves of this neat grass are striped with green, white and yellow. This is a slow-growing, compact plant, forming clumps to about 35cm (14in) high, and it is ideal for a container or for edging the front of a sunny, well-drained border.

plant profile

plant-lover's garden

left: When space is at a premium a cold frame can be used instead of a greenhouse to harden off young plants or for cuttings.

below left: Colourful perennials have been supplemented by tender plants, grown in containers and moved into the border to fill gaps as other plants go over.

Although there is now an increasing trend towards low-maintenance gardens and easy-to-grow plants, there are still many people who love gardening and who do not want an easy-care garden. Growing plants is their life, and they want to use every available scrap of space for their passion. Such people enjoy the thought of growing things and of being in contact with nature, in even a limited way, and they enjoy working in the open air. They also enjoy the results that their efforts produce: a garden full of attractive plants and, if they also grow vegetables and fruit, fresh, tasty produce. There is no question that this is much harder work than looking after, say, a modern garden, which is mainly composed of hard surfaces but then; enjoying the cultivation of each plant is the whole point of having a garden.

PURCHASING PLANTS

It is surprising how many plants can be accommodated in a small garden, and there is an increasing range from which to choose. Some gardeners might prefer to specialize by growing alpines or hardy perennials, while others prefer to concentrate on a particular genus, such as roses, dahlias or fritillaries. Only a limited selection is available from general garden centres and nurseries, but there is a vast array of specialist nurseries, which either provide plants at the nursery or supply them through mail order. There are also specialist societies, which promote a particular area of interest and often have seed exchange schemes that make available to members seeds of plants that are rarely seen elsewhere. Specialization is an exciting world, and a small garden is usually just the right size for a collection.

DESIGNING WITH PLANTS

Few of the gardeners who take time and trouble growing plants are happy to put them just anywhere in the garden. They like to create a pleasing scene, whether this is achieved in an *ad hoc* way by buying or growing plants and just placing them where they seem to fit into a general design, or by adopting what many might regard as a more interesting and rewarding approach by giving some thought to the overall planting scheme. The points to consider are fundamental factors, such as when the plants flower, and the colour, height, spread and shape of the plants. Although it can be fun to add a jarring note into the scheme, most gardeners will prefer to create a wholly harmonious scene.

THINKING COLOUR

One of the most important aspects to consider in a small garden is colour. Some colours go together much more comfortably than others. Pastel shades, for example, blend well together and create a peaceful, hazy atmosphere. Bright colours, on the other hand, are more vibrant and add a touch of excitement to a border, although they can be overpowering in a small space.

Other colours clash and should be avoided unless you deliberately want to make a statement – purple and orange or pink and orange, for example. make unhappy combinations. Other colours clash so much that it is worth using them occasionally just to pep things up and draw the eye: include a plant with bright yellow flowers in a bright blue border, for example, or add a splash of red against a green background.

SIZE AND SHAPE

A border filled with plants of the same size, even if they have been selected to fill a small area, will look visually boring. One that contains fewer plants but with some variations in height will be much more interesting. The classic way to organize a border is to place the taller plants at the back and the shorter ones at the front, so that they build up in tiers. This kind of arrangement can be rather predictable and unexciting, however, and should be relieved by pulling forward a few of the taller plants and allowing the shorter ones to grow towards the back.

The shapes of different plants vary considerably, and use should be made of this. Some lie flat, hugging the ground; others shoot up in narrow columns; some produce rounded shapes; and others are like fountains. All this variation should be taken advantage of to make your small garden as interesting as possible.

plant list:

Hellebors orientalis Ballard's Group

There are now many named cultivars of this hellebore, but they all have the lovely, downward-facing, cup-shaped flowers in early spring. Individual plants grow to about 45cm (18in) high and round.

Paeonia officinalis 'Magic Orb'

The large, fragrant, double flowers have deep pink outer petals and smaller, creamy-pink inner petals. The dark green leaves turn reddish in autumn before they die back. Peonies need support and do best when in rich, moisture-retentive but well-drained soil in sun or semi-shade.

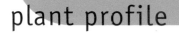

plant profile

SPECIMEN PLANTS

- **Angelica archangelica** (angelica)
  An architectural biennial herb with large, spherical green flowerheads in summer.

- **Cedrus deodara 'Aurea'**
  A small to medium-sized, upright cedar with soft, feathery, golden-green foliage.

- **Cercis canadensis** (Canadian redbud)
  A small deciduous tree with a domed habit with heart-shaped leaves, that are bronze when young and turning yellow in autumn.

- **Crambe cordifolia**
  A clump-forming perennial that produces enormous, airy heads of white flowers in summer.

- **Cynara cardunculus** (cardoon)
  A large perennial with huge, crinkle-edged, silver leaves and large purple flowers in summer.

- **Fatsia japonica**
  An upright, evergreen shrub with large, glossy, divided leaves.

- **Hakonechloa macra 'Aureola'**
  A medium-sized grass forming a fountain of stripy yellow and green foliage that turns red in autumn.

- **Matteuccia struthiopteris** (ostrich fern)
  A large, deciduous fern, which forms a neat shuttlecock of foliage.

- **Miscanthus sinensis 'Zebrinus'** (zebra grass) A large, handsome grass forming upright clumps of stripy foliage.

- **Phormium tenax**
  A large perennial forming clumps of sword-shaped leaves in eye-catching colours.

- **Yucca gloriosa**
  A large perennial with a stiff rosette of spiky leaves.

courtyard garden

Space is always at a premium in small gardens and never more so than in a courtyard, where the area is defined by neighbouring houses and garden walls. In such a garden every opportunity has to be taken to make the space look and feel larger than it actually is, even if it is only an illusion. One of the great frustrations of a small garden is that it usually looks precisely that, small, and this feeling can be intensified when the area is also overlooked from upstairs rooms that may belong to neighbouring households.

These constraints generally affect the courtyard gardener in one of two ways. The first is the practical fact that there is a limit to what can be done in an area that is not only surrounded by walls and fences but also probably has a completely hard ground. The number of activities that can be carried out and the number of plants that can be grown in this space are automatically limited. The other problem is more of a psychological one: the garden often looks and feels cramped.

PHYSICAL SIZE

If you are interested in growing plants there are several things you can do to squeeze a little more usable space from the garden. The first is to use all the walls and grow vertically, planting climbers and wall shrubs that will provide year-round interest and disguise what might be otherwise dull and unattractive walls and fences. Pots and hanging baskets can be attached to poles and posts to create colour and shape at eye level and above.

An alternative approach is to use containers, which offer endless opportunities to grow a large variety of plants because nearly all plants can, at some stage – or even for all of their lives – be grown in a container, irrespective of their natural final size. In some cases, growing in containers will limit plants' spread and growth, making them suitable for use in a garden when, in nature, they would grow too large. *Ficus carica* (fig), for example, is a good container-grown plant that, if left to its own devices in the garden, can spread too much, as can rampant plants such as *Mentha* spp. (mint), which should be grown in containers so that you get the benefits of the plant but not their effect

on the rest of the garden. Herbaceous shrubs and trees are often grown in pots, but it is also easy to grow fruit bushes and dwarf apple trees in containers, too, widening still further the types of plants that can be included in the scheme. You can attach windowboxes and other containers to walls to grow plants that you would normally grow in beds and borders, and containers can also be arranged on

above: Containers, cobbles and colour: lack of space need not limit you. Containers allow a plant lover to create a dazzling array of colour.

tiered shelves and *étagères* so that the plants get plenty of light.

Containers can be bought in a range of materials, including plastic, terracotta, stone and lead, but you can paint and decorate them yourself if you want a particular colour theme. They can be stood individually or in groups to make a display. Because you can move them around so easily, you can create different heights and shapes with the planting, a flexibility that is not possible with flowerbeds.

An obvious way of growing more plants that is often overlooked is to grow smaller plants. It is amazing how many rock plants, for example, you can grow in a trough or an old sink.

Even where there is open ground, the area is often shady and plants must be chosen that will thrive in these conditions. It is pointless hoping to grow sunflowers if your courtyard garden is overshadowed for most, if not all, of the day. Choose plants that grow naturally in a shady, woodland-type environment and make sure you improve the soil so that it is fertile and moisture-retentive.

VISUAL SIZE

Often the intimate atmosphere of a small courtyard garden is appealing, but you may still wish to make it seem larger. The easiest way of overcoming the dilemma is to disguise boundaries by covering them with vegetation so that they cannot be seen. This gives the impression that the edge of the garden could be far away, in the unseen distance. If there is space, a curved

A courtyard garden

The split-level basement courtyard has been transformed into a pleasant, open space. The use of brick for all hard surfaces provides uniformity and continuity throughout the area. Although the plot is basically square, the curve of the steps and of the central raised bed do much to minimize the impact of surrounding walls, while the gently curved beds along one side and towards the back provide space for deep planting to disguise what would otherwise be overpowering boundaries. Shade-tolerant plants are used in the raised beds to soften the edges of the shady area near the back door.

plant list:

FLOWERS FOR SHADE

- **Anemone nemorosa** (wood anemone)
  A low-growing perennial with white flowers in spring.

- **Brunnera macrophylla**
  A medium-sized perennial with bright blue flowers in spring.

- **Eranthis hyemalis** (winter aconite)
  A tiny, yellow-flowered bulb, blooming in late winter to spring.

- **Euphorbia amygdaloides** var. **robbiae** (Mrs Robb's spurge)
  A medium-sized, evergreen perennial with acid green flowers in spring.

- **Helleborus viridis** (green hellebore)
  A low-growing to medium-sized perennial with green flowers in winter to spring.

- **Liriope muscari** (lilyturf)
  A low-growing, evergreen perennial with spikes of blue-purple flowers in autumn.

- **Sanguinaria canadensis** (bloodroot)
  A low-growing perennial with white flowers in spring.

- **Smilacina racemosa** (false spikenard)
  A medium-sized perennial with white flowers in early summer.

- **Trillium grandiflorum** (wake robin)
  A low-growing perennial with white flowers in late spring to early summer.

- **Uvularia grandiflora** (large merrybells)
  A medium-sized perennial with yellow flowers in mid- to late spring.

path that ends behind an object will also further the illusion of space. do not, however, allow a path to end suddenly against a fence or wall.

Another way of creating doubt about the position of the real boundaries is by illusion. The simplest method is to use mirrors. Place a mirror on a wall and disguise the edges so that it cannot be perceived as a mirror, and it will give the impression that the garden goes on beyond it.

An alternative approach is to use paint, and a *trompe l'oeil* scene on a wall can be deceptive. Even a naïve, romantic scene, which will fool no one who sees it close to, can have the desired effect of making a garden look bigger when it is viewed from a distance, as from an upstairs window, but a realistic painting can make it seem as if the garden really does continue on the far side of a painted arch or doorway.

Convallaria majalis (lily-of-the-valley)

This herbaceous perennial is ideal for a damp, shady corner. In late spring the fragrant, white, bell-shaped flowers are borne on gracefully arching stems. The oval, dark green leaves are up to 20cm (8in) long. 'Fortin's Giant' is larger in every respect.

plant profile

low-maintenance garden

above: The ultimate in low-maintenance gardening: gravel, paving slabs and a simple water feature.

It is possible to get carried away when you are designing a garden and to forget just how much work is involved in its maintenance. There is no doubt that the best gardens do need a fair amount of attention – more, in fact, than most people can afford to give them – but with careful planning and forethought it is possible to create an attractive garden that requires only the minimum effort to keep it looking good all year round.

Before you decide on a style of garden, it is important to decide how much time you can spend on it and how this time is to be broken down. If your time is limited to a couple of hours at weekends, it is important to design a low-maintenance garden, especially as some weekends will be lost because of poor weather and holidays. If you can spare an hour a day, on the other hand, the scope is greater and it is possible to introduce borders packed with flowering plants and shrubs that will require more attention.

LAWNS AND HEDGES

One of the great time-consuming jobs in a garden is mowing the lawn. When you add to this the time spent scarifying it, applying fertilizer and weedkiller in spring and sweeping away autumnal leaves you should ask yourself if you need a lawn at all. What do you use the area for? Would an alternative surface be just as useful? A hard surface, such as paving or brickwork, will need hardly any attention apart from the occasional sweep and will be a firm, stable surface for tables, chairs

and sunloungers. Chipped bark, which provides a softer surface than paving stones and is softer even than grass, would make a good alternative play area for children. When you no longer have a lawn, there is no need for a lawnmower or a shed in which to store what can be a big piece of equipment.

After you have spent the afternoon mowing the lawn, you will have to turn your attention to the hedge, which will need cutting at least once a year if it is not going to get completely overgrown and take up twice its allotted space. If you like having a hedge, choose a

slow-growing plant with an erect, narrow habit, such as *Taxus baccata* 'Fastigiata' (fastigiate yew), which will take longer to become established than, say, privet but which will need only a light trim once a year. It is not just cutting the hedge that takes time: you have to clear away the

trimmings and either take them to the tip or shred them so that you can add them to the compost heap. Would a fence be less work?

WEEDS AND WATERING

Some gardeners like weeding – they seem to find it therapeutic – but it is actually a huge waste of time and extraordinarily tedious. If you do not mind using chemicals in the garden, you can use weedkillers, of course; but, apart from the initial clearing of the ground that may be needed in a neglected, overgrown garden, they are not to be recommended in an established garden. It is far better (and much less work) to combat weeds by using a mulch. Remove all perennial weeds and then cover the borders with a layer of bark to a depth of at least 10cm (4in) so that weed seeds cannot germinate.

Another boring and time-consuming task is watering lawns and plants. Mechanical devices, including sprinklers, seep hoses and trickle systems, can be introduced, but it is better to reduce the amount of water required. A thick mulch applied over moist soil will do much to prevent evaporation, or you may prefer to think about a gravel bed planted with Mediterranean-type plants that will thrive in dry, sunny conditions.

PLANTS FOR LOW MAINTENANCE

The choice of plants is important if you want to save time, because some plants require more attention than others. A large number of shrubs and most small trees, for example, require

above: A shady corner surrounded by established trees and shrubs is the perfect retreat from gardening and household chores.

little if any pruning, unlike roses. Check when buying just how much attention each requires. The same is true of many perennials: some need to be staked, deadheaded and divided at regular intervals, while others seem to thrive on benign neglect.

Groundcover plants will also help save time. They will act as a living mulch, excluding light from the soil's surface and preventing weed seeds from germinating. Groundcover will not stop perennial weeds, however, and it is essential to prepare the ground thoroughly and to remove every trace of the roots of plants like bindweed before you introduce the new plants.

Staking perennial plants that need support can take time, so choose plants that are sturdy enough to stand up by themselves and do not flop over at the first breath of a breeze. If you like tall plants, stake them before they are half grown, because it is easier to support them at this stage than waiting until they are fully grown or have fallen over.

LITTLE AND OFTEN

If the amount of work needed to keep a garden looking tidy is allowed to get out of hand, it can be a long, hard slog to regain control. When weeds are plucked out the moment they are noticed it is easier to control them, but if they are allowed to grow away they will soon get among the plants and be more difficult to eliminate. A relaxing stroll in the garden every evening, when you can remove any weeds that have emerged during the day, will save hours of work at the weekend, when you are likely to have many other things to do. Similarly, catching pests at an early stage in their development will not only save time later on but will also give your plants a better chance of flourishing.

Astrantia major (greater masterwort)

The attractive flowerheads have striking green- or pink-veined bracts surrounding the small flowers. The lobed leaves are mid-green. Plants grow to about 60cm (2ft) tall and, once established, will self-seed freely.

plant profile

plant list:

GROUNDCOVER PLANTS

- ***Acaena saccaticupula* 'Blue Haze'**
  A mat-forming perennial with handsome blue, evergreen foliage and red flowers in summer.

- ***Anthemis punctata* subsp. *cupaniana***
  A mat-forming perennial with silvery foliage and white flowers in spring and summer.

- ***Epimedium* x *rubrum***
  A perennial with foliage that lasts through winter and red flowers in spring to early summer.

- ***Geranium macrorrhizum***
  A low-growing perennial with pink flowers in summer.

- ***Lysimachia nummularia* 'Aurea'** (golden creeping Jenny)
  A carpeting perennial with golden foliage and summer flowers.

- ***Pulmonaria angustifolia*** (blue cowslip)
  A low-growing perennial with blue flowers in spring.

- ***Stachys byzantina*** (lamb's ears)
  A mat-forming perennial with silver leaves and pink summer flowers.

- ***Thymus serpyllum*** (thyme)
  A carpeting shrub with evergreen leaves and pink, purple or white summer flowers.

- ***Vancouveria chrysantha***
  A low-growing, evergreen perennial with yellow flowers in early summer.

roof garden

Some people, especially those in flats and apartments, have no garden at all, but many have access to a balcony or a roof, which can be an admirable place for creating a small garden. A roof garden will elevate the gardener heavenwards and make the most of a small but sunny area. From being a potentially dull, possibly overlooked and boring space, the roof can be turned into a beautiful and restful garden, far above the busy streets, where you can escape, entertain and relax.

Because of the sunny, light conditions, a roof garden is the ideal place for plants that might otherwise be difficult to grow, and, once you have provided protection from the wind by erecting a fence or screen, you will find that you can grow a far wider range of plants than you might imagine.

SAFETY CONSIDERATIONS

One of the most important points to bear in mind when considering a roof garden is that the weight of the features, such as large containers filled with moist compost and even a small pool, will be enormous. Before embarking on such a garden, have a structural survey carried out. Keeping the planting and structures near to the sides means that the most weight will be as close to the weight-bearing structures of the building as possible, but a proper survey will identify any potential problems.

MATERIALS

Choose materials that will link the house and garden so that the garden

above: So that the imposing view is not obscured, planting has been confined to one side of this large area. The open metal trellis supports fine safety netting but is otherwise unadorned.

feels like an extension of the living area – which it is. A fence can be used to define the boundary and to obscure unattractive views. Slatted fencing will allow light through while effectively enclosing the open sides of the garden, and wooden fencing often blends in well with the mature brickwork that is often found in roof gardens, especially chimney stacks. The advantages of a slatted fence are that it not only provides privacy but also offers some protection from the elements, and is not very heavy.

Shade will be needed and could be provided by a pergola, possibly made from wooden slats similar to the wood used for the fence. A pergola would also provide support for flowering climbers, and trellis on the wall and a planting hole would make it possible to have a wide range of climbers growing up and over the structure, creating a private, shaded spot for sitting out.

above: Timber decking has been used over the entire roof to create an extension of the indoor space, with matching table and chairs under the temporary canvas awning.

PLANTING

Confining the plants largely to the edges of the garden will create a sense of space in the central area, but the plants also get protection from the elements and help to break up the potentially stark lines of the masonry.

Select plants that have a rich diversity of foliage to make up for the lush green normally provided by a lawn. Evergreen shrubs will give year-round interest, but they should be interspersed with a few fragrant plants that will flower over a long period and help to create a relaxed atmosphere. Using plants that have slender, erect stems will create a

A small roof garden

What might have been a small, unused space has been transformed into a pleasant outdoor area by the use of bold, checkerboard floor paving and bright flowers in containers. Containers have been used to keep the planting low, but a wide range of plants, from small trees to summer annuals, will grow in these conditions. The use of small trays on castors for the containers makes it possible to move them to the sides when the table and chairs are in use. Containers resting on the top of a balustrade like this must be securely attached to avoid them being dislodged by a strong wind.

formal feel, while plants with grass-like foliage, such as *Luzula sylvatica* 'Aurea' and *Phalaris arundinacea* var. *picta* 'Feesey', will add to the visual impact. The containers must be lightweight to avoid putting undue strain on the structure of the roof.

OPTIONAL EXTRAS

Having to water plants regularly in summer can be awkward if you have to carry watering cans any distance. An irrigation system could be used to make sure that the plants get adequate water and to reduce the need for daily watering. Care should be taken that excess water can drain away safely and not seep through to the floors below.

Although a water feature on a roof might seem out of the question, an area of smooth water, which will mirror the sky and the clouds, will be a wonderful addition to the scene. Light playing on its surface will introduce movement, changes in colours and gentle noise.

To extend the use of the roof garden, a lighting system could be installed. A small garden would need a simple system, but the effect would be

instantaneous and you would have an extra room for much of the year. A light in the pool would also highlight the water plants and bring the pool into relief during the hours of darkness. The interplay of light and water after dark is mesmerizing, and lighting would also, of course, make the roof garden a safer place at night.

Myrtus communis 'Variegata'

A pretty shrub for a sheltered spot, this has grey-green leaves, narrowly edged with white. In mid- and late summer it bears white flowers, each flower to 2cm (¾in) across. It will grow in a container in full sun, but needs protection from cold, drying winds.

plant profile

plant list:

SMALL TREES AND SHRUBS FOR CONTAINERS

- **Acacia dealbata** (mimosa, silver wattle)
  A tender evergreen with fern-like leaves and yellow spring flowers.

- **Cordyline australis**
  A tender, palm-like tree with lance-shaped leaves.

- **Cupressus macrocarpa** 'Goldcrest' (Monterey cypress)
  A narrow, conical, evergreen tree with golden-yellow foliage.

- **Juniperus scopulorum** 'Skyrocket' (Rocky Mountain juniper)
  A narrow, upright tree with grey-green leaves.

- **Laurus nobilis** (bay)
  A conical tree with glossy, aromatic, evergreen leaves.

- **Malus x purpurea**
  An erect deciduous tree with purple-pink flowers followed by small, dark red fruit.

- **Olea europaea** (olive)
  A slow-growing evergreen with leathery grey-green leaves.

- **Prunus** 'Amanogawa'
  An upright deciduous tree with fragrant blossom in spring.

wildlife garden

There is something enormously enjoyable and rewarding about being part of nature and being surrounded by butterflies and birds as you work or relax in the garden. There is a world of difference between sitting on a barren, undecorated terrace with only the noise of the neighbours in your ears and sitting near a herb garden, listening to the hum of bees and watching butterflies flit from flower to flower.

Many people enjoy gardening because they feel it brings them a little closer to nature. This may be a cliché, but it is true that working and relaxing in a garden makes you aware not just of the soil on your hands and what lives in it but also of the birds, insects and other animals around you. You become more conscious of what they look like and of the way they live.

AN URBAN SANCTUARY

The multiple pressures on the countryside from housing and roads mean that any extra help that can be provided to both the plant and animal communities are welcome, even – especially – in built-up areas. Providing food, water and habitats for birds and other animals and allowing wildflowers into the garden creates a reservoir that may eventually be used to replenish other areas as they become available. Every little helps in the fight to preserve the countryside, even if your garden is in the centre of a town.

One of the advantages of looking after nature is that it will help you look after your garden. If you grow a wide range of flowering plants, especially

above: A natural pond will be a haven for an enormous range of wildlife. In a small pool choose a miniature waterlily, such as *Nymphaea* 'Pygmaea Helvola', to provide surface cover, and plant species with a naturally arching habit, such as hostas and grasses, around the pool to help disguise the edges.

some old-fashioned ones, these will attract hoverflies, lacewings and ladybirds, which help control pests such as aphids. Encourage birds and other animals to visit your garden, and they will help rid it of a range of pests. Tits and dunnocks, for example, will eat greenfly, and thrushes, hedgehogs and toads help to keep the population of slugs and snails under control. Greenfly and slugs are two of the worst pests in the garden, and anything you can do to encourage nature to help you to control them will make your life easier.

When you are considering a garden makeover there is much you can do to encourage different forms of wildlife to

inhabit or visit your garden. You can make sure there are supplies of appropriate food and drink and places to perch and roost, and you can even supply boxes in which they can nest and bring up the next generations. Part of the garden can be given over to growing wildflowers, partly to play your own part in the preservation of native species and partly to provide food for birds and insects, which generally prefer native plants to introduced ones.

FOOD FOR BIRDS

The simplest way to provide food for birds is, of course, to put out peanuts (make sure they are aflatoxin-free) and wild bird seed. When you are designing your garden, it is worth thinking about where such items as birdtables and birdbaths will be positioned. This is not a problem with free-standing ones, but if you want to have a birdtable that is suspended somewhere you will have to give the siting more thought. From the birds' point of view, it does not much matter where the feeding station is, as long as it is safe from surprise attacks from cats. If you want to enjoy being able to watch birds as they feed, consider placing the birdtable where it can be seen from a window.

Berries and seeds represent the major part of many birds' diets, and these can be provided by including in the garden trees, shrubs and other plants that bear them. Small trees, including *Sorbus* spp. (rowan) and *Ilex aquifolium* (holly), bear berries that are greatly enjoyed by birds in winter. Perennial plants are also a useful source of seeds. Many birds, notably goldfinches, will visit gardens in large numbers to feed on seedheads that have been left. Leaving old vegetation standing throughout winter can make a garden look rather unkempt and untidy, but it is worth leaving at least some throughout winter. The old vegetation is a hiding place for many insects, and insectivorous birds will come for food.

Buddleja 'Glasnevin Blue'

The dense panicles of fragrant, dark, lilac-blue flowers are up to 30cm (12in) long. The flowers appear in late summer and autumn and are irresistible to butterflies. This is a tolerant shrub, which will eventually grow to about 2.5m (8ft) tall.

Fuchsia magellanica (lady's teardrops)

In mild areas, this upright shrub can be used as hedging. The small red and purple flowers are borne all summer long and are followed by dark reddish-purple fruits, which are a useful food source for birds when other resources are limited.

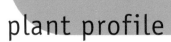
plant profile

plant list:

TREES AND SHRUBS FOR BERRIES

- **Berberis thunbergii** (barberry)
  A deciduous shrub with bright red berries in winter for thrushes, including fieldfares and redwings.

- **Cotoneaster horizontalis**
  Red winter berries attract thrushes of all kinds and waxwings.

- **Crataegus monogyna** (common hawthorn)
  In winter glossy, dark red berries provide food for many species, including starlings, finches, crows, blue tits, thrushes and waxwings.

- **Hedera helix** (ivy)
  Autumn and winter berries are an important food for woodpigeons, collared doves, waxwings, thrushes, jays, starlings and finches.

- **Ilex aquifolium** (common holly)
  The red autumn and winter berries are especially appreciated by mistle thrushes.

- **Leycesteria formosa** (Himalayan honeysuckle)   In autumn red-purple berries attract tits, thrushes, finches and warblers.

- **Lonicera periclymenum** (honeysuckle)
  Glossy red autumn berries are enjoyed by robins, blackbirds, song thrushes, garden warblers, tits, crows, finches and waxwings.

- **Pyracantha 'Orange Glow'**
  Vivid orange fruits in autumn to winter are enjoyed by wood pigeons and thrushes.

- **Sambucus racemosa** (red-berried elder)
  Waxwings and thrushes will eat the autumn fruits.

- **Sorbus aria** (whitebeam)
  The colourful autumn berries are a valuable food for woodpigeons, fieldfares, redwings, blackbirds and mistle thrushes.

3

Many small gardens are in towns, where the problems are not just of finding the room to do all the things you need to do and would like to be able to do outside, and of making the most of every scrap of available space, but also of creating a private and secluded place. Most gardens in towns are overlooked to some extent, and providing an area, no matter how small, that cannot be viewed from your neighbours' windows can be important.

Using the available space efficiently and effectively is also important if you are to get the greatest use and enjoyment from your garden. The value of the third dimension, height, in garden design can never be emphasized enough. It is a vital element in achieving structure in gardens of all sizes, for without it the eye can quickly sweep around the garden and take in everything at a glance. In a small area it is doubly important, for when structure is present the eye is interrupted and things are hidden and must be sought out. Tall structures can be used to provide colours, shapes and textures at varying levels and to introduce shadows. They can also be clad in vegetation, making the garden an altogether more interesting and rewarding place.

One problem with a small garden is that as soon as you start to do anything, whether it is gardening or entertaining, you need somewhere to put things. This takes up space, and so you have even less room to do whatever it is you want to do. It can become a vicious circle, so it is important to make the best possible use of all available storage space.

small issues

maximizing space

If the space in your garden is severely limited it is important to think through the ways you can maximize what is available. This can be achieved both by making the space appear to be larger than it actually is, perhaps by considering new ways of thinking about the boundaries themselves, and by using the space that you do have in innovative ways.

BOUNDARIES

Boundaries determine the physical extent of a garden – that is, the points at which it must end before you enter someone else's territory – and one way to deny their presence is to disguise them: if you cannot see them, they are not there.

Covering the boundaries with plants is the most obvious solution. Hedges are often used as boundaries, but when they are of a plant like privet they usually look regular and like hedges. If you use several different plants, however, each varying in shape and size, the linear effect will disappear, and what is actually a hedge will look like a shrubbery. If there is space, these 'hedges' could be more than one plant deep in places to create an irregular appearance. False paths can be made through the vegetation so that they disappear around a corner before they reach the real boundary, and this will help to foster the illusion that the area is densely planted. Although any plants can be used in this type of arrangement, evergreen shrubs are ideal; otherwise autumn leaf fall will give the game away.

above: A pergola against the house wall can be clothed in a deciduous climber, which will provide shelter and shade in summer, when the garden is in use, but will not cast dark shadows in autumn and winter.

When you are designing the layout of your garden, one of the ways in which you can make the space appear larger is to 'borrow' features, especially trees, from other gardens. If there is a tall, decorative tree in a neighbouring garden it can be made to appear to be part of your own garden as long as the boundary between the two gardens cannot be seen. Planting shrubs in front of a fence or wall, for example, so that the boundary is covered but the tree can still be seen peering over the top of the shrubs, will make it appear to be part of your garden. By implication your own garden will seem to be bigger.

It is always a pleasure to discover small, intimate spaces in a garden where you can be private. One way to achieve this is to create an arbour (see page 56). If you are creating a boundary that is thick with bushes and other vegetation it may be possible to make one or two of these hideaways, simply by growing climbers over a frame or by making 'rooms' in the shrubs, but remember to leave a thick layer of vegetation between you and the boundary. These hidden places will be away from the main part of your own garden where most activity is likely to take place and will give you somewhere quiet and private to relax, if only for a short time.

Not all small gardens are found in the centre of towns and cities, surrounded by other houses. Many small gardens are in rural areas or in areas that verge on the country. In these gardens it can be a good idea to

above: An enclosed urban garden is usually an ideal place to grow species that might be regarded as half-hardy in a more exposed garden.

open up your own boundaries so that you can see the landscape beyond. Bringing what lies beyond into your own garden will help to make your own plot seem larger.

One of the more successful ways of doing this is to open only part of the view rather than all of it, so that occasional glimpses are possible. The classic way to do this is to create a ha-ha – that s, the hedge or fence is sunk into a ditch so that it is hidden from view but still forms a barrier. It makes it look as f the garden continues straight out into the landscape. Building a ha-ha is not usually a practicable solution in a small garden, but someone with ingenuity and energy could possibly achieve it, or a version of it, to great effect.

PLANTING STRATEGIES

In a small garden maximizing space for plants is important. Clothing walls and other vertical spaces is an obvious solution, although it needs to be approached with caution. Arches, for example, generally have a purpose in that they are usually an entrance or an exit through a hedge or fence (see pages 102–3), but they are sometimes erected in the middle of nowhere, simply as a support for climbers. This can look ocd, and if the aim is only to provide height it is better to use a simple pole or series of poles to provide the vertical emphasis. Each pole, which will take up little floor space, must be firmly embedded in the ground. Self-clinging climbers, such as clematis, need something to hang on to

in the form of wire-netting, which can be wrapped and stapled around the pole. Poles are often placed in borders, but they can be used anywhere you want a vertical planting, such as along a path or walkway, where they will provide a rhythmic design. They can also be linked with swags of rope, along which the climbers crawl until they eventually merge. A less permanent solution is to set obelisks and tripods in borders. These can be used to provide support for summer climbers, such as *Lathyrus odoratus* (sweet pea), but can be easily moved at the end of the season.

Someone who is interested in growing the widest possible range of plants might elect to grow small plants (see pages 142–3) – it is surprising how many carefully chosen plants can be grown in a small space. Another possibility is to underplant. Many spring bulbs and herbaceous plants, for example, grow under trees and bushes in the wild, and they flower early in the year so that they can take advantage of the light and moisture filtering through the bare branches. By the time the foliage above them opens, blocking the sun and rain, the plants have flowered and died back below ground to remain dormant until the next spring. This can be used to advantage in the garden. Woodland bulbs and other plants can be grown beneath trees and shrubs in soil that will not be used by other plants later in the year. They will show while there are no leaves on the shrubs, but their tatty remains will be hidden from view later in the season.

STORAGE IDEAS

When you are thinking about the ways in which you can get what you want from a small area, storage can become a major problem. If you have a lawn, for example, you will need a lawnmower and you will need somewhere to keep it. It may be, of course, that you come to the conclusion that you will be better off with a hard surface or even gravel or chipped bark rather than grass so that you do not have to mow anything. Similarly, if you have a fence rather than a hedge you will not need a hedge trimmer. Perhaps you could choose garden furniture that will fold flat, so that in winter it can hang up on hooks in the garage, out of the way of the car, or perhaps it could be durable enough to stand outside all year round so that it does not have to be stored anywhere at all. Think carefully before losing space to storage: do you really need whatever it is you have got to store?

If you have young children, their use of the garden is likely to dominate the layout until they have grown up. Thinking about the long-term use of the garden can make the transition easier, however. A playhouse could be used later for storage purposes, for example, and it could be positioned, designed and constructed or purchased with that later purpose in mind.

SHEDS

In a little garden a small lean-to tool shed can be built against a wall or against a fence if it is substantial enough. (If it is your neighbour's fence you should ask permission before you build.) A lean-to can be big enough to contain the lawnmower and a few tools but will take up little room. A simple frame of 7.5 x 5cm (3 x 2in) timber can be constructed, and the sides and a door can be made either by cladding this with feather-edged boarding or by buying some fence panels and cutting them to size. The door can be made in a similar way but will need a frame of 5 x 2.5cm (2 x 1in) timber to strengthen it. You will not need a window. A simple sloping roof can be made from a sheet of cheap plywood covered with roofing felt. Fill the space where the top of the roof meets the wall or fence with a flexible filler so that rainwater cannot trickle into the shed. Surround the shed with shrubs so that it cannot be seen, or place a climber-clad trellis in front of it.

If your objection to a shed is not so much the space it takes up but its dominant presence, which makes it seem too large for the garden, think about disguising it. Painting it green will help to make it merge into the background, and covering it with climbing plants will make it even less noticeable. The plants will soften the edges and break up its surface. If there is space, placing a trellis in front of it, again possibly covered in climbers, will help to hide it.

SPACE-SAVERS

Although sheds are the ideal form of storage for almost everything connected with the garden, bunkers or large boxes will take up less space and may provide enough room for the few tools that you need in the garden. As long as it is not too heavy to lift in and

left: You do not need a shed to keep your hand fork, trowel and dibber out of the way when they are not being used, although your best tools should stay indoors.

out, a mower can also be stored in it. Old coal bunkers of the kind still found in some gardens are ideal. Storage areas could also be built into other features. For example, if you want a permanent barbecue with a built-in sitting area, the seats could be constructed as lockers, with storage space beneath them. Building a wooden deck instead of a patio might allow you to introduce storage space below it.

GREENHOUSES

Most gardeners hanker after a greenhouse in which to raise a variety of plants. Greenhouses are not only expensive, however, but take up a lot of room, especially as the usual advice for buying one is that you should work out the size you need and double it because you will always need more space than you think. Although it does not have quite the same prestige as a greenhouse, a cold frame can do almost anything a greenhouse can do, apart from keeping the gardener dry in wet weather. It takes up far less space and can be more easily and cheaply made by the gardener with readily available materials than a greenhouse can. It can also be dismantled or moved out of the way when it is not being used.

It is also possible to buy 'mini-greenhouses', which are simply slatted shelves supported against a solid back but open at the front and sides, which are protected by glass or acrylic glazing. Expensive versions are made of pine or even red cedar, but less costly models have aluminium frames and non-shatter polycarbonate glazing. These can be stood against the house wall on a patio, where they will take up little room but provide plenty of space for seedlings or for overwintering tender plants.

above: Narrow, sturdy chests with hinged tops are becoming available. These take up little room, but will hold all the tools you are likely to need.

enhancing space

Few gardeners are entirely satisfied with the size of their garden, but short of moving house there is little that can be done about the physical boundaries that exist. There are, however, several things that can be done to make even the smallest space seem larger.

LAWNS AND PATHS

Although it may seem obvious, mowing the lawn in stripes that go away from the viewer will make a lawn look much longer. Conversely, a very long, narrow lawn can be made to seem wider if the mowing stripes go across the grass.

A similar effect can be achieved with brick paths if the bricks are laid lengthways along the path. This arrangement will draw the eye onwards, giving the impression that the path is much longer than it is. Place the bricks across the path, and the eye is stopped as if by a barrier and the path will appear shorter.

When you are laying out the garden make sure that the whole area cannot be seen in one glance. Design it in such a way that paths curve behind shrubs or trellises to create the impression that the garden goes on and on, out of sight. Skilfully done, it should be possible to have someone walk round in a circle, around the whole garden, thinking they have still not got to the bottom of it.

FOCAL POINTS

Focal points are essential components of garden design, and they can be used in several ways. You may want simply to draw the viewer's attention to a

above: A focal point, such as a statue or specimen plant, will draw the eye along a path, increasing the apparent distance between the viewer and the object.

particularly attractive feature. In a small garden siting a focal point at the end of a path or lawn will help to give the impression that the garden is bigger than it is, because the eye will be drawn down the garden past everything else. On the other hand, a focal point in a border tends to break the monotony and add interest. Another application is to draw the eye away from something else. A container filled with bright flowers will tend to make the viewer ignore an adjacent border that has finished flowering, or a sparkling water feature will keep the eye from wandering off to a neighbour's ugly garage that is visible above the hedge.

Summerhouses and gazebos make good focal points, and people are always attracted to them, even if they do not linger there for long. When such features are used as focal point, it is important that they are well designed, because they will be prominent in the garden and the subject of closer scrutiny than a similar feature tucked behind a trellis screen. A gazebo standing at the end of a broad path or at the edge of the lawn should be of higher quality than one that is hidden among trees and shrubs.

Even a humble bench can be used to draw the eye. A white-painted wooden or metal seat placed at the end of a curve in the path will attract the eye as well as providing a restful place to sit and admire the vista in the other direction. Pieces of sculpture are increasingly widely available, although the quality is variable. They are often positioned at the end of a path or lawn,

above: In a small, little-used garden, it can often be fun to create a talking point, such as this artistic sundial, offset on a circular lawn.

plants, standing by themselves, will also always draw the eye. A solitary, columnar conifer, for example, such as *Taxus baccata* 'Standishii' (golden yew), will make a fine focal point, as will a stand of the vivid red grass *Imperata cylindrica* 'Rubra'.

Plant colour can be used to achieve the opposite effect. If, instead of drawing attention to the planting, colours are chosen that merge into the distance, a border will seem to be longer than it is. Pastel shades, especially misty blues, will make the plants look further away, just as hills look further away on a misty day than on a bright, sunny day. In the same way, bright colours – reds and oranges – will seem nearer to the viewer.

but they also work well when partially hidden among foliage.

Large containers, such as urns, can be used instead of sculpture, especially if they stand on plinths, and smaller containers, filled with bright flowers, can be stood in borders and along paths to create interest for the eye.

PLANT POWER

The cheapest way of creating a focal point is with a plant, although it must be one that is distinctly different in shape, texture or colour from its neighbours, or it will simply disappear into the background. A bright yellow lily growing among the green foliage of a group of shrubs or a blue delphinium in a border of predominantly yellow flowers will always stand out. Specimen

plant profile

Meconopsis betonicifolia (Himalayan blue poppy)

The brilliant blue flowers are borne in clusters in early summer above the rosettes of blue-green leaves. This perennial, to 1.2m (4ft) tall, is hardy, but often short-lived.

plant list:

BLUE FLOWERS

- *Agapanthus* cultivars (African blue lily)
  A perennial with spiky foliage and rich blue flowers in summer.

- *Aster amellus*
  A late-flowering perennial with daisy-like flowers.

- *Campanula persicifolia*
  (peach-leaved bellflower)
  A perennial with bell-shaped flowers in summer.

- *Delphinium grandiflorum* **'Blue Butterfly'**
  A sturdy perennial with spikes of bright blue flowers in summer.

- *Eryngium alpinum*
  A small to medium-sized perennial with little daisy-like flowers in summer.

- *Felicia amelloides*
  Vivid blue, yellow-centred daisy flowers are borne in summer.

- *Veronica spicata*
  A dainty, low-growing perennial with bright blue flowers in summer.

YELLOW FLOWERS

- *Achillea* **'Coronation Gold'**
  A medium-height perennial with flat, golden flowerheads in summer.

- *Aurinia saxatilis* (gold dust)
  A low-growing, spring-flowering annual.

- *Cephalaria gigantea* (giant scabious)
  A tall, summer-flowering perennial.

- *Cestrum parqui*
  A medium-tall shrub with flowers in summer and autumn.

- *Fremontodendron californicum*
  A large, sprawling climber with golden-yellow, cup-shaped flowers.

- *Hemerocallis* **'Corky'** (daylily)
  A summer-flowering perennial with lovely flowers opening from reddish buds.

- *Lysimachia nummularia* **'Aurea'**
  A carpeting perennial with yellow foliage and summer flowers.

above: In modern gardens mirrors can simply be used for reflection, but there is no reason why they should not be ornamental features in their own right.

MIRRORS

Mirrors are the greatest illusionists of all. They may tell the truth in the bathroom but in the garden their role is to fool people into believing that the plot is bigger than it really is.

A mirror fixed to a wall will simply reflect what is in front of it, giving the appearance that it continues behind the wall. If the mirror can be clearly seen to be a mirror the illusion is ruined and the reflection is seen for what it is. If the mirror is disguised, however – by vegetation growing around the edges, for example – it may be so unexpected that the image it reflects truly appears to come from behind it, thereby making the garden appear larger.

The mirror must be positioned in such a way that it reflects something worth showing. It should also ideally be at an angle to the viewer so that they do not simply see themselves, which will ruin the illusion. Try to have a bush or shrub between the mirror and viewer, with something beyond it – that is, behind it from where the viewer is standing – that cannot be seen except in the reflection. Even if it is the same scene, the angle of the reflection will usually be sufficient to fool the eye into seeing something different. Paths or paved areas that seem to go on beyond the mirror can reinforce the illusion.

In a modern garden the presence of mirror will be unremarkable. In a more traditional scheme it would be much better to disguise it so that the viewer will be unaware that it is there and will not be expecting a reflected scene. A simple method of hiding the edges is to

points to remember:

FIXING A MIRROR

A mirror must be firmly fixed to a wall or fence. It should be made of thick glass and have a waterproof silver backing. A mirror used outdoors will not last for ever because the backing will eventually break down, but its life will be extended if water can be prevented from getting down the back. The edges can be sealed with a mastic filler, similar to the material that is used around baths, or the mirror can be fitted into a frame, which, in turn, can be screwed to a wall. Cementing it to a wall is another solution, but this creates problems in future years should it be necessary to remove it. It will also cause the mirror to crack if the wall moves or sinks. Special mirror plates, available from hardware stores, are a better option. These allow the mirror to be held against a wall without any screws showing because the bottom ones are fixed to the wall, with the mirror resting in a U-shaped channel, while at the top the channel slides downwards to hold the mirror fast.

left: The view glimpsed through the partly open door is enticing, but both it and the door have been painted onto the garden wall amid a real trellis.

below: The brick arch serves the dual purpose of holding the mirror in position and fostering the illusion that the path continues through the arch.

unchanged all year round. To give the appearance of extra space, you could have a vista down an avenue leading to a folly or a painting of a summerhouse or other structure, seen as if from a distance. The real problem is that few of us are capable of painting a convincing picture, and a successful *trompe l'oeil* is probably best left to a professional. Alternatively, you could use the grid system of enlarging illustrations to transfer a scene you have seen in a book or magazine to your garden wall.

SAFETY FIRST

Mirrors are extremely effective, but they can also be dangerous if they are broken. It is not a good idea to include them in a garden in which children play, or if it is likely that elderly and infirm people might fall against them and cut themselves. Gardeners who prefer to encourage birds to visit their gardens will not want to include mirrors among their plants for obvious reasons.

grow a climber or some other vegetation around it; alternatively, put a trellis framework or even a doorframe around it so that it appears to be an entrance to another part of the garden.

TROMPES L'OEIL

The purpose of a *trompe l'oeil* is to deceive the eye, and although it is a painting it is supposed to look as if it is real. The subject of the picture can be anything you like, such as a doorway in a wall that appears to be ajar with beds and borders beyond. If you use plants remember that most would, in reality, change with the seasons, so to be realistic you must choose plants such as evergreens that are largely

creating privacy

One of the problems of turning a small garden into an outdoor room is that, unlike an inside room, it is not enclosed. Most of us like our private lives to be private and to feel that we can act in the garden in the same way, within reason, that we can in the privacy of our home.

In a garden, however, there is little privacy. There are neighbours just over the fence, looking out of their windows, making a noise and holding barbecues, with the associated sounds and smells. There are people and cars passing by and aircraft flying overhead. A garden can be a nightmare combination of prying people, noise, smells and other pollution and not the relaxing oasis that we would like it to be. We are social animals, but we all like our privacy as much outside as inside. There is little we can do, short of moving, that will totally obliterate our neighbours' presence, but it is possible to reduce their impact to some extent.

It is important to be able to turn a garden into your own private space, an area in which you are able to relax and recharge your energies. The first step is to get rid of your neighbours, and the easiest legal way to do that is to hide them, building up your boundaries so that they simply vanish behind them. This may take time, but in the long run it will be well worth it. Once the boundaries begin to thicken up, the noise and smells will begin to diminish. You will never get rid of them completely, of course, but you will begin to make life more tolerable and your garden more of a haven.

above: A barrier does not have to be solid to provide privacy. Placing trellis along the top of a low wall makes a previously exposed corner of a town garden a secluded spot for relaxing.

EXTERNAL BARRIERS

One obvious way of coping is to erect solid walls or fences, which will certainly help to keep out prying eyes, especially if they are about 2.1m (7ft) high. If a fence already exists, try to establish whose it is before you rip it down. If it is not yours you cannot expect your neighbour to replace it unless it is unsafe, and so you may have to erect another one on your own territory. This is not usually necessary with wooden fences, but if, for example, the existing fence is no more than a few strands of wire, a solid fence will serve your needs much better. If you do erect a fence against a neighbour's, do not use their posts because they will be entitled to remove them, which would leave you with a bit of a dilemma. It is, in any case, always a good thing to consult your neighbours, or least let them know, when you erect fences, walls or hedges.

INTERNAL BOUNDARIES

Using plants rather than fences and walls to create privacy is the gardener's solution. These plants may form a hedge, but they could equally be plants set further into your garden so that they form a thick barrier of foliage between areas where you sit or entertain and the boundary. Virtually any plants will suit the latter purpose, although shrubs make a more permanent feature. Tall grasses and herbaceous plants will make a screen in summer but will be of little use in winter, when it might not matter anyway. The advantage of using herbaceous material is that it creates a constantly changing scene, unlike one that is composed entirely of shrubs.

Evergreens make a year-round barrier and are especially valuable next to noisy roads. *Taxus* spp. (yew) and *Ilex* spp. (holly) are slow-growing but eventually form a dense hedge, which will absorb sound as well as creating visual privacy.

KEEPING THINGS IN PROPORTION

Do not go to extremes and raise a high hedge of x *Cupressocyparis leylandii* (leyland cypress), or you may end up with court battles on your hands. This plant is the most widely used conifer for hedging as it grows quickly – up to 1.2m (4ft) a year. However, be warned – individual plants will grow to 35m (over 100ft) tall and more than 5m (15ft) wide. There is no need to antagonize your neighbours by making their garden unpleasant. Tall hedges not only cut out the light but are hungry and can make it impossible to garden anywhere near them. They can also overpower the house and make it dark, and the root systems can do damage to foundations. Nor should you fall into the habit of thinking that anything your neighbours can play, you can play louder. It is possible to drown noise locally by creating an alternative – for example, a tinkling waterspout will do a lot to displace more distant noises from a neighbouring garden. This will not drown out anyone who is determined to make a lot of noise, but it will make life easier in more normal situations.

above: Dense planting in a walled garden creates a green hideaway. Evergreen shrubs need only light trimming to keep them under control.

above: Even in a courtyard garden, where it may not be practicable to use plants as an overhead screen, it is still possible to construct a private, secluded seating area.

BOWERS AND ARBOURS

One way of providing privacy from overlooking neighbours can be created by constructing a framework over which climbing plants are allowed to grow. The classic Mediterranean plant for this is *Vitis* spp. (vine), which is ideal because, although the individual leaves are large, there simply are not enough of them to provide complete coverage, so the shade is dappled. You could choose varieties of vine that will produce grapes or those that are grown for their attractive foliage. There are plenty of other climbing plants to choose from, including roses and honeysuckles, which will add fragrance to your hideaway.

CONSTRUCTING A SIMPLE ARBOUR

Construct a sturdy framework of tanalized timber, sinking the bases of the posts into the ground to a depth of at least 45cm (18in). Plant one climber on three sides of the arbour, leaving the fourth open to create a space with an intimate, enclosed feeling. Alternatively, plant on one side only. This will create an arbour with a greater sense of space. A paved area within the framework will provide a firm, stable surface on which a garden bench or seat can rest.

PERGOLAS

Pergolas are generally larger and lighter than arbours, and they are usually constructed over paths and walkways. The same principle can, however, be used for making dining areas. Again,

the structure is based on posts with a 'roof' to support plants, but in this case the sides are much more open – a pergola is, in effect, a leafy roof supported on posts. Vines make excellent plants for growing over pergolas, which are perfect for filtering out the sun and also for providing a screen from neighbours who may be able to see into your garden from their upstairs windows.

AWNINGS

In areas where the sun is an infrequent but welcome visitor the need to provide privacy and shade arises infrequently, and a temporary screen might be more appropriate. There are numerous garden umbrellas and parasols available, but these often need a table or a secure hole to keep them steady and there is rarely sufficient space for a group of people to sit comfortably together beneath them.

CONSTRUCTING A SIMPLE AWNING

An awning is an attractive way of providing shade and privacy from above, which can be permanently attached to the house or garden wall and pulled out when required, or it can be hung from hooks on one side and supported on poles on the other and removed and stored when it is not in use. Cut and hem a piece of canvas or other sturdy material to the size of awning you want and add eyelets in each corner and in the centres of two opposite sides. At the appropriate height, drill and plug holes in the house

left: Overhead cover can be for effect as well as screening. A canopy of vine leaves provides a relaxing Mediterranean-style setting for a summer's evening.

wall at the same intervals as the eyelets and insert a cup hook in each. Hang the awning from these. Knock an 8cm (3in) nail in each end of two or more poles. Place the nail at one end of the pole into an eyelet in the free end of the awning. Pull the awning tight and insert the nail in the other end into the ground or into a crack between the paving slabs beneath. Tie a rope from the top nail back to a peg in the ground to form a guy rope. A more attractive finish would be achieved by sewing a pelmet around the front and side edges of the awning.

A free-standing awning away from a wall can be made with posts at each corner (and one in the middle if necessary), each of which should have two guy ropes.

Hydrangea anomala subsp. *petiolaris*

This vigorous deciduous climber produces beautiful clusters of creamy-white flowers in summer. The large, heart-shaped leaves are dark green. It will do best in moist, rich soil in semi-shade.

plant profile

plant list:

CLIMBING PLANTS

- ● ***Akebia quinata*** (chocolate vine)
  A large plant with purple flowers in spring.

- ● ***Campsis radicans*** (trumpet vine)
  A very tall climber with orange flowers in summer.

- ● ***Celastrus orbiculatus*** (bittersweet)
  This vigorous plant has small greenish flowers in summer, and these are followed by small yellow fruits, which open to reveal the red-coated seeds.

- ● ***Clematis montana***
  A large, reliable, popular plant with a profusion of pink flowers in spring to early summer.

- ● ***Cobaea scandens*** (cup-and-saucer vine)
  A large annual climber with exotic-looking purple and white flowers.

- ● ***Eccremocarpus scaber*** (glory flower)
  A medium-sized climber with tubular red flowers in summer.

- ● ***Humulus lupulus*** 'Aurea' (golden hop)
  A deciduous climber with golden-yellow foliage.

- ● ***Ipomoea tricolor*** 'Heavenly Blue'
  A fast-growing annual, this has vivid blue flowers in summer.

- ● ***Lathyrus odoratus*** (sweet pea)
  A small, annual climber with scented flowers in a range of colours.

- ● ***Lonicera periclymenum*** (honeysuckle)
  A large climber with scented, pink-yellow flowers.

- ● ***Passiflora caerulea*** (passionflower)
  Lovely blue, white and purple flowers are followed by orange fruits after a hot summer.

- ● ***Wisteria sinensis***
  A large climber with racemes of white or lilac-blue flowers in summer.

disguising essentials

A garden is a bit like a kitchen or a bathroom: it may be well decorated, but it is still a working space and there are always bound to be a number of functional bits and pieces around that are not particularly elegant or attractive to look at. When you are designing the garden, the whole of the outside space around the house must be included in the scheme, even if it is not going to be used for growing plants. You cannot leave a couple of dustbins standing on the edge of the patio and hope that no one will see them, even though you may have become so inured to their presence that you have long since ceased to notice them.

HIDING UTILITIES

Most of the items that will need to be disguised are likely to be utilitarian. Dustbins are an obvious example of this: every household has at least one, and it must be stored somewhere. Other features that you need to think about are drains, washing lines, oil tanks, garden sheds and garages. You might store bicycles or even a cement mixer near to the back door, and most households seem to accumulate odds and ends that are rarely if ever used but never seem to be thrown away. Sometimes the area in question is part of the garden that is used as a 'service' area rather than for growing plants. You may, for example, have rows of plants in pots waiting to be planted out or potted up, or there may be cuttings in frames. Alternatively, you might want to devote some space to propagating or bringing on seedlings.

above: Every house has drainpipes, but carefully positioned shelves or even purpose-built piers will support containers to hide them.

So that new garden features do not look out of place, consider your new design carefully. A garage, for example, can be designed and built in such a way that it is attractive and needs no disguise. In the same way, garden sheds and greenhouses can be made to look pleasing in their own right. Compost bins are rarely attractive, although there is no reason they should not be designed so that they fit into the overall garden design. Many gardeners, however, will not be able to afford to spend much money on a new garage or they will have inherited one from the previous owner and not be able to afford to replace it. There are, however, several ways of hiding objects from view or of transforming them into something more attractive.

Depending on the overall shape and design of your garden, one solution would be to scatter the features around the garden, disguising each in a different way, so that they are less obvious. Another approach would be to concentrate all the eyesores in a single spot and cordon off the whole area with a fence or trellis screen. You might even decide that one side of the garden needs to be fenced off and used as a storage area. Do not fence things off so effectively that there is no access. You will need to get to compost bins with your garden and household vegetable waste, and access to the shed or greenhouse should not be so convoluted that you cannot easily get the lawnmower or wheelbarrow into the main part of the garden. Not all houses are beautiful, and in extreme

TRELLIS SCREEN

Even if you have a garage or shed, you may still have garden equipment, such as a wheelbarrow or large flowerpots, that you simply cannot keep under cover. A temporary screen, which can be moved and removed as needed, can be used to hide such items from sight.

Panels of trellis screen, about 1.8m (6ft) high, are available in diamond and square patterns. Use these cut to size or make your own trellis from lightweight slats of 25 x 6mm (1 x ¼in) timber spaced about 4cm (1¾in) apart.

Make frames for each panel from 2.5 x 2.5cm (1 x 1in) timber. There is no need to mitre the

corners: butt them neatly and nail them in place. If you want to paint the trellis, do it before you fasten the individual pieces together.

For stability, use three hinges to join two panels together. Make sure that the hinges are positioned so that the panel can be folded up concertina-fashion when it is not needed.

circumstances the appearance of the garden or the effect you are trying to create might be compromised by the house itself. There may not be much that can be done, short of rebuilding the house, but it is surprising what a covering of creepers or climbers will do (see page 57 for some useful climbers). The house need not be hidden – colourful windowboxes, filled with trailing plants, can be used to draw the eye from the house itself.

above: Finding space for a compost bin can be a problem in a small garden. A sturdy trellis screen will both look neat and keep the compost together so that it breaks down quickly.

USING PLANTS

The time and effort spent disguising services and utility areas within the garden will be worth it in terms of the overall appearance of the plot. It is possible to hide all manner of objects, either by constructing a simple screen or by using plants, which are often the most natural and easiest means of concealment.

A classic method of hiding an object is to grow a climbing plant over it. A climbing plant can be trained over a fence or trellis that is erected in front of the object in question. One of the most useful plants in this respect is *Hedera* (ivy), which is available in a wide range of colour and leaf forms, is reliably hardy and is self-clinging. Garden sheds and garage walls can often be quickly hidden by a climbing plant if a trellis or network of wires is attached to it. Positions against a wall or fence are ideal for wall shrubs that might not otherwise be reliably hardy, and these can be trained to provide year-round cover and interest. Choose the shrubs in the same way you would for plants in the wider garden, taking their colour, texture and habit of growth into account.

FENCING IT OFF

A fence can be used to hide all kinds of eyesore, and a simple panel fence – inexpensive to buy and easy to erect – will totally hide them from view. Often, however, a plain panel will look as dull and unappealing as the object you are trying to hide. Covering the fence with a climber or wall shrub is

the obvious solution, but sometimes erecting two, slightly staggered panels, one slightly behind the other so that a path seems to disappear from view behind the front section will give an impression of depth as well as hiding the object. Remember to leave room for access between the two panels.

PAINTING AND DECORATING

A quick and simple way of disguising something is to paint it. An oil tank, for example, that has been painted dark green is more likely to merge with the background than one painted red or left an unattractive shade of off-white.

There is no reason why the most should not be made of a flat surface by painting it. Expanses of panel fencing can be painted blue, green or even purple if that suits your garden style. You could decorate a flat surface with something unconnected with the garden, or, if you have the skills, you could paint a view of a garden to give the impression that there is another section of the garden to explore. Some additional ideas for decorating walls and fences are given in chapter 5.

Another useful hint for diminishing the impact of an unattractive feature is

right: *Hedera* spp. (ivy) is invaluable in the garden but is often overlooked in favour of more 'glamorous' plants. Choose a variegated form to provide a year-round disguise for the roof of your shed.

above: In a cottage-style garden plants can naturally be allowed to hide potential eye-sores, especially ones like fox-gloves, which can be planted or allowed to self-sow.

to place something eye-catching nearby, so that the viewer's attention is drawn from the eyesore. A bubble fountain or small pool will draw the eye away from the neighbour's shed roof or a featureless expanse of wall.

INSPECTION COVERS

Manhole covers can be a gardener's nightmare. They are usually ugly, but they cannot be removed or permanently

covered because access might be needed to a mains service at any time. One way of coping with the problem is to disguise the metal cover by placing a container of plants on it. Do not choose something so heavy that it can never be moved. You could use a group of small containers, which can easily be moved around and replanted as necessary.

On a patio or path a better solution is to use a purpose-made 'tray' which can be filled with the hard surfacing material you have chosen – small pavers or tiles or gravel would be adequate – and placed over the cover. If necessary, the pavers or tiles in the tray can be arranged to match a pattern, or the tray can even be filled with compost for sowing grass or even low-growing plants.

When an inspection cover is in a border, it can be effectively and quickly disguised by planting a mat-growing plant, such as *Acaena* spp. (New Zealand burr), which will spread across the cover but can be easily cut back if you ever need access to the mains service beneath.

CLEARING THE DECKS

Before you spend time and money on building fences and erecting trellis screens, look at the eyesore and see if you really need it at all. Do you need a garden shed if there is room in the garage to store the lawnmower and your spade and garden fork? Are you ever likely to use the caravan or cement mixer again? Can the pile of rubbish be cleared away in a skip and never allowed to mount up again?

points to remember:

SAFETY FIRST

Sometimes the appearance of a corner of the garden is not the only reason for wanting to screen it or fence it off. If children play in the garden you might want to find a way of protecting a greenhouse or cold frame so that there is no danger that they will cut themselves on broken glass.

plant list:

WALL SHRUBS

- *Abelia* x *grandiflora*
  The dark green leaves are evergreen or semi-evergreen, and fragrant white-pink flowers are borne from midsummer to autumn.

- *Berberis* x *stenophylla*
  A vigorous evergreen plant with yellow flowers in late spring followed by blue-black fruits.

- *Ceanothus thyrsiflorus* (blueblossom)
  The glossy, mid-green leaves are evergreen, and in spring mid-blue flowers are borne on the arching branches.

- *Chaenomeles* x *superba* 'Knap Hill Scarlet'
  In early spring to summer this deciduous shrub bears large, long-lasting, bright red flowers on spiny stems.

- *Chimonanthus praecox* (wintersweet)
  Sweetly scented yellowish flowers appear in winter before the glossy, mid-green leaves.

- *Escallonia* 'Donard Seedling'
  The glossy, dark green leaves are evergreen, and pink flowers are borne in early to midsummer.

- *Fremontodendron* 'Pacific Sunset'
  The dark green leaves are evergreen, and large, orange-yellow flowers last from summer to autumn.

- *Itea ilicifolia*
  An evergreen shrub with greenish-white flowers in 'catkins' from midsummer to autumn.

- *Myrtus communis* subsp. *tarentina*
  The narrow leaves are evergreen, and the white-pink flowers, borne in late summer, are followed by white fruits.

- *Pyracantha* 'Golden Dome'
  The glossy, dark green leaves are evergreen, and the small white flowers are followed by golden-yellow berries.

4

Today's small garden is a hard-working area, which will be used for a wide variety of outdoor activities. The days when a garden was used exclusively for growing plants are long gone, and most people now want gardens that have an area that is paved in some way to provide plenty of space on which tables and chairs can be used for meals and entertaining, as well as having room for barbecues, sunbathing and children to play on.

Although most surfaces can, as long as they are not concreted down, be moved, it is a difficult and expensive job. It is important, therefore, to be certain that you get it right the first time. Take your time to plan the area. Draw the space to scale on paper and outline it on the ground with spray paint. Walk around the area and look at it from every angle, including upstairs windows, and view it in your mind's eye to check that it is right before you begin. If you are uncertain, consider a few alternative ideas before you commit yourself and, if at all possible, visit gardens where different types of surface can be seen *in situ*.

In the past, large areas were put down to grass, and there is no reason why this should not still be so. There are tough grasses that will withstand children's play and the regular passage of feet along paths, just as there are softer grasses that are aesthetically more pleasing if you like perfect lawns. The main disadvantages are that you cannot use grass in winter and it needs cutting, which means you need a lawnmower, somewhere to keep it and time to use it. These requirements place demands on a garden that may already be short of space and on a gardener who may be short of time. Nevertheless, lawns have many advantages and are still the perfect place for relaxing on a sunny day.

If you decide against grass there are plenty of other surfaces available, and although most are more expensive in the short term they are easy to maintain, do not involve owning and using a lawnmower and can be used in winter.

the garden floor

design considerations

Most gardens consist of a mixture of lawn, hard surfacing and plants in varying proportions. Deciding on how much space you devote to each will depend on your lifestyle and on the demands that will be placed on the garden by your family, but whatever their proportions, areas of lawn and hard surfaces will form the framework of the garden design, and it is only when their size and position have been determined that you can begin to add the decorative details, such as arches and pergolas, garden furniture, water features, statues and other ornaments and, of course, the plants.

PATIOS AND PATHS

Paved patios tend to look better when they are laid in symmetrical, formal designs, while wooden decking is an ideal choice for curved, flowing layouts. Decking usually has a much more relaxed, informal feel to it than paving. Wood is a material associated with outdoor living and leisure and, because it is relatively soft, it is a better surfacing material for a garden in which children will play.

While decking blends in with plants much more sympathetically than paving, paving provides a strong contrast with living material: the one is hard and solid, the other is light and full of movement. The two work well together in any garden, and there are few things more attractive than the straight edge of a patio softened by a profusion of trailing plants.

The straight edge of paving can also be used in conjunction with curved

flowerbeds and lawns within a single design. The overall effect will be one of contrast: straight and curved lines and squares and circles are important elements of all garden layouts, and combining them provides interest and movement in the garden.

From the point of view of appearance, a potentially dull-looking area of hard surface can be made more interesting and attractive by a careful choice of colours, by breaking up the floorscape (with tubs or a small water feature, for instance) and by attention to the detailed finishing, both within the surfaced area and around its margins. Paving made up of small units,

such as brick pavers, can both add character and create an illusion of space within a small garden. If the same type of brick is associated with materials also used in the house or its boundaries a pleasingly co-ordinated look will be achieved.

Paths should be used sensitively and for a reason. A path that leads nowhere will look out of place. Use curved paths in an informal design and straight ones in formal schemes. Rather than using a path to divide a garden into two equal sections, consider running it along the shadier side of the garden or curving it around shrubs so that it disappears from view.

above: One of the most versatile of all surfacing materials, decking can be shaped to fit a wide range of spaces and looks sympathetic with other materials, including concrete.

LAWNS

The ideal lawn is both ornamental and practical, and there is a great deal of scope to create an individual and interesting design based on grass. Make sure the shape of the lawn harmonizes with flowerbeds, ponds and other features, but you should avoid complex shapes with sharp angles, which not only look fussy but are also difficult to mow and edge.

Most lawns are a fairly standard shape – either rectangular or square – but in a small garden such a shape will merely reinforce the overall lines of the garden and bring the boundaries into focus. A gently curved lawn is a much better proposition, giving the gardener greater freedom to design the areas around it. A lawn flowing through a garden can be used to link up the separate parts to create a unified whole.

Grass is the ideal surface for children because it is so soft, but children and adults with sporting tastes can do serious damage to lawns. A sandpit can be a good option for very small children, but it may be better to discount grass altogether and opt for a mixture of paving and borders until the children lose interest in the garden.

If you want a lawn make sure that you choose a grass mix that will withstand heavy wear. Look out for turves or grass seed that contain a high proportion of rye grass, which is more robust than a lawn of bent or fescue. You will not have a smooth, dense 'bowling-green' lawn, but regular mowing will keep it looking attractive and even.

left: Using the same type of decking for the patio, steps and a small sitting area provides a unifying element that holds together the disparate elements of the small garden.

points to remember:

SUCCESS WITH HARD SURFACES

- *Problems such as unevenness, sinking or breaking up that are encountered once an area is in regular use are nearly always due to poor foundations or bad drainage. Tree roots are another potential source of problems. Weed growth can be both unsightly and damaging, but can be largely prevented if you prepare the ground thoroughly before laying the surface.*
- *Make sure that the hard surface is laid on a well-drained, stable base to avoid problems with sinking and waterlogging.*
- *Remove all topsoil because it contains organic matter that will decompose and settle over time.*
- *Although surfacing material can be laid on well-compacted subsoil if it will receive little wear, it is usually better to use a well-consolidated layer of hardcore covered with sand, ash or screened gravel (hoggin).*
- *Plan for effective drainage of rainwater, including under-drainage systems where appropriate.*
- *Always lay the surface with a fall of about 1 in 40 away from the house wall to prevent rainwater forming in puddles and to help keep the surface dry.*

hard landscaping materials

Of all the hard surfaces available to gardeners, paving slabs are probably the easiest to deal with, and the results are immediate. Bricks and pavers are the other most often used hard-surfacing materials, and they provide an attractive, if expensive, surface.

PAVING

If it suits your lifestyle and mood and the style of the garden, straightforward, four-square paving slabs, which are quick and easy to lay, are the obvious choice, but there are now so many variations available that you can probably devise a wholly original and interesting arrangement.

If you want to use basic slabs, consider laying them in an alternative arrangement to the conventional grid pattern. One option is simply to stagger them or turn them through 45 degrees so that they make a diagonal pattern – a simple but attractive alternative. Another possibility is to use a combination of slabs of different sizes. This needs careful planning or you will find you have too many of some slabs and not enough of another. Work out the layout to scale on squared paper before you begin.

Another simple but effective way of ringing the changes is to use coloured or textured slabs. Textured slabs now come in a range of patterns. Some are simply the uneven surface of riven stone, but others are imitations of other materials, such as stable bricks. These can be arranged in circular patterns as well as the more conventional squares. The slabs can be made more interesting

if you cast them yourself, which gives you an opportunity not only to make different shapes but also to incorporate things like shells, pebbles and other objects in the surface.

NATURAL STONE

York stone, limestone, granite and other kinds of natural stone have one major advantage over other hard-surfacing

above: Incorporating the patterns or colours that have been used indoors into the surfacing of a patio will emphasize the sense of continuity between indoors and out, and make both areas seem larger.

materials: once laid they look instantly mellow and as if they have been in place for a long time, and this could be a good selling point if your house is an old one. They are, however, extremely costly, even when bought second-hand, and they are not always readily available. If you are buying second-hand from a demolition yard, which is usually the cheapest source, you may find that the slabs vary greatly not only in size but also in thickness, and this must be taken into account when they are laid.

BRICKS AND PAVERS

Bricks are a traditional form of paving or hard surface, but, like all good materials, they transcend their age and still have the ability to look modern and stylish. This is partly because they are versatile and can be laid in a wide variety of patterns, especially if you mix colours and textures. This characteristic makes it possible for anyone who wants to do so to create an individual shape and pattern for patios and paths. Bricks tend to be slightly irregular, both in shape and colour, whereas pavers are much more regular in both respects and have a more modern look.

Both bricks and pavers can be laid on a bed of sand in the same way as paving slabs (see page 72), but for heavy use, especially if they are to be used on a drive, an underlying layer of concrete should be laid first. Hiring an impactor will help to compact the soil beneath the area to be covered as well as making sure that all the bricks or pavers are tamped down into the sand, creating a perfectly level surface.

above: Polished glass nuggets are not cheap but they are a stylish and easy way to add colour to a corner of a patio.

COBBLES

These smooth, rounded stones look attractive when they are used on a small scale – set around a tree, for example, or used to infill a small corner, where it might be difficult to cut larger paving materials. They are not suitable paving materials, however, because they are not only rather uncomfortable to stand on but also become dangerously slippery when wet. They are not a good choice for areas where you want to stand furniture because the surface is completely irregular, and tables and chairs will rock intolerably.

Cobbles do look attractive when they are used to break up a large expanse of concrete – set in a circular swirl, for instance, or arranged in a square. Granite setts can be used in the same way to provide patterns on what might otherwise be a dull expanse of paving or concrete. Bed both cobbles and setts carefully to give as flat a surface as possible.

TILES

Tiles are made of hard-fired clay and, depending on the composition of the clay and the temperature of the firing, they can be very durable. Quarry tiles are popular for paving; these are unglazed, geometric in shape (usually square or octagonal) and regular so they can be used to make formal, smooth surfaces. They are, however, difficult to cut, so should be reserved for areas with long, straight edges rather than being used for complicated curved perimeters.

A more eye-catching effect can be achieved with glazed paving tiles, which are available in different shapes and colours, often with painted motifs and designs. The more decorative tiles look best in the strong sunlight of hot climates. Glazed tiles are fragile and relatively expensive, so it is best to use them in small quantities. Fragments of tiles can always be used to make floor mosaics.

CONCRETE

Used *en masse* as a garden surfacing material, concrete is hard, durable and fairly easy to lay. Once laid, it is more or less permanent, so you may want to think twice before laying a large area. Colouring agents can help to relieve the tedium if the concreted area is fairly small and the colours are chosen with care, but a more interesting effect can be achieved by modifying the surface texture.

Alternatively, you can mark it out into mock paving squares, although if this is not done neatly it is likely to look worse than a plain surface.

Concrete can be made to look more acceptable and less harsh if the surface is brushed while it is still damp to reveal a pebble or gravel aggregate. This mellow, soft appearance is especially appropriate in the garden itself rather than on a patio.

MIXED MEDIA

Mixing different materials always produces a much more interesting surface. Paving slabs, especially stone ones (if you can afford them), work well with traditional bricks as well as with gravel or larger stones, in the form of pebbles. Patterns can be created in the surface with flat pieces of tile, or tiles or slate stood on edge.

Such decorative effects often produce a somewhat irregular surface to walk on and should therefore be used only in areas that are not much used for walking. They are, however, ideal for use as guides to indicate a path across a patio or as ornamental 'tramlines' on a path.

points to remember:

USING PREFABRICATED SLABS

Prefabricated slabs are the most commonly used hard-surfacing material in the garden. They are available in a wide variety of colours and textures, ranging from the ordinary grey slab measuring 60 x 60cm (2 x 2ft) to circular and polygonal forms. All are about 5cm (2in) thick. If you are laying a large area use two colours, checkerboard fashion, to avoid monotony, but be careful not to choose colours that do not sit happily next to each other. More expensive types are made of reconstituted stone, and some slabs have a textured finish that resembles weather-worn stone. Make sure that you choose slabs with a non-slip surface.

MAKING SLABS

If you have time it can be worth making your own paving slabs. This gives you an opportunity not only of using imaginative shapes but also of rendering or colouring the surface in a variety of ways. Pebbles, pieces of mosaic or old brick – more or less anything you wish, in fact – can be added to the surface of the concrete. If the concrete is brushed before it is fully cured – that is, while it is still soft – the aggregate (stones) will be exposed, giving the slabs an interesting finish.

changes of level

easiest simply to ignore it. On the other hand, standing on a slope or constantly walking up and down a slope can be tiring, and a whole garden on a slope seldom works visually. The solution to this is to remove the gradient and make two or more flat areas with steps between. In a small garden the upper level could be a terrace, especially if it is immediately outside the house, while the lower level becomes the lawn or flower and vegetable beds.

A more complicated approach is to remove the main slope and turn it into a series of level areas and random slopes. This makes a much less formal picture and can be quite exciting, especially if you prefer a more informal style of gardening. Yet another approach is to have a series of terraces, and this arrangement works especially well if the slope is steep, giving a series of level or gently sloping paths across the slope, each one backed by a wall or deep bed, which can be tended from a path.

TERRACING A SLOPE

When you are terracing a slope it is important to remember not to get topsoil and subsoil mixed up. The last thing you want is heavy clay sitting on top of fertile topsoil.

On a shallow slope with a reasonable depth of good soil it is possible to adjust the slopes simply by moving the soil around. If the slope is pronounced, however, hire a digger to help you move the soil around. There are small, self-drive ones that will pass down the side of a house on a relatively

above: Changes in level can be exploited to produce additional spaces for planting as well as quiet sitting areas away from the main patio.

A garden that slopes or is on different levels requires more planning and work to get the structure right, but once it is done the difference in levels can provide variety, producing a much more interesting garden than one that is completely flat. On the other hand, a level garden is much easier to work

and move about on, especially for elderly or infirm gardeners.

COPING WITH SLOPES

There are many ways of dealing with a slope, depending on the kind of space you want to create. If part of your garden is on a gentle gradient it may be

above: In an informal garden plants can be allowed to spill over the steps to soften the edges of the stone. Remember to remove all lichen from the surface of the stones in winter.

narrow path. Push all the topsoil to one side and sculpt the ground as you want it before replacing the topsoil. This can be done by hand with a spade and wheelbarrow, but it is hard work.

MOVING AROUND

When your garden is arranged on more than one level, it is necessary to have a means of moving from one area to another. It is possible to build steps, but it may also be necessary to build a ramp so that you can easily move things like wheelbarrows and lawnmowers about. Bear in mind that flights of shallow steps are not comfortable to ascend or descend. A ramp is a much better idea for such areas.

Steps must be solidly constructed. The style will largely depend on the style of the garden – formal steps will look out of place in an informal garden, for instance – and this will also dictate

your choice of material, whether it be brick, stone, concrete or wood.

MOVING WATER

A major advantage – indeed, one of the attractions – of having a sloping garden is that you can create convincing streams and waterfalls. The steeper the garden the more dramatic the water, which can descend from a 'spring' or pool at the top and fall or run to a pool or reservoir at the bottom, from which it is pumped back to the top. The stream can be lined with concrete or a pond liner, but if you use liner make sure that it is hidden or completely disguised. The edges of the stream can be densely planted with ferns and hostas, which will thrive in the moist conditions there. Their trailing leaves will hide the artificial edges of the stream and allow a natural transition into the beds and borders in the rest of the garden.

points to remember:

RETAINING WALLS

In order to create two flat areas from a slope you will need to build a retaining wall between them. The wall can be of the dry-stone type or built from brick or blocks. Unless you are skilled in this type of work, however, it may be safer to employ a professional, because retaining walls have to withstand great pressure. It is essential that proper foundations are dug and filled with concrete before the wall is erected. For walls up to 60cm (2ft) high the foundations should be 35cm (14in) deep with 15cm (6in) for concrete; for walls that are higher than this the concrete should be 25cm (10in) deep. Brick and blocks will need a mortar bonding, and weep holes should be left in the base of this to allow water to run out from behind the wall. Fill the space between the wall and the bank with a layer of rubble to aid drainage before backfilling with soil.

STEPS

In a sloping or split-level garden steps are generally needed to give access to the various parts of the garden, and they also provide a visual link between the different elements of the design.

The material you choose should blend in with the other materials used in the garden. There are many types of bricks, blocks, pavers, walling blocks and paving slabs that are suitable, and you could combine materials to great effect. Bricks and blocks can be used for both risers and treads, or you could mix textures so that faces are smooth or pitted, or you could use decorative concrete blocks that resemble split stones. Slabs are, however, suitable only for the treads, although they may be smooth-faced, riven or even geometrically patterned.

PLANNING

Sketch out the position and shape of the steps on squared paper to help you determine how they will look and how they will fit in with your existing garden plan. Even more important is to draw a side elevation of the steps, which will show how steep they will need to be. You will need this information to work out the number and depth of the steps. If the steps are too steep, they will be tiring to use, but if they are too shallow they can cause accidents through tripping. Bear in mind that risers should normally be 10–13cm (4–5in) deep, although a depth of 15–18cm (6–7in) is acceptable. Treads should never be less than 30cm (12in) from front to back so that they will take the ball of the foot

when you are descending without the back of your leg scraping on the previous step.

To work out how many steps you will need, measure the vertical height and divide the figure by the height of a single riser plus the tread. On a

above: Planks with a ridged surface are ideal for the treads. Make sure the treads are wide enough to accommodate the full length of your foot.

terraced site measure the height of the retaining wall. On a sloping site the calculation is more complicated: drive a peg into the ground at the top of the slope and a length of cane into the ground at the base of the slope. Tie a length of string between the peg and the cane and establish the horizontal with a spirit level. Measure the distance from the base of the cane to the string to give the vertical height of the slope, and divide this figure by the depth of the riser plus the tread to give the number of steps that will have to be cut into the slope.

In addition to working out the number and height of the steps, you also need to work out the width. Consider who will be using the steps. Treads that are 60cm (2ft) wide will accommodate only one person. Two people, walking side by side, will need treads at least 1.5m (5ft) wide.

CUT-IN STEPS

This type of step is used if you need to be able to negotiate a slope or bank easily. The shape of the steps is cut out of the earth itself, and a range of materials can be used for the treads and the risers. Cut-in steps may be formal, regular flights or informal and meandering.

Work out how many steps you will need to make by using a peg and a cane to measure the vertical height of the slope as above. Divide the figure by the depth of the riser plus the tread of the steps you plan to use, and this number will give the total number of steps you can fit into the area.

project: railway sleeper steps

1   2   3   4   5

MATERIALS AND EQUIPMENT

railway sleepers
wooden pegs
hammer
saw
drill
screws

6

In a small garden there will probably be only a small change in level over the entire plot, but rather than trying to level the garden take advantage of the slope to incorporate one or two steps into the design. This will create a definite break in the garden, allowing you to have two different styles. The raised area will provide an additional opportunity for growing trailing and creeping plants. Railway sleepers, which have been used here, are readily available, but make sure that you do not buy ones that have been treated with creosote, which will seep out of the wood and contaminate the surrounding soil.

1 Excavate the area, forming the outline of the risers and treads in the earth. Remember to include in the depth of each tread the width of the railway sleeper that will form the next riser. Put the excavated topsoil on a thick sheet of polythene for the time being.

2 Hammer in the posts to which the sleepers will be fixed. If your soil is soft, make sure the posts are firmly bedded in concrete. Use a line of string attached to pegs and a spirit level to check that the steps will be perfectly level.

3 Cut the sleepers to fit the width of the steps. If the steps are an extension of, say, a raised bed also created with railway sleepers, mitre the corners at the front to create strong, neat angles.

4 Screw the sleepers to the posts. It's important that the sleepers are fixed securely because the weight of the earth behind them, especially in wet weather, will be considerable.

5 Add some ballast to level the area of the tread, tamping it down firmly, then cover the surface with sand.

6 Top the area with gravel, making sure that the surface of the gravel is slightly below the top edge of the front sleeper so the gravel does not get scattered over the rest of the garden. Alternatively, if the steps will be little used, you could grow a carpeting plant such as *Thymus serpyllum* or *Chamaemelum nobile* 'Treneague' in the treads. Wood tends to get slippery over time, and for safety it is a good idea to attach chicken wire over the exposed surfaces of the sleepers used for treads and to staple it in place. It will scarcely be visible but will stop you from slipping on the algae and lichen that will inevitably grow on the wood over time.

paving

Before you can lay the paving of your choice, you should think carefully about the foundations that may be necessary. Whether you are constructing a solid footing on which to build a brick boundary wall, laying the base for a new greenhouse or planning a new path, the principles are similar.

FOUNDATIONS FOR PAVING

Paving slabs, block pavers and other paving materials must be laid on a surface that is firm, flat and stable. A base of well-compacted subsoil covered with a layer of sand about 5cm (2in) deep is sufficient for laying paving for a path that will take little wear, but for large, well-used areas or in gardens where the soil is soft, it will be necessary to have a layer of compacted hardcore (broken bricks and stones) to prevent the paving from sinking and cracking. Hardcore contains many hollows, even after it has been consolidated by a garden roller. These have to be filled by spreading a layer of sand over the surface and levelling it with the back of a garden rake, a procedure known as blinding.

Paving slabs or other small-scale pavers can be laid directly on the layer of sand, with mortar to keep them in position. Some block pavers, however, can be laid loose on the layer of prepared sand and do not require additional mortar.

Before you begin doing any excavation work of any kind check where all the service pipes and cables run so that you do not do any accidental damage.

STRIP FOUNDATIONS

Small structures, such as brick planters and masonry garden walls, must be built on strip foundations, which consist of a trench filled with a layer of hardcore topped with fresh concrete. The foundation must be wider than the wall, so that the weight of the wall is spread out at an angle of 45 degrees from its base into the foundation and on into the subsoil. In general, a foundation for a wall should be twice the width of the masonry.

The depth of the concrete foundation depends on the height and thickness of the wall and on the condition of the soil, but it should be half as deep as it is wide and project beyond the ends of the wall by half the width of the masonry. A wall over six courses of bricks high would require a trench about 40cm (16in) deep.

DRAINAGE

Patios and paths can be made wholly impassable by every shower of rain if

above: Large paving slabs emphasize the calm, cool atmosphere of a small courtyard garden. Keeping the planting to raised beds and containers around the edges creates a spacious, restful feel in the confined area.

they are not constructed so that they shed water. When you are making a paved or concreted area, build in a slight slope so that the water can run off and does not form pools. A fall of about 1 in 40 will move water quite quickly to a border or into a shallow gully, which can lead to a soakaway or drain. Construct the gully from half-round ceramic pipes bedded in cement or simply from cement that is trowelled to form a runnel.

If a hidden gully is desirable on a patio or path, lay half-round ceramic pipes down the centre of the area and slope the paving or concrete very slightly towards the gully, overlapping the edges. A gap of 1cm (½in) in the centre will allow the water to run into the channel from where it can be carried away from the patio.

PATIOS

The actual size of the patio will depend on what you intend to use it for and on the size of the garden – you do not want it to overwhelm the rest of your garden, but if you have only a small, walled yard at the back of the house it would be appropriate to extend the patio to cover the entire plot.

As a guide, a patio measuring 3.6m (12ft) square should be regarded as the absolute minimum. However, there is no reason why it should be square, however: bear in mind the shape of the garden and the house, the slope of the ground and the materials you intend to use to pave the surface. Always make a sketch plan of the garden to show the position of the

above: Coloured paving can be used to provide accents and to signal changes in level. When several materials are combined, it is important to keep to a limited palette of colours to prevent the scheme from looking busy and over-complicated.

patio in relation to the house and the position of patio doors.

Patios can be constructed from many different materials to complement the constructions of your house and blend in with the overall theme of your garden. They can be arranged in style from a simple paved square to complex arrangements on various levels, incorporating a built-in barbecue and seating and a water feature. Practically all types of paving materials are suitable for surfacing a patio – bricks,

pavers, stone or concrete slabs, setts, cobbles and gravel – but do take care in selecting a surfacing material, as you will laying a large area, and some textures or colours could be too much.

You might want to use the same materials to pave a patio as those that are used for paths elsewhere in the garden, which helps to give a unified appearance to the garden, and this is desirable, especially in a small area, where a mixture of materials can look cluttered and busy. Alternatively, you could match the materials used in the construction of the house to emphasize the idea of the patio being an additional room.

Regardless of the material you use to surface the patio, it can look very stark if the surface is unbroken by decoration. To provide visual interest in the surface consider adding sections of other materials that may be present elsewhere in the garden – areas of gravel or cobbles in a patio paved with slabs or bricks, for example, or a combination of pavers and slabs. Any patio will be made more attractive if pots of flowering plants are placed around it.

In an informal garden holes can be left in the surface of the patio into which flowers and small shrubs can be planted, or the patio can be laid up to the edge of the lawn, provided it is slightly below ground level to prevent damage to the mower blades. To soften the transition between the patio and wider garden, shrubs can be planted for form a low hedge along the garden side of the patio, or you could lay paving at the edge with increasingly wider gaps between the individual pieces and allow the lawn to grow in between so that the patio appears to blend into the lawn and vice versa.

In a more formal garden, the patio can be divided from the garden by a low wall of screen blocks or by the use of a low, narrow, raised planter of brick or walling blocks.

Another idea is to build raised planters as part of the patio, possibly linking them with a seating area or a barbecue, or you could use the main

left: When it is well laid, crazy (or random) paving provides a long-lasting, stable surface. It can also be used to face walls built of concrete blocks.

material of the patio to edge an integrated water feature.

CRAZY PAVING
Crazy paving consists of pieces of broken paving slabs laid to produce a complex, decoratively patterned surface. Despite the apparently random effect of the paving, however, the pieces must be laid according to a strict formula, both for symmetrical appearance and for strength. Although crazy paving has often been sneered at, there is a great deal to be said in its favour, provided that the broken stone of which it is constructed is natural and also that it is properly laid. The style has been given a bad name by the bits of broken concrete or synthetic paving, the stretches of concrete marked out in a random pattern and the poorly fitted

project: contemporary crazy paving

1   2   3   4

A combination of coloured tiles and crazy paving can be used to add interest to a small area near a back door or even as a small patio in a basement garden. Before you begin, remove the topsoil to a depth that will give you a level surface when you have laid not only the paving but also the foundation. If the area is not going to take heavy wear, allow for a base of ballast to a depth of 5–7.5cm (2–3in).

MATERIALS

ballast
16 square slate tiles
broken stone (York stone, porphyry, slate and so on) to fill about 1sq m (1sq yd)
sharp sand
cement
soft sand

1 The outside edging of slate should be laid on a bed of mortar made up of 2 parts sharp sand,

2 parts soft sand and 1 part cement. Gently tap the slate level, checking with a spirit level placed across both dimensions. Slate is fragile and will splinter, so work carefully. Leave overnight for the mortar to set.

2 Arrange the crazy paving pieces in the inner square, making sure they fit well together and that there are no large gaps between them. The stone is laid on a similar mortar to the slate edging.

3 Point the pieces with a mix of 3 parts sharp sand to 1 part cement and leave to dry for about an hour.

4 Brush a dry mix of sand and cement over the surface so that there are no trowel marks. Avoid walking on the paving for at least two days until the mortar is completely dry. Cracks in the mortar could cause the stone to become uneven and lift, which could be dangerous.

paving with ugly, thick mortar joints. When it is properly laid, random paving can perfectly suit the informal garden, although it often seems out of place in towns or near very modern houses.

The sides of the paved area should be formed by a row of fairly large slab pieces, which have at least one straight edge, which is placed outermost. Similar sized pieces with irregular edges are positioned along the centre of the area, while smaller, irregular pieces are used to fill in any spaces remaining between the slabs.

If you intend to use natural stone for crazy paving, bear in mind that the pieces are likely to vary considerably in thickness. Prepare the ground carefully so that the paving presents a flat, even surface. Dig out the topsoil, and if the subsoil is not firm dig this out too and replace it with 7.5–10cm (3–4in) of hardcore. Top with 5cm (2in) of sand, raked and levelled. Bed the slabs on dabs of mortar and point the joints between the slabs with mortar, taking care to bevel the mortar to allow water to drain away efficiently.

decks and decking

In many countries wooden decking is the preferred method of creating a sitting area. It is a natural extension of the idea of having a veranda running along the back of a house, but a deck can be built anywhere in the garden and does not have to be immediately adjacent to the house.

SITING THE DECK

The main advantage of a deck is that because it is made of wood it can be constructed anywhere. There is no need to level the ground and no need to disturb the surrounding garden. A deck can also be built at any height, from ground to roof level. It can jut out from a high point in the garden to create a viewing platform, or it can be positioned so that it extends over a pond so that you can sit on the edge and watch the fish. A deck also has the advantages of being permanent, so it will not wash away, does not need mowing and can be easily kept clean. At the same time, the wood is relatively soft and yielding, unlike concrete, brick and stone, and, although it will deteriorate over time, as long as good-quality, pressure-treated timber is used and it is maintained regularly, it should last for many years.

The site and size of a decking platform will depend on a number of factors. Because it is likely to be a popular surface for outdoor events, such as alfresco meals or entertaining, make the proposed area as large as you can afford in terms of space and resources. If there is an existing patio with paving slabs that have been down

above: Laying decking planks in different directions is a simple but effective way of signalling a change in level, which might otherwise be a potential danger.

for some time, this will make an excellent solid and level base for duckboard decking, which will provide a refreshing change of texture. The increase in height from the paving could be used to advantage if a small pool is to be built on one side, but check that there is sufficient clearance for any doors opening from the house if you are going to use existing paving as the base.

SHAPE

Many decks are square or rectangular because these are the easiest shapes to make. If the decking is going to fit comfortably in the overall garden design, however, it should fit the available space no matter what that might be, even if this means spending extra time and money getting it right.

Because wood comes in long planks and strips, it is easy to think of things made of it invariably being composed of straight lines. Most decking has got a straight edge, but there is no reason why it should not be cut to make curves. A series of circles, perhaps at different levels, for example, could be extremely attractive, or the edge between the deck and a shrubbery or lawn could consist of a long, sinuous line.

Because wood can be cut and shaped, holes can be made in the deck through which plants can grow. It would be possible to create a space or spaces for one or more small beds, perhaps with foliage plants or bushes growing in them, and it also means that established trees or bushes that are growing in the area that is to be covered by decking need not be cut down: simply work around them. This approach can be especially effective on steeply sloping ground, where the deck might jut out into the trees and shrubs growing below, and it could be equally effective on level ground, where the trees will provide natural shade.

helps to prevent slipping, but the surface of the ribs can be quite lethal once they are coated in green algae.

ROOFING IT OVER

While trees make a natural canopy, it is possible to build a slatted roof over the decked area, which would let in a certain amount of light but filter out the sun. It could be constructed in such a way that an awning could be pulled over it to provide additional shade when required. Another possibility would be to build a pergola over all or part of the deck and grow climbing plants over it to provide shade, colour and perhaps perfume, depending on which plants you choose. *Vitis* spp. (vine) will produce a wonderfully dappled light, which is perfect for eating under.

above: Because decking is laid on piers, it can be an excellent way of having an extended sitting area at a higher level than the garden beneath, which might be too steep to be usable.

SIZE

Decking can be made of decking tiles or decking planks, which are long lengths of timber, 3–4m (10–12ft) long and 15–20cm (6–8in) wide, and some decking timber has ribbed surfaces. The tiles are normally 45cm (18in) square and can be arranged with the timbers fixed across the frame diagonally or at right angles.

Make sure you buy pressure-treated timber with a minimum thickness of 2.5cm (1in) for the decking planks. If thinner timber is used you will have to increase the number of cross-supports under the deck to prevent the timber from warping. Several types of timber are used for decking, from the more expensive hardwoods to some very cheap softwoods. It pays to shop around for such an expensive feature, because it is not only longevity at stake but the quality of the construction. The decking surface should be kept meticulously scrubbed and free from algae. Decking with a ribbed surface

points to remember:

USING DECKING

Decking can solve problems as an alternative to paving if you are laying a patio over several different levels or a very uneven surface. If you cannot afford to deck the entire area, see if a corner of the patio could be decked. You should use hardwood or, if you must use softwood, get timber that has been thoroughly treated with preservative, and the very best-quality fastenings. Decking is quite easy to construct yourself, unless it has to be built high off the ground, when you should seek professional advice. Experiment with different patterns by arranging the planks in different designs and at different levels.

location, set in the angle between two walls that meet at right angles.

Draw a scale plan of the garden on graph paper and mark in the intended position and size of the deck. Remember to indicate access arrangements and other features that might influence the design. Draw a side elevation of the site to illustrate the way the ground slopes: the deck can be constructed on sloping ground by adjusting the length of the timber posts so that the deck surface is horizontal. Use the plans you have drawn to work out the amount of timber you will need.

Set up string lines and pegs to mark the perimeter of the proposed deck so that you can imagine the visual impact it will have on the garden and the house.

DECKS AND WATER

Decking not only introduces a large area for outdoor living as an alternative to hard paving in a patio area but is also a good choice for edging a pool. As well as being a highly ornamental surface and a sympathetic edging to water, it has many practical advantages. Because it is slightly raised above the ground, there is a moist and shaded environment underneath for amphibians, such as frogs and toads, to hibernate in winter and search for food, notably slugs and snails, in summer.

Rainwater passes through the decking timbers and is not directed to the drains as it would be with a concrete patio, which makes better use of rainfall in areas prone to drought. In addition – a factor particularly relevant

in a small garden – the space under the decking can also be a useful place to hide pipework, filters, switches and water clarifiers.

From an aesthetic viewpoint, the design of the decking edge allows the water to be overlapped by timbers, creating the impression that water passes underneath and thereby making the pool seem larger. The piers for decking can be extended into shallow water to create jetties.

BASIC DUCKBOARD

If you already have a level concrete base in place, a basic timber slatted duckboard platform can be constructed entirely from lengths of pressure-treated sawn or planed softwood measuring about 7.5 x 2.5cm (3 x 1in). Assemble the duckboard on site. It is extremely easy to build, consisting of lengths of timber, which form the bearers, spanned by timber slats.

Space lengths of timber about 75cm (30in) apart and parallel with each other. They should run in the direction of the slope. Cut slats of the same timber to span the width of the platform and place them at right angles across the bearers. Set the slats 5–10mm (¼–½in) apart, using an offcut of wood as a spacer so that the gap is constant across the length.

Lay full lengths of timber across platforms that are up to 3m (10ft) wide. For a wider platform butt-joint the lengths. Stagger the joints at each side of the platform in alternate rows so that there are no continuous break lines. Secure the slats to the bearers to

PLANNING THE STRUCTURE

Decide what you are likely to use the deck for, because this will help you determine its overall size. If you intend to dine outdoors, for example, it must be large enough for a table and chairs with space for people to pass behind when serving a meal. If the deck will be used as an area for sunbathing, space must be allowed for loungers.

When planning your decking you need to consider how it will appear when it is attached to the house wall. If it is fairly narrow – about 3m (10ft)

above: Take advantage of the fact that timber can be easily cut to shape to create curved areas that take up less room in a small garden.

wide, for example – and projects out from the wall by about 6m (20ft), it will not sit easily. A deck of this width running along the wall of the house would probably appear to be in better proportion. A squarer deck, on the other hand, is more in keeping with a corner

project: laying decking

1   2   3   4   5

A raised timber deck adjoining the house provides an ideal space for relaxing and entertaining. Drainage is not a problem, because water passes directly between the gaps between the timber, and slight variations in the surface level of the ground beneath can be easily accommodated. Steps and a handrail, a pergola and even a balustrade can be added to make an imposing structure, or the timbers can be left as a simple platform.

MATERIALS

3 x 2in (8 x 5cm) treated timber
  joists
wallplate
decking timber (boards)
bituminous felt
4 x 4in (10 x 10cm) timber posts
masonry bolts
cement
ballast

1   Attach a wallplate to support the joists along the side of the house abutting the decking. Use masonry bolts to hold the wallplate in position. The ends of the joists sit in notches in the wallplate.

2   If the ground is very uneven, the joists can be supported on posts, which themselves rest on concrete pads. The posts are cut to length so that the joists are horizontal. On a flat surface, the joists can rest directly on concrete pads, which are about 45cm (18in) square and 10cm (4in) deep and have a groove in the top in which the joists sit.

3   Protect the joists by covering the area with bituminous felt or a similar waterproof material. Cut the joists from tanalized timber about 2 x 3in (5 x 8cm). Place the joists in the wallplate and in the grooves in the concrete pads so that they are about 1m (3ft) apart.

4   Place the decking planks, which should be of 12 x 3cm (4¾ x 1¼in) timber, across the joists, making sure there is a gap of about 6mm (¼in) between each plank to allow for expansion.

5   Screw the planks to joists and then screw a timber fascia board vertically to the ends of the bearers to hide the rough edges from view. Make sure that any additional end-pieces are screwed into the joist as illustrated. Grooved decking planks are an attractive alternative to plain wood and can help to prevent slipping.

4cm (1½in) long floorboard nails, using two to each bearer position.

RAISED DECKS

Raise the deck on low brick walls or concrete piers about 30cm (1ft) high and spaced at intervals of about 1.2m (4ft) across the site. Make sure there is some form of damp-proof course (such as a bituminous felt) beneath the supports to prevent damp from rising up through the brickwork and attacking the wood. For neatness, it is a good idea to build a continuous peripheral wall too, so that

the underside of the deck is not accessible to pets and inquisitive small children. Make sure the tops of the walls are level with each other, because they provide the supports for the deck's main supporting joists. It is important that the surface of the deck remains at least 15cm (6in) below the house damp-proof course to prevent damp from penetrating the walls.

Simply rest the joists on top of the low walls or concrete piers, and construct the deck as for the basic duckboard above.

gravel

Gravel makes a relatively inexpensive and quickly laid surfacing material. Curves are much easier to form with gravel than with paving slabs, slight changes in level are readily accommodated, and the surface makes a good contrast with other materials.

USING GRAVEL

Gravel offers the advantage that it can be easily taken up and later re-laid if underground pipes or other services have to be installed at any time. Moreover, if you become bored with it, the gravel is likely to form a good base for an alternative surface. One disadvantage is that, unless it is carefully graded, the surface will be loose: pieces of gravel spilling onto an adjacent lawn could cause serious damage to a mower, and they are easy to bring into the house on the soles of the shoes. Avoid gravel spilling over by creating a firm edge, such as a kerb of bricks on edge.

Gravel is available in two main forms: crushed stone from quarries and pea gravel from gravel pits. The former is of better quality, but will be very expensive unless the stone is quarried locally. Gravel occurs in a variety of attractive natural colours, and your choice should, if possible, complement any stone used in the garden for walling or rock gardens. The alternative, washed pea gravel, comes in shades from near white to almost black. Whichever type is used, make sure that the stones are neither too large, which makes walking uncomfortable, nor too small, when the stones will stick to the

above: The stiff, needle-like leaves of *Festuca gautieri* (bearshin fescue) make dense clumps, which are an ideal contrast to the mulch of bright, glass-like gravel.

soles of your shoes. For most purposes the best size is in the range 10–20mm (½–¾in) in diameter. Check that the gravel stones are all one grade as mixture tends to settle into layers and looks less effective.

The main advantage of gravel is that it is good at suppressing weeds. The only maintenance it should need is an occasional raking over to keep it looking trim and to remove any bumps or indentations in the surface.

In addition to the traditional grey and cream-coloured gravels, decorative stones, in metallic shades of blue, green, grey and even pink, are available. Nowadays it is also possible to buy coloured glass 'gravel', which can be blue, green or brownish-orange as well as translucent. Coloured gravel is especially effective when it is used around water features or as a mulch for spiky grasses and sedges: try the small blue fescue *Festuca glauca* 'Elijah Blue' with translucent or blue gravel or the stately *Pennisetum setaceum* 'Burgundy Giant' with amber-coloured glass chippings.

left: Herbs, such as lavender and thyme, which originate in Mediterranean countries, will thrive in a bed covered with a mulch of river shingle, which will act as a weed suppressant and help to conserve moisture in the ground.

below: Gravel is a perfect surface on which to stand containers. Water can easily drain through the container, and, when the containers are moved, the gravel can be raked to remove all signs of their previous position.

GRAVEL PATHS

Gravel can be a very useful material for paths in many styles of gardens, and it is easy to lay and maintain. It is important to provide some form of positive edging, such as bricks laid on edge or concrete kerb stones bedded in sand or concrete or even stout, preservative-treated boards, secured by stakes. The gravel can be laid on compacted earth or it can be laid on sheets of perforated horticultural polythene, which will prevent weeds from coming through. You will have to top up the level from time to time, no matter how carefully you edge the path, and gravel always looks better if it is raked occasionally.

points to remember:

CHIPPED BARK

Chipped or shredded bark or wood chippings are a popular material for creating visually and physically soft surfaces. Its somewhat unruly appearance makes it unsuitable for formal areas, and, because of its natural affinity with wood, it is generally used in wilder parts of the garden. Bark is particularly suitable for woodland areas, where its colour and texture blend in well with trees. Bark is a good choice for areas where children play because it is relatively soft. Heavier pieces of bark are better than composted bark, which is more like peat in consistency and can be more difficult to control.

lawns

A well-maintained lawn will enhance the appearance of any garden, but it is no use pretending that a lawn is anything but hard work. Getting a good lawn in the first place involves careful preparation of the ground, and throughout the year the lawn needs feeding, scarifying, aerating, weeding and, in dry weather, watering. In addition, of course, in the growing season grass has to be cut regularly – two or three times a week for a good lawn – and then edged to give a neat finish. Surprisingly, most gardeners think that the effort is worthwhile.

PREPARING THE SITE

Ideally, a lawn should be positioned where it will be open to the sky, with no large overhanging trees. If that is not possible, the area should not be shaded for more than half the day in summer. The soil should be reasonably well drained. If your soil is waterlogged and you hanker after a first-class lawn, you will have to introduce some form of drainage system.

If you are going to sow grass seed by hand, use string and stakes to mark out the lawn in strips about 1m (3ft) wide. If the soil is very fertile and has been weeded once or twice beforehand, allow 15g of seed per 0.8 sq m (½oz per sq yd). If the soil is less fertile and has not been weeded before sowing, double the quantity. Nothing need be done until the seedlings are well grown if the soil is moist, but if the surface dries out before germination use a fine spray or lawn sprinkler.

above: No matter how well designed your garden is, if you plan to have a large area of grass it will look jaded if it is not properly watered during the drier seasons.

USING FERTILIZERS

Lawns have to be fed to keep them growing well. Towards the end of spring apply about 100g per 0.8m sq m (2oz per sq yd). In autumn lay a special lawn dressing appropriate for the season – make sure it is low in nitrogen in relation to potash and phosphoric acid so that you do not encourage lush growth. While you are doing this, also lay a fine top-dressing of peat over the lawn at a rate of about 100g per 0.8 sq m (4oz per sq yd) and then brush this into the ground.

WATERING

Watering the grass in dry weather is essential to prevent the lawn from turning yellow and then brown. If the lawn is closely mown it will also need to be watered more frequently because the soil is more exposed to the hot sun. Apply water gradually in sufficient amounts to soak about 2.5cm (1in) into the soil. If it is applied too quickly the water will cake the surface and run off. Fine sprinklers are better than harsh jets as they give an even distribution.

SCARIFYING AND AERATING

Raking the lawn is important because it removes debris and moss, scatters wormcasts and works fertilizers and top-dressings into the ground. Gather up the moss as you go so that you do

project: laying turf

1   2   3   4   5

You should measure out the quantity of turf beforehand, but remember to buy a little more than is required for off-cuts. Turves are usually sold by the yard.

Turf can be laid at any time between autumn and spring, although it should not be laid when the soil is waterlogged or frozen. Make sure you buy them from a reliable source: some suppliers simply skim turf from meadows and numerous weeds may appear. You should also specify the type of grass you want: hard-wearing utility grass for a family with children, for example, or a finer fescue if the appearance is important. Measure the area to be grassed and buy rather more than you will need to allow for curves or awkward corners. The area in this project is defined by a mowing edge of bricks, but if you are turfing an area in the wider garden mark the edges with string, spray paint or your garden hose.

MATERIALS AND EQUIPMENT

turves from a reputable supplier
plank
breadknife or half-moon edging tool

1   The best soil for lawns is a well-drained, fertile loam, 20cm (8in) or more deep. Dig over the site and remove all stones and perennial weeds. A few days before you lay the turves apply a dressing of fertilizer to the ground unless the soil is already rich. Rake in the fertilizer and incorporate it thoroughly into the soil.

2   Make sure the site is level by stretching string or garden twine between pegs. Add or remove soil to level the ground, then tread over it to tamp down the soil. Level the surface with the back of a garden rake.

3   Lay the turves in straight lines, making sure that each turf is close to the preceding one and allowing a 2.5cm (1in) overlap at the edge. If necessary, stagger the rows by laying half turves. Lay the turves so that they are above the level of the mowing edge so that the blade of the lawnmower is not damaged.

4   Do not walk on newly laid turf. Lay down planks to stand on to help spread your weight evenly as you work.

5   When you have finished laying the turves, trim the edges with a breadknife or half-moon edging tool to give a neat, sharply defined edge. Water regularly in dry weather until the grass is growing strongly. If possible, do not walk on the grass for about two weeks after laying.

not scatter it from one area to another. Using a spring-tine rake, first work in one direction and then at right angles so that all the area is covered. This should be done about once every two weeks from spring until late summer. Thoroughly rake again before applying the autumn fertilizer. Aerating the lawn will promote healthy growth. The

easiest way is to spike it with an ordinary garden fork, pushing the tines in to at least 7.5cm (3in) and levering the fork backwards on the handle so that the turf is raised slightly repeat the process every 15cm (6in) or so over the lawn. Aeration is usually done in early autumn, although it can be performed whenever needed.

WEEDING

Although regular mowing will keep annual weeds under control, special lawn weedkillers can be applied in spring and early summer, a few days after the fertilizer has been applied. For persistent coarse weeds you may have to repeat the application every two or three weeks.

MOWING

Mowing a lawn keeps the grass short enough to be neat and attractive without hindering its growth. If you mow too close you will weaken the grass and allow moss and lawn weeds to become established. On the other hand, if you allow the grass to grow too long, coarser grasses become increasingly dominant, and finer grasses deteriorate. The best approach is to mow regularly but not too closely.

Increase or decrease the frequency of mowing according to the rate of growth, which varies from season to season and which may be affected by the weather, feeding, irrigation, the varieties of grass being grown and the general health of the turf itself.

Different types of lawn require a different frequency of mowing. Fine lawns, for example, should be mown every two or three days, while average lawns should be cut every five days and other turf should be cut at least once a week.

If your mower has a grass box it will automatically collect the mowings. Otherwise, use a spring-tine rake to collect up the clippings for composting. Leave the mowing on the lawn only if the weather is especially hot and dry, when it can be a good idea to leave them in place because they will act as a mulch and help to conserve moisture in the ground.

EDGING

Trim the grass growing horizontally over the edge of the lawn using a mechanical edge trimmer or a pair of long-handled shears. Cut the edge of the lawn with a half-moon edging tool or a sharp spade.

above left: The mat-forming *Thymus serpyllum* var. *coccineus* is a mass of pinkish-red flowers in summer and is a wonderfully fragrant and decorative alternative to grass. Thyme can take very light wear.

above: A striking cover for an area that will not be walked on can be created from a checkerboard effect of blue glass chippings and low-growing, spreading *Soleirolia soleirolii* (baby's tears). The cultivar 'Variegata' has silver leaves.

above: One of the best known non-grass plants is the non-flowering form of camomile, *Chamaemelum nobile* 'Treneague', which has aromatic foliage that can be clipped back to keep the plants dense and neat.

When you are planting close to a lawn, it is useful to lay a line of flagstones or something similar between the flower borders and the lawn, or to leave a channel about 5cm (2in) wide and 7.5cm (3in) deep, so that the verges of the lawn can be trimmed easily. Paths that abut lawns should be laid so that they are 1–2cm (about ½in) below the level of the lawn so that the lawnmower can be used over the edge. Leave a channel between the lawn and path.

RENOVATING NEGLECTED LAWNS

The first task is to cut the grass with the lawnmower blade set as high as possible. A rotary mower is best for long, straggly grass, and if the grass is very overgrown a scythe or auto-scythe will be needed. Work over the area with a wire spring-tine rake to remove the dead grass, thatch and moss. Add a proprietary lawn fertilizer in late winter and water if needed. If there are any broad-leaved weeds, dig them out by hand. Apply lawn weedkiller immediately after raking. Some bare patches may appear after you have weeded and used weedkiller. If this is the case, loosen any compacted soil, rake it smooth and either insert turf or sow some seeds. Once an abandoned lawn has been carefully tended, it should be back to a healthy normal state after one growing season.

points to remember:

ACHIEVING 'BOWLING-GREEN' LAWNS

Getting and keeping a good-quality lawn takes time and effort, and regular mowing is an important part of the process.
- *Always plan the direction of mowing to minimize overlapping, reversing and abrupt changes of direction.*
- *Mow in dry weather, because wet mowing will clog the machine and grass box and make the job take longer.*
- *Scatter wormcasts before mowing.*
- *During the colder months do not mow when cold winds are blowing because the leaf tips may be scorched by the wind.*
- *Rake before mowing if the grass contains weeds.*
- *Repeated backward and forward movements result in uneven cutting.*
- *Always mow at right angles to the line of the previous mow as this helps to control weed grasses.*

NON-MOW GRASS

If a low-maintenance surface is a high priority for you, it might be worth considering artificial grass. This is not the kind of thing you see on greengrocers' stalls but the material that is used for all-weather sports surfaces. This can be laid over an existing terrace, although a smooth surface with no cracks is really needed.

5

In a small garden you are never far from the boundaries, which therefore play a much more significant role than they do in larger areas. Because they are so prominent they need attention, either to make them disappear into the background or to make a positive, interesting feature of them.

In the past fences and walls were erected to keep out other people's animals and to keep in your own livestock. A boundary was also a way of marking the edge of your territory. It is still true that boundaries are used to restrain animals, but now it is pets rather than farm animals that we try to keep in or out of our gardens. Boundaries have other functions, too. Keeping out unwanted people has become important, particularly in the search for privacy and security. Tall boundaries keep out prying neighbours and help to deflect sounds and smells, such as from traffic and other people's barbecues.

Boundaries can be ugly, and they can intrude into the garden. One way of coping with this is to disguise them. Using climbing plants is one solution, especially if you use something evergreen, such as ivy. This can, eventually, look rather boring, but the expanse of green can be enlivened by growing flowering plants, such as honeysuckle and clematis, through it to relieve it at different times of year. Another solution is to paint the boundary, either so that it retires into the background – by painting it green, for example – or by making it more noticeable by using bright colours.

Not all gardeners are fortunate enough to have solid walls and fences, even ugly ones, marking their boundaries. They may have to start from scratch, either because there is nothing at all or because what is there is falling down and needs replacing.

walls, hedges and fences

walls

Walls and fences always sound desirable objects to have in a garden, but they often turn out to be pretty boring and have few redeeming features, apart from their ability to keep out the neighbours. A little judicious use of paint will, however, give them a new lease of life. There may well also be functional reasons for painting a wall. Many small gardens, for example, tend to be shady and dark, sometimes even too dark to grow plants or ever to look attractive. Painting the walls white or another pale colour will help to reflect the available light into the space.

USING VERTICAL SPACES

In small gardens every scrap of space should be used to the best advantage, and so, although you can disguise walls and fences, it does seem a shame to waste them. A lot can be done to enliven them and either make them a feature in their own right or use them as the starting point for something more interesting. *Trompes l'oeil*, for example, can be painted on walls to make a garden seem larger than it actually is or just to provide visual interest. The surfaces can be hung with a variety of objects, plaques and plant containers. At one extreme there might be a bright mosaic, including glittering pieces of mirror, and at the other a series of windowboxes filled with bright red geraniums to create the effect you want to achieve.

If you are interested in growing plants but have only a limited amount of space, vertical surfaces become

above: A brightly painted wall can be a good foil for white-flowered plants and for foliage plants and grasses. The theme can be continued with gravel.

particularly important. There is a wide range of climbers and wall shrubs that will happily take advantage of a wall: some will climb to the eaves, while others are suitable for growing under windows or over low walls. Climbers with fragrant flowers, such as some roses, *Lonicera* spp. (honeysuckle) and jasmine, are good plants for growing up a house wall, and they should be sited so that the fragrance wafts in through the open windows.

If you are simply using the plants to cover an ugly wall or building, foliage plants are likely to be the best choice, as these have a denser covering power than those grown for their flowers. Evergreen plants, such as *Hedera* spp. (ivy), give the best year-round cover. On the other hand, although they lose their leaves in autumn, many deciduous climbers, such as *Parthenocissus quinquefolia* (Virginia creeper), form a dense pattern of branches and shoots, which is sufficient to provide interest in winter, and the autumn colour can be breathtaking.

CREATING A BACKGROUND

In gardens where plants are the most important features, walls and fences tend to be simply either a background to, or a support for, plants. A well-built brick wall is perfect in its own right for this, but if the wall is constructed from unattractive bricks or from concrete blocks it can detract from the plants. One way to deal with this is to paint the surface dark green. This will allow it to merge with the foliage and be far less conspicuous. Shades of blue-green

project: painting dull walls

1   **2**

are popular, and although they stand out more than plain green they can still be sympathetic tones to use with a range of plants.

BRIGHTENING UP THE LANDSCAPE

Plants may not be the dominant feature, either in the garden as a whole or in the vicinity of the wall. If this is the case, the wall can be treated in such a way that it becomes a positive feature. Depending on the mood you want to create, you can use soft or bright colours. It can be painted all one colour or it can be several, possibly in bands or some other pattern. Colour can be used to pick out specific areas – for example, the wall might be mostly red, but a green area could be used behind pots containing red geraniums.

Exterior paintwork is exposed to the weather and therefore must be repainted regularly to keep it in good condition. Garden walls and fences are, however, usually painted for decorative effect rather than to protect them, and so it does not matter if the paint becomes a little chipped or flaked. Indeed, this may be desirable, and the wall can be painted in such a manner that it looks as if it has not been painted for years. This intentional distressed look can bring age and character to a setting.

PUTTING ON THE PAINT

The type of paint you will use depends on the effect you want to achieve. For a long-lasting cover you should use an exterior wall paint that contains sand

to make it hard-wearing and weatherproof. This is rather conventional, however, and exterior paints are available in only a fairly limited range of colours. For more decorative effects, therefore, you should consider using ordinary

household paints. Emulsion paints will not wear well in the open, although they are perfect if you want the weathered look. Oil-based gloss paints will last much longer but will need to be regularly repainted if you want to keep the wall looking pristine.

MATERIALS AND EQUIPMENT

wire brush
exterior filler
sealant
water-based emulsion or primer
oil-based gloss paint

Although ordinary household paintbrushes can be used on brick, a special masonry brush for applying paint to stone and brickwork will make it easier to get into all the pores and crevices. As with any painting job, for best results the first task is to prepare the surface.

1 Thoroughly clean the wall. Brickwork can be brushed down with a wire brush. Unless you really want a perfect finish it is unlikely that you will need to fill any gaps, but, if you do, make sure you use an exterior filler that will withstand the weather.

If the surface is dusty or flaky it should be sealed with a sealant designed for outdoor use before painting. The sealant will also prevent the wall from absorbing the paint like a sponge and therefore help to make the paint go further.

2 Paint on a dry day and preferably one on which there is no wind so that dust and other debris does not get blown against the still-wet paint. Emulsion paints can be applied direct to the surface, but oil-based gloss paints will need primers and undercoats to make sure the best possible adhesion is achieved.

above: A brick wall against a narrow passage can be decorated with mosaic. Use cement or exterior-quality adhesive and grout for a long-lasting and eye-catching feature.

MOSAICS FOR WALLS

Mosaics can be used to brighten up a wall as well as to provide intrinsic interest. A mosaic needs plenty of planning, imagination and a bold hand, but if you are willing to give it a try you will be rewarded with something completely personal.

The idea has been around for centuries. Mosaics were originally used mainly as floor decoration and were made up of thousands of small coloured tiles made from fired clay. These small tiles, *tesserae*, are still available from craft and specialist suppliers, and they can be used for a mosaic in the classical style. You can, however, use a much wider range of materials, and one of the best as well as one of the cheapest sources is broken pottery. Fragments of colourful ceramics are ideal for modern mosaics, and they can be used with pieces of old tiles and coloured glass. You could also include three-dimensional objects such as shells and pebbles.

CHOOSING A DESIGN

Although a mosaic can be placed against any background, it is worth making sure that the design is seen to its best advantage. Some of the brightest and most eye-catching mosaics are seen in Mediterranean countries, where the colours contrast with white-painted walls, which seem to illuminate the design. Much pottery has a shiny glaze, and when shards are used light is reflected back from the mosaic itself, usually changing as the sunlight changes throughout the day or even when it is seen from different viewpoints, an effect that can be intensified by setting the pieces at different angles. To make the most of reflected light, small pieces of mirror and glass can also be used.

Some people can create their own original designs, but if you need help decide on the style – classical, abstract or figurative – and look at examples in books and magazines. Abstract schemes are probably the easiest, especially if you select a geometric pattern, but you could decide on a swirling, freestyle arrangement. When you find a design or pattern you like, use the grid system to enlarge it and draw it on the wall.

AFFIXING A MOSAIC

The wall on which the mosaic is to be created should be sound and preferably flat, unless, of course, you want to make a three-dimensional mosaic, which can look striking on a wall. If you want to do this, sculpt the wall to the required contours before starting the mosaic. If you want a perfectly flat surface you may have to render the area before you begin. Brush the wall thoroughly to remove any loose material, then wash it to remove the dirt and traces of grease. Seal the surface with a brickwork sealant. Draw the pattern on the wall and begin to apply the mosaic, working on a small area at a time. Because the mosaic will be outside in all weathers it must be weatherproof, so use cement rather than an interior adhesive. The grouting between the pieces should also be

left: A small wall-mounted water spout can make a charming feature in an otherwise plain wall. Make sure that the pipe returning the water can be safely housed on the other side of the wall.

waterproof and should fill all gaps and crevices so that rainwater cannot get behind the design. If water does work its way between pieces, it may freeze in winter and force pieces away from the wall.

WALL DECORATIONS

A garden wall can be used as a gallery for all manner of objects, from items that you have collected over the years to those you have found and want to keep as a memento or that suddenly take your fancy. They can be as ephemeral as a dead branch or they can be a relic of the past, such as an old bicycle frame or piece of farm machinery. The objects could be related – a collection of old horticultural tools, for example, would be appropriate in a garden. The subject will depend on your own taste, but objects of this sort often look best if they appear to have been left hanging around, almost accidentally, where they are now found – as if they were last used years ago and have simply been overlooked – rather than having been only recently put on display.

Although bizarre objects can be amusing, they are not to everybody's taste. Many feel that terracotta plaques or face masks are more appropriate in a garden. There is an extremely large range of these, as well as cement, stone-substitute and lightweight, weatherproof resin versions, which are available from garden centres and other specialist outlets. Popular designs include classical motifs and lions' heads.

The word windowbox suggests that such containers should be used only on windowsills, but there is no reason why they should not be attached to a blank wall or fence. Boxes in neat rows or at staggered intervals or even placed at random, all filled with tumbling red *Pelargonium* 'Roi des Balcons Impérial' or trailing rose-pink *Petunia* Supercascade Series, will transform the ugliest of walls. As well as full-sized containers, there are a number of smaller wall-mounted planters into which you can simply place the plant in its flowerpot. Containers of this sort will need watering once, even twice, a day in summer, so unless you have a pump-action watering can make sure they are within easy reach. Remember that water will trickle from the containers and down the wall, leaving a dirty stain, so do not use them if this is going to be a problem.

points to remember:

FIXING DECORATIONS TO WALLS

Many objects can be nailed directly to walls and fences. Use masonry nails for brick, but wear protective goggles because bricks can shatter as you strike them. For other surfaces it may be necessary to drill and plug a hole before using screws or expanding bolts to make a more permanent fixture. Make sure that the object is securely fastened to the wall so that it cannot fall or be blown off. Unless you want the object to be loose so that you can take it with you when you move house, the best way of fixing masks and plaques is with cement. Make sure that you can support them while the cement sets, or you may find that the mask slides down the wall while the cement is still wet. For loose fixing, use screws or bolts.

stylish fences and simple screens

Like walls, fences have several uses in the garden, notably, of course, as a barrier around the edge of your property but also as a means of dividing sections of the garden from each other. Fences are cheaper and easier to erect than walls, creating almost instant boundaries, and there are sizes and styles to suit every type of garden.

CHOOSING A FENCE

There are many styles of fence to choose from, but it is important to select a style that is appropriate to your property and your needs. Picket fences, for example, will look more at home with older properties, whereas ranch-style fencing will be better suited to modern buildings. A tall, solid fence will afford privacy, shade and shelter from the wind, while one with a more open construction will allow light and breezes through. Screens and trellises are similar to fences but are principally used for concealing or dividing one area from another, and they can be adorned with climbing plants for a more decorative finish.

Although it is not as sturdy and long-lasting as a wall, a fence is much cheaper and quicker to erect, and it will make an ideal temporary barrier while a natural one of shrubs and trees grows to maturity. Even so, a well-built fence can be expected to last for many years, especially if it is regularly treated with wood preservative.

Traditional fences often consisted of nothing more than posts with single wires or wooden rails between them.

above: Screens, such as these woven wood panels, can be used as features in their own right. The panels are used to frame and limit the view of the small tree behind them.

These are effective for marking a boundary, but they are not much use for keeping out people or animals or for creating privacy. Introducing additional lengths of barbed wire will overcome part of the problem but is a far from attractive solution. An alternative approach is to disguise an old wire fence as a 'fedge', which is a combination of a fence and a hedge, by planting ivy along the fence so that it climbs up and covers the wire (see page 94).

Most types of fence need to be constructed piece by piece on site, and they can be tailored exactly to your needs. It is, however, possible to buy ready-made fence panels in a range of standard sizes and styles, and these speed up construction considerably, although they will not be as sturdy as a custom-built fence. In addition, the length of the fence required will rarely be the equivalent of a whole number of panels, which means that you will have to cut one to make it fit. Another type of fence that is sometimes also available in ready-made form is the picket fence, which is supplied as a kit of prefabricated parts ready to be nailed together.

FENCING MATERIALS

You can buy ready-made fencing panels and kits from garden suppliers and timber yards, and a timber yard will also supply the necessary wood if you want to make your own fence. Whatever your source, the wood you use should be tanalized – that is, it should have been pressure-treated with a preservative that acts against fungal and insect attack. Make sure that the preservative is suitable for garden use before you buy. Some wood is treated with creosote, which is not only poisonous to plants (especially when it is freshly applied) but also has a limited lifespan and has to be reapplied every two or three years, which is clearly not practicable if the fence has plants climbing over it. If you are applying wood preservative, look out for solvent-based products, which are longer lasting than creosote and can be painted over. For safety's sake never burn scraps of pressure-treated timber, and wear a mask when you are cutting wood so that you do not inhale the dust, which may be toxic.

If you are using untreated timber, make sure that the posts are allowed to stand in preservative for a few days so that the ends are well protected. The rest of the wood can be treated by brush or spray once it has been erected. Knots in wood can be a problem, especially if resin oozes out, which can make painting the wood later on difficult. Apply a special knotting compound, shellac, to the wood. Occasionally, dry knots simply fall out of the wood, leaving a hole in the timber, so do check all wood carefully before use.

When you buy nails and other fittings for fencing work always make sure that they are galvanized, which will prevent them from rusting.

FENCE POSTS AND FENCE SPIKES

Fences must be supported on stout posts, and if these are of wood they should be at least 7.5cm (3in) square for low fences and about 10cm (4in) square for taller ones. Precast concrete posts are also available, some with slots to accept ready-made fence panels, and both these types should be set into the ground by at least 60cm (2ft). Alternatively, use fence spikes to support the posts. The spikes, which are made of galvanized metal, have a square collar at the top into which the post fits. They are available in a range of sizes to suit different heights of fence and size of post. For a fence that will be over about 1.2m (4ft) high you should use a spike that is at least 75cm (30in) long, and for higher structures you will need correspondingly longer spikes.

If you choose fence posts, dig a hole and prop the post in it on a brick, using temporarily pinned-on braces to hold it steady. Make sure that the post is vertical, checking each side in turn with a spirit level. Ram hardcore into the hole around the propped-up post to support it firmly. Stop the hardcore about 15cm (6in) below ground level. Trowel in freshly made concrete around the post and compact it to dispel air bubbles. Shape the mound so that rainwater will run off quickly.

Metal fence spikes are much easier to use. Drive the spike into the ground at the appropriate place, using a sledgehammer and an offcut of wood fitted into the collar. Some types of spike are supplied with fixing accessories into which the offcut is fitted. Check that the spike is vertical as you work and continue to drive it into the ground until the base of the collar is level with the ground. Insert the post into the collar of the spike and tighten the integral bolts to hold it firmly.

left: The painted posts and frame of the waterfall are a surprising, but not unsympathetic, backdrop for hostas. Repeating the posts elsewhere in the garden provides height and rhythm.

PANEL FENCES

In small town gardens wooden panel fences are widely used; they are economical and easy to erect, and they are a reliable means of creating a solid barrier. There are several styles to choose from, and they vary in cost. The cheaper styles often look cheap and do not last long. Interwoven or basketweave panels are a popular choice, which are made from thin slats of pine or larch about 7.5cm (3in) wide and woven horizontally around vertical slats. The finished panel is usually framed by softwood battens. The panels are usually 1.8m (6ft) wide and are available in a range of heights between 0.6 and 1.8m (2–6ft).

The panels are simply nailed between the posts. It is sensible to erect the first post (see page 93), offer the panel to it and then erect the second post, and to continue working in that way along the desired line. Prop

left: Rather than covering a trellis with plants, paint it the same colour as other elements in the garden, such as a wooden bench, and transform it into an attractive feature.

each panel on bricks or off-cuts of wood so that it is level before driving the nails home. You can prevent the panel edging from splitting by drilling pilot holes for the nails first. You can also buy U-shaped brackets that are nailed to the posts. These allow the panels to be dropped into place and then secured with nails driven through the brackets. If concrete posts are used, the panels simply slot in from the top.

Most ready-made panels are held together by short, thin nails or even staples, so if a panel has to be shortened it is a relatively simple task to prise off the edging, cut the panel to length with a hand or power saw and nail the edging back on.

Finish the fence by capping the post tops to protect the endgrain. You

points to remember:

MAKING A FEDGE

A fedge is a cross between a fence and hedge. It takes up less space than a hedge (so is useful where space is limited), is less greedy and is easy to create and maintain. First, erect a wire fence using chain-link or wire-netting. Knock posts into the ground at intervals of about 1.8m (6ft). Stretch a length of galvanized wire between the tops of the posts, another halfway down and a third just above the ground. Attach wire-netting to the main wires. Plant ivies 60cm (2ft) apart along the fence and allow them to scramble up, over the wire. The ivy will eventually cover the structure completely, creating a narrow hedge. Trim it back each spring, as you would a normal hedge. Among the ivies that can be used are the large-leaved, vigorous forms such as Hedera colchica 'Dentata Variegata' and H. colchica 'Sulphur Heart', H. canariensis 'Gloire de Marengo', which has white-cream variegation, and H. helix 'Angularis Aurea' which has white-cream variegation, and H. helix 'Manda's Crested' with large, curled leaves.

above: When a screen is used to disguise an unattractive part of the garden, painting it a bright colour will distract attention from the eyesore.

can get specially made caps, which are square pieces of bevelled wood that overhang the sides of the post so that rainwater can run off. Alternatively, cut the post tops at an angle so that rainwater will be dispersed.

With tailor-made fencing, horizontal supporting rails are usually added at the same time as the posts are erected. Know as arris or split rails, these are triangular in section so that water will run off, and their ends fit into slots cut in the posts. The upright palings or boards are then nailed to the faces of the rails.

With vertical close-boarded fences it is customary to fit a gravel board (a length of timber) between each pair of posts at ground level to protect the cladding from rising damp and from rotting through contact with the ground.

It should be nailed to two short pieces of wooden batten nailed to the posts. When horizontal close-boarded fencing is being erected, or if some form of post-and-rail arrangement is used, the board or rails can be nailed directly to the posts.

Adding trellis to the top of a fence is a simple and effective way of increasing its height. If you are erecting a new fence, take the additional height into account when you are calculating the dimensions of the posts. If you want to add trellis to an existing fence, you will have to attach vertical battens

to the inner faces of the existing fence posts to provide a stable support for the additional height and weight.

PICKET FENCING

Picket fences have a particular charm, and they are especially suitable in a small garden. Although ready-assembled picket panels are available, you may prefer to make the fence up from scratch so that you can vary the design to suit your own preferences and the style of your garden. The pickets (pales) are normally spaced between 3.5 and 5cm (1½–2in) apart, but you may want to fit an arrangement of alternating long and short pales to give a curving or zigzagging top to the finished fence.

Assemble the picket fence on a flat surface by laying out the horizontal rails and securing the pales over them. Use a spacer to make sure that the pales are evenly spaced. Nail the picket panels to the fence posts, driving in two nails to the horizontal rails at top and bottom. Make sure that the rails are horizontal by checking with a spirit level. If you have to turn a corner, use a corner post and nail the horizontal rails of the two lengths of fencing to the post at right angles.

The tops of individual pickets or pales can be shaped in various ways to give a more decorative finish. The simplest designs are square, pointed or rounded, but more complex ones include intricately carved Gothic and ornate Queen Anne styles. The slats are often painted white, but they can be left a natural colour or painted an attractive soft blue-green.

above: Bamboo screening is sold in rolls and is light enough to be nailed directly to a trellis. The gaps between the canes allow light to filter through, ideal for woodland plants.

NATURAL SCREENS

One way of getting something more individual is to make your own screens, and there are several ways of doing this, some having a more obviously do-it-yourself look than others. Bamboo fences provide a sympathetic backdrop in a small garden, and the simplest way to create a screen is to nail a roll of bamboo matting over an existing fence. It is best if only the framework of the fence is used, so that light can filter between the individual canes, but the bamboo can be used over a solid fence to disguise it as long as none of the original fence is visible. In addition to rolls of split and whole bamboos, peeled reed, coppiced willow and heather screens are now widely available, the individual strips held together with plastic-coated or galvanized wire. The rolls, to 5m (about 16ft) long, are available in heights of 1m (3ft) and 1.5m (5ft).

Larger bamboo canes can be nailed individually to wooden rails held between posts. The canes can vary in thickness to provide interest, and they can be placed in a regular pattern or at random. The height can also be varied.

In rural gardens it might be appropriate to introduce a touch of the countryside by using traditional hurdles of the kind that were once made for enclosing sheep and cattle. These panels, which are made of woven hazel or willow, are highly decorative. The craft of hurdle-making is being increasingly revived for the garden market, and more and more individual designs are becoming available. Some of the open-weave panels are attractive

points to remember:

WILLOW HEDGES

If you can get hold of freshly cut wands of Salix spp. (willow) use them as hardwood cuttings and plant them straight into the ground between late autumn and early spring. An alternative, but more expensive, option is to buy individual willow plants and reduce each one to four stems. Place four cuttings next to each other in a line, spacing them about 20cm (8in) apart and arranging them so that two slope one way and two the other. Weave each pair into and out of other pairs to create an open diamond pattern. Cut off the tops at the required height and weave several extra wands horizontally along the top to hold it all together. The wands will take root, and sideshoots and leaves will appear. Once a year, in spring, remove all sideshoots. The wands will eventually graft themselves together to create a strong, living hurdle, and as long as the sideshoots are removed each year it will retain its appearance without turning into a bulky hedge.

project: trellis

1

2

and suitable for internal screens, although they are not practical for external boundaries, and they are ideal in informal and wildlife gardens. The hurdles are about 1.8m (6ft) wide and are 1–1.5m (3–5ft) high. Willow is non-durable, and if they are left untreated the hurdles will last for only 5–10 years.

SCREENS AND TRELLIS

Although sitting in the sun can be pleasant, there are times when a little shade is welcome. Some plants do not appreciate being in the sun all day, either, and several plants do best in complete shade. If your garden does not have any naturally shady areas it is a good idea to create some, and an easy way is to erect some form of screen that will allow sunlight to filter through but create enough shade to provide comfortable conditions for both people and plants. Normally, screens are erected as part of a pergola or a similar structure bordering a patio and are fixed between the supporting uprights. There is, however, no reason why they should not be constructed as a form of fence between normal fence posts. Just as a garden without shade can be uncomfortable, an entirely flat garden can be boring, but again, screens of some kind can be erected to create a vertical element that will break up the garden.

A popular and readily available screen is the trellis, a latticework of narrow wooden or, less often, plastic slats that form open squares, diamonds, rectangles and so on or are even arranged in a herringbone

pattern. Trellising is a gift for the gardener. It is an ideal barrier between different parts of the garden as it effectively blocks off one part of the garden from another but allows tantalizing glimpses of what lies beyond, and it can be clothed to

greater and lesser degrees by plants to give more or less shade or more or less seclusion. In addition to its value as a support for plants, trellis can be added to the tops of fences, fixed to walls (as above) or used to build pillars for ornamental arches.

Ready-made trellis panels are widely available from DIY stores and builder's merchants, but they are not difficult to make, and if you have a small or oddly shaped area it will be more cost-effective to make your own. The softwood slats are simply nailed to the framework, which can be made to any dimensions you wish. The arch formed here is used to frame a display of containers, and it has been fixed to the wall on battens, which hold the trellis slightly away from the wall.

MATERIALS AND EQUIPMENT

softwood timber for slats, 25 x 6mm (1 x ¼in)
softwood timber for frame, 25 x 25mm (1 x 1in)
plywood
saw
hammer
panel pins
woodworking adhesive (optional)

1 Cut the appropriate number of slats to the required lengths and paint them. The shape of the arch is made from a strip of plywood. Paint this and the wood that will form the outer frame. Leave all pieces overnight for the paint to dry.

2 Nail the horizontal and vertical slats to the framework, using an offcut of timber to make sure that the pieces are parallel and evenly spaced. Woodworking adhesive can be used if wished to give extra security to the joints. Use 25mm (1in) nails to secure the curved strip in place.

hedges

Hedges have both a functional and an aesthetic role in a garden. In the Middle Ages they were solely used to keep out wandering animals and people, while miniature box hedges were later used to create neat, raised edges to borders. Today many of the hedges planted along the perimeters of gardens still have a defensive nature, but there are also informal hedges, some abounding in flowers, others with attractive leaves. Internal hedges, perhaps separating one part of a garden from another or just acting as a decorative feature along a path, are also popular – *Lavandula* spp. (lavender), for example, will make an attractive and scented internal hedge.

CHOOSING A STYLE

The range of hedges is wide, but those with a formal outline are usually grown for their foliage, and informal types with irregular shapes are planted for their beautiful leaves or flowers. Some hedging and screening plants are evergreen conifers; others are shrubs and may be deciduous or evergreen. For many years the all-green or golden-leaved *Ligustrum* spp. (privet) was the most widely planted hedge. Although privet still has a role in gardens, there are many other hedging plants to consider. Evergreen shrubs and conifers with attractive foliage are still the most popular plants for hedges, although increasingly flowering shrubs are being employed. Part of this change of allegiance from the use of privet has been the trend away from 'boxed-off' front gardens to open-plan designs. If a defensive or view-blocking hedge is not

left: A hedge need not be a purely functional barrier. Blocks of dramatic architectural hedge make the boundary itself the main feature in this formal garden.

above: The slow-growing *Buxus sempervirens* 'Suffruticosa' (box) is the traditional edging for herb and knot gardens. It can be clipped back hard and will maintain a neat, dense shape.

needed, a front garden with a width of 9m (30ft) can save up to 8.5sq m (90sq ft) of space. This is because an overgrown privet hedge can easily form a barrier about 1m (3ft) thick. Such hedges also impoverish the soil around them. Nevertheless, alongside roads and in cold, wind-exposed areas they are invaluable for deadening noise and giving protection against wind. In exposed areas, evergreen hedges are frequently the first features to be established in gardens. Many shrubs and conifers can be encouraged to form hedges, either as a boundary alongside a road or to divide one part of a garden from another – or even as a decorative feature, such as in a knot garden, where dwarf hedges line paths and beds of herbs or flowers. Evergreen, semi-evergreen and deciduous plants can all be used. Formal hedges have clean, crisp outlines, and they are invariably formed of evergreen conifers, small-leaved evergreen shrubs or deciduous shrubs, such as *Fagus sylvatica* (beech), *Carpinus betulus* (hornbeam) and *Crataegus monogyna* (hawthorn), which can all be clipped.

FLOWERING HEDGES

There are flowering hedges for boundaries as well as decorative internal ones. For many years *Crataegus monogyna* (hawthorn) was used to create hedges in rural areas, where its thorns prevented the entry of animals and its white, heavily scented flowers provided a welcome display in late spring and early summer. It still has its uses, but in urban gardens the evergreen and winter-flowering *Viburnum tinus* (laurustinus) creates an attractive feature from late autumn to late spring or early summer. In areas with a mild climate *Hibiscus rosa-sinensis* (Chinese hibiscus) forms a spectacular hedge, but colourful flowers are also possible in temperate regions, and escallonias, lavender, shrubby potentilla, rhododendrons and rosemary can be used to provide bright, highly scented screens.

BAMBOO HEDGES

Wonderful informal screens can be made from several types of bamboo, which will eventually form dense thickets without the need for any pruning, except as a remedial treatment should they become damaged. *Pseudosasa japonica* (arrow bamboo), for instance, grows to 4.5m (15ft) high and has dark, glossy green leaves. *Fargesia nitida* (fountain bamboo) is less vigorous and has purple stems and bright green leaves. For a lower hedge *Sasa veitchii* is a better choice: it forms a dense thicket to 1.2m (4ft) high. The large, green leaves have light, straw-coloured edges. The only pruning necessary with bamboos is to cut out stems that have been damaged after heavy falls of snow have been allowed to remain on top of them for several days.

points to remember:

MAINTENANCE

Hedges are often the most neglected plants in a garden, but they actually need as much attention in their infancy as other plants, as well as regular clipping and training in their adult life.

- *Small-leaved hedging, such as Ligustrum spp. (privet), is traditionally trimmed with hand shears. Modern hand shears are lighter to use than earlier models and do not judder wrists and hands so violently. Nevertheless, for many gardeners they are still difficult to use, especially on a large hedge. The alternative is to use an electrically powered trimmer: some cut on both sides of the blades, others on one side only. Use ear-muffs to reduce the risk of damage to ears and wear goggles to protect your eyes.*

- *Large-leaved evergreen shrubs must be pruned with sharp secateurs rather than hand shears, which will chop leaves in half and create an unattractive mess. Always cut shoots back to just above a leaf joint. Fresh shoots will develop and hide the cuts. Do not position the cut so that a short piece of stem is left. This is not only unsightly but it may also cause the onset of die-back.*

left: An attractive alternative to formal hedging are these neat cones of *Buxus sempervirens*. The elegant topiarized spirals and graceful swags under the front windows add interest to the all-green planting.

ESTABLISHING A FORMAL HEDGE

Deciduous, formal hedging plants must be cut down by about half and have all sideshoots cut back by a similar amount immediately after being planted. When bought as bare-rooted plants, planting is from late autumn to early spring. For container-grown plants, plant at any time when the soil is workable. In the following year, from late autumn to early spring, again severely cut back the leading shoot and sideshoots by about a half. This may appear to be too drastic and to lose much of the plant, but unless pruning is severe the base of the hedge will be unsightly and bare of stems and leaves in summer. In the third winter cut back all new shoots by a third. In the following season, shoots that develop will be bushy and start to form a solid screen of leaves. During a hedge's infancy, water it regularly and feed it in spring and midsummer to encourage the development of fresh young shoots.

SHAPING A HEDGE

Creating a uniform shape along a hedge's entire length is essential. To establish a uniform height, a taut string stretched between stout poles is ideal over a short distance, but a better way is to use a template, which can be made from sturdy cardboard or, for extensive hedges, from hardboard.

Rain cleanses hedges of dust and dirt, but heavy snowfalls often cause irreparable damage because the weight breaks shoots and splays branches outwards. Instead of a square top, choose a rounded or a sloped outline, so that snow can more easily fall off. In areas where there is little risk of snow the top of a hedge can be cut with a squarer outline.

RENOVATING OLD HEDGES

Hedges in old gardens often become neglected, too large and bare of shoots and stems at their bases. They encroach into beds and borders and they screen and swamp neighbouring plants. They also impoverish the soil, as well as obscuring the light and becoming full of old, dusty leaves and stems. They also often harbour weeds.

If the hedge is too wide it can be cut back hard in spring. Often, however, this may be too drastic to do all at once, and it is generally better to spread the work over two or three seasons. In the first year cut back the top to the desired height, using a line to get a uniform height. In the second year prune back hard one of the sides. The following year cut the other side back. Hedging material is rarely suitable for the compost heap unless you have a shredder, and it is often better to burn it or take it to a municipal tip. When you have cleared away the cuttings and removed any weeds that were growing at the base of the hedge, apply a fertilizer and, when the soil is damp, a mulch to encourage new shoots to develop and to keep down weeds at the base.

Not all hedging plants that are cut back can be guaranteed to regrow. Those that can include *Aucuba japonica* (spotted laurel), *Fagus sylvatica* (common beech), *Buxus sempervirens* (box), *Elaeagnus* spp. (deciduous forms), *Forsythia* x *intermedia*, *Ulex europaeus* (gorse), *Crataegus monogyna* (hawthorn), *Ligustrum ovalifolium* (privet), *Pyracantha* spp. (firethorn), *Rhododendron* cultivars and *Taxus baccata* (yew).

Rosmarinus officinalis (rosemary) and *Lavandula angustifolia* (lavender) are often used for hedging, especially around herb gardens, but both eventually become tall and straggly, especially when they are not trimmed annually. New growth will not develop when the pruning cuts have been made into the old wood, and, rather than cutting them back severely, they are best replaced with young plants. When you replace the plants, replace some of the soil at the same time. Prune the new, young plants in mid-spring to encourage them to adopt a neat, low habit, and every subsequent year remove 2–3cm (1in) of the previous season's growth to encourage bushy, even growth. With the exception of *Taxus baccata* (yew), overgrown conifers should not be drastically cut back as this will completely spoil them.

project: creating a topiary bird

1　　2　　3　　4

However, the tops of conifers can be removed from young hedges when the desired height has been reached.

DECIDUOUS HEDGES

Deciduous plants may not be everyone's first choice for a hedge. The year-round privacy and screening provided by evergreen plants means that they are often selected automatically when a boundary is to be marked by a hedge. The value of deciduous hedges should not be overlooked, however, especially when areas within a garden are to be divided by hedging. There are many suitable plants, but two of the most reliable and, for many gardeners, the most attractive are *Fagus sylvatica* (beech) and *Crataegus monogyna* (hawthorn).

HEDGES AND TOPIARY

There is a certain romance about topiary, whether it is seen in a classical setting and depicts various geometric shapes or in a cottage garden, where a more fanciful shape has been created out of *Buxus sempervirens* (box) or *Lonicera nitida* (shrubby honeysuckle). Topiary does not have to be on the grand scale to be fun: a small sphere is just as satisfying for a novice as a more ambitious animal shape for an experienced enthusiast. In earlier times large-leaved evergreens, such as *Laurus* spp. (laurel), were used, but this created features too large for cottage and other small gardens. Also, laurel is difficult to clip without damaging the leaves.

Topiary is usually created from evergreen shrubs, but deciduous shrubs, such as forsythia, crab apples and laburnums, are sometimes employed. A cone formed by a conifer, such as *Taxus* spp. (yew) or *Thuja* spp. (arborvitae), is an ideal subject for beginners. Use only one plant, tie it to a support and when a shoot reaches about 15cm (6in) above the top cut it off. Trim it to shape regularly.

PLANTS TO TOPIARIZE

Several small-leaved evergreens can be used to form topiary subjects. One of the most reliable is *Buxus sempervirens* (box), a slow-growing plant with small, aromatic, glossy green leaves. It is ideal for forming birds and animals as well as geometric shapes to 1.2m (4ft) high. It grows very well in containers. There are several cultivars with variegated leaves.

Ligustrum ovalifolium (privet) has shiny, green leaves, but it can be semi-evergreen in cold regions. There is a golden-leaved form. Privet is not suitable for planting in containers. The leaves are larger than those of *Lonicera nitida* (shrubby honeysuckle). This is a prolific grower with small, shiny, dark green leaves clustered around stiff stems, and it is ideal for subjects up to 75cm (30in) high and long. The cultivar *L. nitida* 'Baggesen's Gold' has golden

Topiary can be used to create focal points or simply as a conversation piece in the garden. Simple cones, spirals and spheres are easy and elegant, but if you want to try something more unusual use one of the wire frameworks (formers) available from garden centres. This is a long-term project, and your topiary will take several years to achieve its finished state. We used a form of *Taxus baccata* (yew), but any small-leaved evergreen will do.

MATERIALS AND EQUIPMENT

wire frame from garden centre
two young privet bushes
ties
pruning shears

1 Add several large stones to the bottom of the pot to provide ballast, then plant the two shrubs in a large container, spacing them carefully apart and half-filling the container with good-quality compost.

2 Insert the wire former into the container, taking care that you do not damage the plants' roots, and fill the container with compost to about 2.5cm (1in) below the top.

3 Tie the shoots to the former and cut any straggly shoots. Continue to do this as the plants grow.

4 As the plants grow, continue to tie in shoots to the former and clip back shoots to the required outline. Yew is one of the few conifers that will reshoot from old wood, and regular clipping will encourage dense, bushy growth.

leaves. Both forms can be grown in tubs.

Taxus baccata (yew) is a small-leaved evergreen conifer bearing dark green leaves. It forms topiary subjects to a height of 2.4m (8ft) and will grow in containers.

Thuja occidentalis (arborvitae) and its many cultivars are evergreen conifers, which are ideal for simple topiary sculptures and suitable for growing in containers. It can be used for topiary subjects to 1.5m (5ft) high.

entrances, exits and paths

Entrances and exits are important parts of any garden. Not only do they provide security, but they are also the visual threshold to the garden – the first and last places that people see when they visit. Their appearance, therefore, tends to create a lasting impression of the garden. Consider the view framed by the entrance: it may be the path and front door or it may be the garden itself. No matter what is framed, it gives an immediate impression of your space and, by implication, of yourself. Stand at the entrance to your own garden and think about the impression you want to give to visitors.

GATES

A gate is an essential part of a wall, hedge or fence if you want a continuous barrier with access through it. Gates are usually made of wood or wrought iron, and it is important to choose one that fits in with its surroundings. A very ornate wrought-iron gate would look out of place in a simple country garden, just as a simple picket gate would be inappropriate in a patio garden.

Constructing a gate from scratch is not easy, and if possible you should buy a ready-made kit consisting of all the parts that can be glued or screwed together. In general, metal gates should be hung from metal posts or from brick piers, whereas wooden gates should be used in wooden fences that, wherever possible, match the style of the fence.

All gates need hinges and some form of latch and handle. There is a wide range available to match the style

left: The front gate is the first thing that visitors to your garden will see. Make a statement about you or your garden with a specially made gate and alert visitors to the type of plants they are likely to encounter.

of the gate, many of which are designed to be decorative as well as functional. When you buy fittings, select those that are durable and are in proportion with the gate.

Metal gates with widely spaced bars may pose a security risk if there are young children in the garden; but,

whatever material and style you choose, make sure that the uprights are well concreted in or they will soon move and the gate will stick or constantly swing open, which will defeat the object of having a gate. Internal gateways can be more frivolous. They need not even be designed to shut but can be used to

draw the eye to another part of the garden or become a focal point in their own right.

Security is a necessary if tiresome consideration. You can adopt a cavalier attitude towards keeping out intruders, but if you have children it is essential that there are adequate, safe gates

above: A hedge can be trained to create an archway over a path, although you will have to wait several years to achieve a neat, dense arch.

ARCHWAYS

A complete archway, whether it is solidly made of brick, wood or iron, or living, in the form of a hedge, is the ultimate way of framing entrances and exits as well as of linking different areas of the garden. A glimpse of what lies beyond is often tantalizing enough for people to abandon the area they are in and move on to the next. The simplest way of creating an archway is to buy one of the many plastic or metal ones that are available from garden centres and the large DIY stores. Plastic usually looks like plastic and will not last long, so metal is a more economical choice for the long term.

Many of the ready-made arches are narrow. When you are buying an arch, always imagine what it will be like when it is clothed with climbers and how little space will be available between the uprights to allow you to pass comfortably through, especially if you are pushing a wheelbarrow or manoeuvring the lawnmower back to the garden shed.

Depending on its situation, it may be better to leave the arch unclothed. In a small garden, however, where space is at a premium, an archway can be used as an excuse to grow a few more climbing plants. Roses are a popular choice for this type of situation, and you may want to look for a thornless cultivar, such as *Rosa* 'Zéphirine Drouhin'. Many roses will produce flowers all summer long, but by running a clematis up through the rose you will have a double season of flowers. Both the rose and clematis

should be planted in spring and tied in to the uprights. *Clematis alpina* 'Frances Rivis' has pretty mid-blue flowers, while *C. florida* 'Sieboldii' has lovely white blooms. Keep the shoots inside the arch trimmed or tied back so that the plants do not become an obstacle.

ERECTING AN ARCH

An arch must be able to withstand a lot of pressure from the wind, especially when it is covered with a leaf climber, and it must, therefore, be firmly implanted in the ground. The uprights should be embedded in the ground to a depth of at least 45cm (18in), and they should, ideally, be concreted in, especially if the arch is in an exposed position. Dig the area where the climbers will be planted and add plenty of well-rotted organic material. Set the plants at the same depth as they were in their pots. Tie them in to the frame of the arch, spreading them out so that they make an effective cover.

HEDGE ARCHES

Arches can be constructed out of hedging. These are usually simple to look at because it is not possible to grow climbers over them. Instead, allow the hedge on either side of the entrance to grow up until it the stems are long enough for you to pull them over to form the arch. You can use a metal former within the hedge so that you can tie in the shoots to form the shape, or you can just pull them over the space between and tie them together. Eventually, they will fill out, and the arch will look like a hole in the hedge.

through which they cannot slip. Secure, out-of-reach catches are essential. Self-closing devices are useful to make sure that gates shut after visitors, such as the postman, but unfortunately they can compound the problem because if a child does manage to slip out they can not get in again.

PATHS

Arches and gates have a practical purpose in that they give access to the garden itself or to another part of the garden. Alone, however, they are rather pointless: they need to be combined with the paths and walkways that take the gardener or visitor through the garden, towards the house or simply to the compost bin or greenhouse. Although the shortest distance between one point in the garden and another may be a straight line, that does not necessarily mean that the path you lay between the two points should be straight. A straight path may fit in with a garden that has a rigid geometric design, but in most gardens it will serve only to split the garden needlessly.

Straight or angular paths will tend to segment the garden and give a formal appearance, but if you incorporate curves you will produce a more natural effect. You should also take into account the profile of the ground itself, both for the appearance of the path and for practical considerations. A path sloping towards the house or an outbuilding, for example, will create a direct route for heavy rainwater to flow to the house walls rather than soaking into the ground as it would normally.

Where paths need to change direction it is generally better to make that change in the form of a curve rather than of a sharp angle, unless the latter fits in with the overall design of the garden. However, avoid the other extreme and do not construct a path with sharp curves and squiggles: they will be a nightmare to build and to use.

PLANNING A PATH

As with so many other garden projects, a scale plan drawn on graph paper will be of tremendous help in planning the position and width of your path. Draw in all the major features and then try different positions for the path. Another possible way of doing this is to take a photograph of the garden from the house and then use tracing paper to add overlays showing possible positions for the path.

Any of the following materials can be used for paths, either on their own or in combination: bricks, cobbles, concrete pavers and slabs, gravel and sawn logs. You can make attractive patterns to give interesting variations in texture and colour. If you intend to use bricks or slabs as a paving material you can sketch these in on your plan, too, to give a much better idea of how the finished path will look. The pattern in

below: The attractive bamboo gate, with its simple fastening, is a fitting accompaniment to the fine *Acer palmatum* 'Garnet'. The path is neatly edged with wooden stakes.

Paths that are to receive little wear and tear can be laid on a firm, level base of compacted earth and a layer of sand 5–10cm (2–4in) deep, without the need for a firmer foundation. Ram down the exposed subsoil with a stout timber post or compact it with a garden roller. Lay the sand and check that the base is level with a spirit level placed on a piece of timber. If you live in an area with soft soil or if the path is to support heavier than normal loads, you should lay a foundation of compacted hardcore, consisting of about 10cm (4in) hardcore rammed down over a 2.5–5cm (1–2in) layer of sand.

When you are laying bricks or pavers set them out in your chosen pattern, keeping the gaps between each unit uniform and no more than 1cm (½in) wide. After you have placed a few, lay a wooden straightedge across them and tap it down with a heavy hammer until the faces of the bricks or pavers are all level. Ideally, if the path does not run downhill naturally you should arrange a slight drainage fall or 'pitch' to one side or the other of the path so that rainwater will run off. Check this with a level laid on top of a second straightedge held across the path. A small wooden wedge underneath one end of the level will allow you to obtain a consistent fall by keeping the level's bubble in the middle of its tube. Tap the bricks or pavers down more on the side to which the rainwater must drain, but make sure the tops of all the bricks remain in line so that they will not cause a hazard.

which you lay the paving may require that some pieces are cut, in which case a carefully drawn scale plan of the path will show you just how many will need cutting and allow you to adjust this figure by moving the pattern here and there before you actually start to do the work.

LAYING THE PATH

When it comes to laying out the shape of the path on the ground, use pegs and cords for straight stretches and lengths of garden hose for the curved areas. As a rule, paths should be about 1m (3ft) wide, but there is no reason why you can not make them narrower or wider if you wish, provided they are not so narrow that they make you feel that you are walking a tightrope. Remember what the paths will be used for: manhandling a wheelbarrow or lawnmower around flowerbeds and borders because a path is too narrow will be an irritation that could have been avoided with a little forethought.

above: Gravel is an excellent material for paths, especially when laid on a weed-suppressing membrane, but it must always be edged so that it does not spread into neighbouring borders.

105

6

The decorative features you introduce to your garden, just as much as the plants you use, will help to reinforce the style you have chosen. As with any room in your home, you need to think about how you will furnish the outside room. You may want to consider using some of the same colours in the garden as you have chosen for indoors to enhance the feeling that you are simply stepping into another room when you pass through the back door or patio doors. Alternatively, you may prefer to use your garden as somewhere to experiment with a style and ornamentation that you would not necessarily want to have in your sitting room. Yet, whether your garden is a scene of colourful chaos or is a pared-down, minimalist landscape, treat it as a personal space, a relaxing haven, a restful retreat full of fragrance or just somewhere you can doze to the sound of running water or bird song.

The 'furniture' you introduce into the garden can be permanent structures – pools, rock gardens and the like – or they can be temporary items, such as willow obelisks or sculptures, which you can move around or even discard as the mood takes you and as your garden matures and changes. There is something immensely satisfying about using attractive objects in a garden. Even a garden that is dominated by plants will benefit from the occasional piece of sculpture, urn or even an old, gnarled tree stump. Such objects provide something on which the eye can rest. The feature you choose should not, however, be any old object: a dustbin or abandoned, rusty wheelbarrow will not have the same effect as a thoughtfully placed sundial or elegant urn. There are dozens of possibilities, some expensive but others less so or even available for free.

decorative
touches

water features

In a small garden some form of self-contained, re-circulating fountain can be very satisfying, for it combines the appealing trickling sound of moving water with the absence of open water, which can be dangerous if children play in the garden. It is also possible to create a small-scale, modern version of a classical wall fountain, with an ornamental spout from which water cascades into some form of collecting trough before draining away to a concealed tank or sump. Alternatively, you may want to create a brimming pool to bring light and reflections into a dark corner. Whichever type of feature you choose, make sure that it is in proportion to its surroundings and that the style and materials you choose are in keeping with the garden as a whole and your house.

MOVING WATER FEATURE

One of the most popular of the self-contained water features, providing the maximum sound of tinkling water with the minimum chance of drowning children, is the bubble or pebble fountain. This type of feature is suitable for a patio or for the wider garden, where it can be made, for example, into the centre of a small natural area, surrounded by ferns and hostas and other shade- and moisture-loving plants. You will need to excavate a hole sufficiently large to accommodate the water reservoir or sump. If this is to be positioned on a patio, bear this in mind from the start and consider if the work involved in excavating beneath what may be a paved surface is worth it. A

bubble fountain does not really lend itself to being raised too far off the ground, which would be necessary if you could not accommodate the reservoir below ground level, and you might want to consider an alternative feature for such a position.

Because it will not be visible, you can use an old plastic dustbin or any other, large watertight container for the

above: Whether the feature is made with stylish blue spheres or cobblestones, all bubble fountains work on exactly the same principle: a small pump raises water from a reservoir to pour over the feature and return to the underground reservoir.

reservoir or sump. A submersible pump will stand on bricks in the bottom of the reservoir, and the pipe through which the water is forced upwards is fed through a hole in the centre of a sheet of galvanized mesh. The mesh is laid over the reservoir and is itself covered with a mass of cobbles or a single millstone with a hole through the centre and surrounded by smaller stones. The water is forced up through the feed pipe and cascades over the stones and cobbles, to run back into the reservoir beneath the mesh. The cable to the mesh can be easily hidden under the stones and gravel.

Another popular form of self-contained water feature, which again requires a reservoir of some kind, is the wall-mounted fountain. Such features can have water cascading into a small pool at the foot of a wall or the water can fall down a wall and into a hidden reservoir. Safety considerations might suggest that the latter arrangement is selected, but even a small pool offers opportunities for water plants – not waterlilies, of course, which do not appreciate continual splashing, but there are many other water and marginal plants that will enjoy such a situation.

There are many different styles of wall-mounted spouts, ranging from the traditional gods' and lions' heads and dolphins to modern, geometric styles in metal. Some styles incorporate a small basin beneath the delivery spout, in which the water collects before trickling down into the larger pool or disappearing into the hidden reservoir, and you can even get chains, down

project: leaf fountain

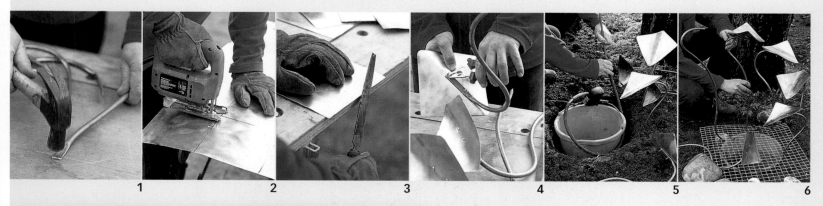

1 2 3 4 5 6

It is possible to buy kits, which include a submersible pump, for water features that have a trickle of water descending from one small receptacle to the next, with the water falling into a submerged reservoir before it is returned through an upright pipe to the top receptacle. The basic principle, however, can be easily applied to a fountain that you can design yourself.

MATERIALS

3 2m (6ft) lengths of 15mm copper pipe
thin copper sheet 45 x 30cm (18 x 12in)
10 2.5cm (1in) nuts and bolts
sharp sand
bucket for reservoir
submersible pump
2 bricks or blocks
hose clip
galvanized mesh wider than the bucket
washed cobbles of various sizes

1 Cut individual 'stems' of gradually decreasing height from the copper pipe. The longest will carry water from the pump, while the others will support the copper leaf shapes. You will have to experiment to find the appropriate distance between each 'leaf'. Bend each 'stem' slightly and flatten one end of each 'stem' so that the 'leaves' can be held in position.

2 Cut out four or five shapes from the copper sheet. Aim to create a shape that will hold a small amount of water but that will look in proportion to the 'stems'.

3 Slightly indent the centres and curl up the lips of the 'leaves', except for the area forming the spout. Each 'leaf' must be able to contain water when the pump is switched off but not so deep that the 'leaves' contain more water than can be held in the reservoir.

4 Attach the 'leaves', using two nuts and bolts for each 'leaf'.

5 Excavate a hole to accommodate the bucket and line it with sand to create a flat, stable base. Stand the submersible pump on two blocks in the base of the reservoir so that any debris that falls into the container does not clog up the pump. Connect the pump to the rigid pipe that will deliver water to the top of the fountain. You should use a short length of flexible hose that is slightly greater in diameter than the copper pipe. Hold it in place with a hose clip.

6 When the water is circulating, check that the flow of water is appropriate, adjusting the flow regulator on the pump to ensure that the flow of water is even. Cover the reservoir with mesh and arrange cobbles over the top.

which the water drips before being returned via the pump to the top of the chain again. Fibreglass is now widely used, which means that such features are not only relatively inexpensive but also comparatively light and do not need an exceptionally sturdy wall to support them. Do not, however, be tempted to mount such a feature against an existing house wall, since the continual presence of water may cause damage, no matter

how carefully and thoroughly you have prepared the surface.

The water spouts are as simple to erect as the bubble fountains, but you should bear in mind that you need access to both sides of the wall – the pipe delivering the water to the spout will run up one side and be angled through a hole in the wall. The lion's mouth, if that is your choice, should be positioned over the end of the pipe.

The water runs through the pipe, emerging as if from the lion's mouth, down the wall and into a reservoir or pool, from where it is pumped up, behind the wall, to fall again.

STILL WATER

Although many people like the tinkling sound of water as it trickles from a spout or over a collection of pebbles, in a small garden a reflective or brimming pool will not only provide a wonderful opportunity to grow a wider range of plants than would otherwise be possible but will also reflect the sky, bringing light and making visible the reflections of the clouds as they chase above the water's surface and increasing the apparent space.

A garden pool that is large enough to have good visual impact and ample space for a modest collection of plants and fish will require a surface area of 4.5–5 sq m (50–55 sq ft). The importance of creating a pool of an adequate size is not only related to the variety and numbers of plants and fish that may be accommodated but also, more importantly, to the pool's ability to become a self-sustainable environment that is clear and healthy. Increasing the surface area by excavating only a shallow basin would be a recipe for disaster. Small garden pools require a minimum depth of 45cm (18in); they are better still if 60cm (24in) can be reached. This additional depth will provide a zone of water near the bottom that is reasonably constant in temperature and is filtered from the immediate glare of sunshine.

PLANTING

For a pool to be healthy and clear, the conditions that cause green algae to flourish should be avoided – that is, strong light and adequate foodstuffs in the form of mineral salts dissolved in the water. The aim of the design of a garden pool, therefore, is to provide an environment that will deny them mineral salts and shade out bright summer light.

Conveniently, this is achieved in a well-balanced pool by other plants: submerged plants (oxygenators), which use up the mineral salts, and surface-leaved plants, like waterlilies, which shade out light. Marginals play a part in both roles but are mainly used as decorative plants in the shallower fringes of the pool. In order to provide a suitable depth of water for the marginal plants the profile of the hole should include a shelf about 23cm (9in) deep and wide. Submerged plants and waterlilies grow from the bottom of the deeper zone, which remains free of frost in temperate winters.

CONSTRUCTING A POND

It is essential that the sides are absolutely level for a brimming pool, so when you have identified a suitable site knock in pegs in the corners and two intermediate pegs along each side, about 80cm (30in) apart. Starting at one corner, knock in the peg to the level that will be the same level as the surrounding paving to the pool. Knock in the adjacent peg so that its top is level with the first corner peg. Use a spirit level placed on top of a straight-edge that is long enough to sit

above: The rill, which is contained in a metal canal, is reflected in the mirror, which not only apparently increases the length of the rill but also enhances the level of light in the shady corner.

on the adjacent peg. When you are sure that the second peg is level with the corner peg, continue to work round the square, making all the peg tops level. Dig out the soil to a depth of 23cm (9in). If the soil is light and unstable, stop the sides falling away by sloping them slightly so that they are at an angle of no more than 20 degrees. The topsoil can be spread on the garden borders or stored for future use.

Once the pool outline has been dug out to 23cm (9in) all over, use sand to mark the deep area of the pool. The areas left at 23cm (9in) deep will make shelves for the containers of marginal plants if required. Because a reflective pool may be more effective with few or no marginal plants, the shelves need not go all the way around the edge. Dig out the deeper zone of the pool, which should have a finished depth of about 60cm (2ft). Use a flexible butyl liner over an underlay. The liner will move about until some water is added, so half-fill the pool before laying the paving or decking around the edge. The pool is finished by taking the liner up vertically between the edging paving stones and the paving that surrounds it. This allows the pool to be filled to the top of the paving stones.

WATER AND ELECTRICITY

Many water features require electricity to power a submersible pump. Safety regulations are being constantly tightened in the garden, and all electrical equipment must be protected by a residual current device (RCD, sometimes known as a contact circuit breaker). The trip switches in RCDs are extremely responsive, and electrical storms or power cuts often mean that they need to be reset. If the pump appears to have stopped for some reason, check that this device is not

above: A small brimming urn water feature, easily installed and available in kit form, is ideal for a small patio.

plant list:

WATERSIDE PERENNIALS

- *Aruncus dioicus* (goat's beard)
  A medium to tall plant with cream flowers in summer.

- *Astilbe x arendsii*
  A low to medium-sized plant with feathery foliage and cream, pink or purple flower spikes in summer.

- *Caltha palustris* (marsh marigold, kingcup)
  A low-growing plant with yellow, cup-shaped flowers in spring.

- *Cardamine pratensis* (lady's smock)
  A low-growing plant with lilac flowers in spring.

- *Iris ensata*
  A medium-sized iris with blue flowers in summer.

- *Lobelia cardinalis* (cardinal flower, Indian pink)
  A medium-sized plant with spikes of scarlet flowers in summer.

- *Lythrum salicaria* (purple loosestrife)
  A medium-sized plant with upright spikes of purple flowers in late summer.

- *Onoclea sensibilis* (sensitive fern)
  A handsome, medium-sized fern with divided, pale green foliage.

- *Persicaria bistorta* (bistort, Easter ledges)
  A vigorous, low-growing plant with pink flowers in summer.

- *Primula japonica*
  A rosette-forming plant with pink or white candelabra flowers in summer.

points to remember:

PLANTS TO AVOID

It is as well to be cautious about the type and number of plants you introduce to a pool, especially a fairly small one. Among the plants on offer from many garden and water centres are several especially pernicious plants, including Hydrocotyle americana *(floating marsh pennywort),* Azolla filiculoides *(water fern) and* Myriophyllum verticillatum *(milfoil). These plants are not only fast-growing and will quickly swamp a small pool, but they are also almost impossible to eradicate once they are established. A small pool is not a suitable home for* Typha latifolia *(bulrush) nor for* Nymphaea alba, *a beautiful white waterlily that will spread to 2.1m (7ft) or more.*

the cause and simply requires switching on again.

Regulations are increasingly leaning towards the use of low-voltage lighting wherever possible in the garden. Fortunately, low-voltage electricity is easier to install than mains voltage cable, but it does require a transformer, which can be an indoor model or a special waterproof type for outdoor use.

Submersible pumps are easy to install and easy to connect. They can be used to run not only small bubble features and wall-mounted water spouts but also fountains and streams. A larger, more complex feature might require a surface-mounted pump, which would need a separate ventilated chamber.

gravel gardens

There has been a great revival of interest in growing plants in Mediterranean-style conditions – that is, hot and dry for most of the summer with just the occasional downpour of rain – and climate change is extending the geographical range of gardens in which such weather occurs. Even in areas as yet unaffected by global warming, where it is not possible to replicate the exact climatic conditions, it is possible to simulate the physical conditions. The resulting garden – which can be a large or small bed or border – can look quite stunning and will certainly look very different from conventional herbaceous and mixed borders.

PREPARING THE SITE

Although a mainly dry and sunny climate is desirable for this type of garden, it is not essential. What is essential, however, is a free-draining soil that will prevent any stagnant soil from settling around the plants' roots. In addition, although the soil should be free-draining, it should allow only excess water to be lost: the soil should contain sufficient humus to hold enough water for the plants' use. In the wild the humus is likely to be in the form of detritus and old plant material, but in the garden it can be any well-rotted organic material as long as it is not too rich in nitrogen, because most of the plants that thrive in this type of garden are not heavy feeders.

The area should be in an open position, where there is plenty of sun and freely circulating air. It should not be enclosed and humid. Ordinary garden soil can be used as a basis as

left: In a warm, sheltered garden *Agave americana* 'Variegata' will make an eye-catching, if not necessarily hardy, front-of-border plant. The blue slate chipping mulch is an attractive alternative to ordinary pea shingle.

long as it is not too heavy. First, in autumn dig over the soil, removing all perennial weeds. In spring dig the area over again, removing any weeds that have regenerated and this time incorporating some leafmould and plenty of grit or gravel. The leafmould will help to retain moisture, and the grit will help excess moisture to drain away.

If you garden on very heavy clay soil, digging such a bed is likely to create a sump, with water collecting in it rather than draining away. In these conditions it will be necessary to lay drains of some sort to remove any water that is likely to lie in the bed. A heavy soil will take a lot of breaking down. Grit, gravel and sharp sand are the best materials to add to aid the process. Even these, however, may not improve the situation, and it may be

better to import a load of good-quality topsoil and replace the heavy clay with it, or to build a raised bed, again filled with good topsoil, so that the bed is above the heavy ground and will drain onto it. The resulting bed should drain so easily that if you were to throw a bucket of water on it the water would immediately seep away and not stand in puddles.

PLANTING

There is a wide range of plants that will thrive in the conditions offered by this type of bed. Many of them, naturally, come from Mediterranean regions, but there are also other plants that are found in colder areas but that grow in well-drained situations, such as along shingle seashores and in sandy soils. Most of the plants with silver or grey

foliage will do well in Mediterranean-style borders, but many bulbs will also enjoy the conditions, especially members of the *Allium* genus.

The plants should not be positioned as close together as they would be in a 'normal' bed, partly so that there is adequate moisture and nutrients for every plant and partly so that air can circulate freely around them.

FINISHING TOUCHES

Once the plants have been planted it is a good idea to top-dress the entire area with gravel or small stones. This will not only create an appropriate background against which the plants can be seen to best effect but will also help to improve the growing conditions by providing a mulch that will help keep weeds down. The gravel also ensures that there is a

project: mini gravel garden

1　　　　　　　　　　2　　　　　　　　　　3

plant list:

PLANTS FOR A DRY GARDEN

- **Acaena saccaticupula** 'Blue Haze'
  A carpeting perennial with blue foliage and red summer flowers.

- **Allium hollandicum**
  A medium-sized bulb with purple drumstick flowers in spring.

- **Cistus x purpuresu** (rock rose, sun rose)
  A rounded shrub with purple flowers in summer.

- **Euphorbia characias** subsp. **wulfenii** (spurge)
  A statuesque perennial with green flowers in spring and summer.

- **Lavandula angustifolia** (lavender)
  A small, fragrant shrub with silver-grey foliage and blue-purple flowers in summer.

- **Onopordum acanthium** (cotton thistle)
  A tall, thistle-like biennial with silver foliage and purple flowers in summer.

- **Ophiopogon planiscapus** 'Nigrescens'
  (black lilyturf)
  A low-growing perennial with black, grass-like foliage.

- **Papaver somniferum** (opium poppy)
  An annual poppy with red, pink or purplish flowers in summer.

- **Salvia x superba**
  A small shrub with violet flowers in summer.

- **Sedum** 'Herbstfreude'
  A fleshy perennial with pink flowers in autumn.

MATERIALS

semi-permeable membrane
mesh
gravel
washed cobbles of various sizes

1 Remove all perennial weeds, stones and other debris from the area and dig in plenty of well-rotted, humus-rich compost. After preparing the ground, cover the area with semi-permeable membrane.

2 Stand the plants in their pots over the area to make sure they are well positioned, and then make X-shaped cuts in the membrane through which the plants can be inserted into the soil.

3 Cover the area with gravel to a depth of 4–5cm (1½–2in) and add some large graced pebbles. You should allow about 60kg (1cwt) of gravel per square metre (yard).

A gravel garden provides the ideal environment for a wide range of plants. The gravel is an excellent method of protecting the delicate crowns of plants such as alpines and many Mediterranean species from winter wet, and the semi-permeable membrane on which the gravel is laid prevents weeds from germinating. We used a collection of grasses, which will eventually form dense clumps. Any annual weeds that do appear in the gravel can be quickly and easily removed by hand.

well-drained 'collar' around each plant at the very point at which it is vulnerable to rotting in damp conditions. Because there is space between and around the plants, it is

important that the surface is attractive, and gravel, available in a range of colours, is the perfect material for this purpose. If possible, choose a colour that will harmonize with the hard

landscaping elsewhere in the garden.

A Mediterranean bed can be a simple, flat affair, or it can be undulated to make the surface more interesting. To add additional interest, a dry river

course could be integrated with the gravel garden. This could be decorated with larger stones and weather-worn pieces of wood or driftwood in intriguing shapes.

raised beds and scree beds

Many gardeners who enjoy growing alpine species find that the conditions provided by raised beds and scree beds are ideal for their preferred species. These features need not be confined to the specialist gardener, however, and raised beds in particular have an important part to play in gardens that are designed for people who are disabled or who, through age or illness, are becoming less mobile.

RAISED BEDS

Raised beds are nothing more than borders that are raised above ground level, with a low brick, concrete block or wooden wall to hold the gritty, free-draining soil in place. They are good places for growing alpines and rock plants, which can be better viewed and appreciated in a raised bed than in a larger border, but they have a much wider use than simply offering the ideal conditions for many alpine species.

As we grow older it is not always possible to achieve all the things we have previously taken for granted, and this can be devastating after a lifetime's gardening. There are also many people who, through accident or illness, cannot achieve as much as they might wish. As well as considering turning borders and beds over to more low-maintenance ones (see pages 38–9), it is also possible to raise some areas of the garden to more manageable levels.

The walls of raised beds can be built with any suitable material. They look best when they are the same material as the other hand landscaping.

above: Painted timber is an attractive material for a simple raised bed. The top edges have been decorated with tiny mirror squares, which will sparkle in sunlight.

Railway sleepers are appropriate in informal gardens, for example, while bricks or paving slabs would be more suitable for gardens where paths or patios are a similar colour or texture. Do not make the raised bed so wide that you cannot comfortably reach across the top, and vary the height according to your needs: a bed for someone in a wheelchair will be lower than one for someone who prefers to work standing up. Make sure there are weep holes around the base and put plenty of drainage material in the bottom. The depth of soil will depend on what you want to grow: alpines will grow in much shallower soil than herbaceous plants.

SCREE BEDS

Rock garden plants that require extremely sharp drainage are best cultivated in scree beds, which are designed to simulate the naturally occurring conditions at the foot of mountain slopes where there is a deep layer of finely broken rock and a certain amount of humus.

A scree bed is essentially a raised bed with much of the soil replaced by stone chippings. Retaining walls of sandstone brick or broken paving slabs may be used to support the sides of the bed, and these should be arranged with an inward slant to make them stable. Lay the lowest stones on a concrete base. The upper courses may be dry or filled with soil to accommodate plants that enjoy growing in vertical crevices – these should be inserted as building progresses. Leave drainage holes in the

below: A permanent raised bed with brick or stone walls must have built-in weep holes around the base. Cover the bottom of the bed with stones or rubble to improve drainage.

base of the wall at frequent intervals. The bed should be at least 60cm (2ft) high over clay soil to ensure good drainage and at least 30cm (1ft) high over sandy soil. Place a 10–15cm (4–6in) layer of broken bricks and rubble in the bottom of the bed and use the following compost mix to fill the rest of the space: 10 parts stone chippings 1 part loam, 1 part peat substitute or leafmould and 1 part sharp sand. Plant up in autumn or spring.

STONE SINKS AND TROUGHS

Although they are on a much smaller scale than raised beds, many plants can be grown in square and rectangular containers, including many of the rock garden plants listed on page 117. Old animal feeding troughs are rarely available these days, but old stone sinks can be successfully converted into miniature gardens and alpine troughs. The old-fashioned, glazed white sinks, which can still occasionally be found, can look rather stark, and coating them with hypertufa provides a more sympathetic surface, especially for informal gardens. The sinks are extremely heavy, so do not try to lift one by yourself. Like all containers, they need to be raised slightly off the ground so that excess water can drain away, so take this into account before filling the finished sink with compost.

project:

CONVERTING A STONE SINK

Before you begin, roughen the shiny surface of the enamel glaze as much as possible by scoring the surface with a glass- or tile-cutter. This will help the layer of hypertufa and glue to adhere better. Mix thoroughly a mixture of 1 part sharp sand and 1 part cement with 2 parts sphagnum peat. You will need sufficient materials to nearly fill a builder's wheelbarrow. Paint the outer sides of the glazed sink and a generous area over both sides of the top rim with heavy-duty industrial glue. Leave the glue to go tacky, and in the mean time add a little water to the hypertufa ingredients, mixing it thoroughly to make a stiff paste.

Wear strong rubber gloves for the next stage. Pick up a small quantity of the moist mix and, starting at the bottom, press small amounts of the mix to the sides, kneading with your fingers to give a rough consistency. Continue adding the mix until the whole glued area is covered, and then leave the sink for at least 24 hours to set.

The fresh mix will darken and grow algae more quickly if the outside surface is painted regularly with sour milk, liquid fertilizer or a proprietary antiquing fluid available from specialist firms that manufacture reconstituted stone.

Before adding the compost, place a piece of mesh over the plug hole so that the compost does not simply get washed away.

rock gardens

Gardeners who are seriously interested in alpine plants grow a wide range of species, many of which are ungrowable in the conditions found in most gardens. They grow plants from high mountain ranges that require specialized cultivation techniques and that will not tolerate the hurly-burly of an ordinary border. There are, however, many gardeners who simply like the effect that a rock or gravel garden gives to the garden and are content to grow the many easy and attractive plants that enjoy such conditions.

CHOOSING A SITE

A rock garden, with its layers of large rocks and colourful alpine plants, can make an extremely striking feature if properly executed. When it resembles a rocky outcrop on a mountainside or cliff-face, it is the ideal partner for a water feature and a good way to link different levels in the garden and display a whole range of unusual plants.

One of the most important features of a rock feature is that it should look like a natural outcrop rather than a heap of large stones with plants growing among them. This requires considerable skill, both in selecting the site and the stones and in laying the rocks so that they look as if they belong together. Ideally, little soil should be visible in a rock garden. It should be packed into crevices between and in the rocks and is even better if covered with a layer of grit or gravel. This will help not only to disguise the soil's presence but also to retain moisture in summer.

As with so many features in the garden, it is important to choose the correct site for a rock garden. Do not forget that you are trying to reproduce a natural setting, so it really should not have a wall, fence or your house as a backdrop if this can be avoided. A hedge or trees would be suitable.

Although you can build a rock garden on flat ground, it is much better if you can build it into the face of an existing slope, which might not be practicable in a small garden unless you are deliberately introducing a change in level and are planning to move earth from one section of the garden to another. It should be in a sunny position, although it should not be in full sun all day long. It should definitely not be in shade, nor should it be under trees, which will drip rainwater on the plants. The site and the rock garden itself should be well drained and built on firm foundations.

MOVING STONES

One of the important factors about building a rock garden is to make sure that you do not strain your back as you attempt to move the rocks. Even apparently small pieces will be very heavy; if you are able to lift them, do so by bending your knees and keeping your back straight.

There are a number of ways in which you can move the rocks over the ground. Smaller pieces can be moved by wheelbarrow, but larger rocks will need to be rolled along using stout wooden levers or crowbars. You may be also able to move them using wooden rollers on a track made of wooden planks laid on the ground. Rope slings can also be fashioned and fitted around rocks so that they can be lifted by two people.

BUILDING A ROCK GARDEN

Mark out the shape of the rock garden on the ground. Strings stretched between pegs or a garden hose are ideal, or you could use spray paint specially designed for garden use. A shape with a curved front will look most natural.

Dig around the perimeter with a spade, then dig out the topsoil within the area of the rock garden and keep the fertile soil separate for mixing with grit for the growing medium. Compact the base by treading lightly – trampling hard may impede drainage. Begin by positioning the largest rock, the keystone, and build V-shaped arms from it using smaller rocks. Fill the lower outcrop of rocks with a mix of topsoil and grit. Rake out the bedding material and compact it by light treading, but do not dislodge the stones.

Build the second outcrop of rocks on top of the first tier but set it back from its edge, leaving adequate space for planting. Remove the plants from their pots and place them in holes dug in the planting medium between the rocks. Introduce plants in crevices between stones.

left: The aim of a rock garden is to create a habitat in which alpine species would naturally occur. In general, the larger the stones the more successful the planting.

above: A well-planted rock garden will fit happily into your garden if you use stones of a type that occur naturally in your part of the world.

points to remember:

CHOOSING STONE

Whenever possible use local stone because this will be most in keeping with the area in which your garden is sited. If stone is not available locally choose sandstone or limestone, because these weather well into attractive shapes. Ask your local stone merchant or mason's supplier, garden supplier or quarry for a selection of sizes, telling them that you want the material for a rock garden. They may sell by weight or size, and you will need a lot – several tonnes for a decent size rock garden. Think about how you are going to get the rocks to your site. If you have access you could rent a mechanical digger (backhoe) and a driver to move the rocks from your front drive, which is where they will be dumped on delivery unless you have made other arrangements.

plant list:

EASY PLANTS FOR A ROCK GARDEN

- *Aquilegia flabellata*
  Pretty blue-grey leaves are surmounted by pale bluish-purple nodding flowers in late spring to early summer.

- *Armeria maritima* (sea thrift)
  A clump-forming perennial with narrow green leaves and round white, pink or purple flowerheads.

- *Daphne arbuscula*
  A dwarf, evergreen shrub with fragrant pink flowers.

- *Dianthus* 'Inshriach Dazzler'
  An alpine pink with deep pinkish-red flowers with fringed petals.

- *Draba mollissima*
  A hummock-forming evergreen perennial with bright yellow flowers in late spring.

- *Dryas octopetala* (mountain avens)
  A mat-forming subshrub with creamy-yellow flowers in early summer.

- *Leontopodium alpinum* (edelweiss)
  Conspicuous silver-grey bracts surround the little yellow-white flowers in spring.

- *Lewisia cotyledon*
  An evergreen perennial with panicles of pink, purple, white, cream or yellow flowers in spring and summer.

- *Oxalis adenophylla*
  Pretty grey-green leaves are finely divided and are surmounted by pink-purple flowers in late spring.

- *Primula alpicola*
  A rosette-forming perennial with white, yellow or violet flowers in summer.

- *Silene acaulis* (moss campion)
  An evergreen perennial with deep pink or white in summer.

pergolas and arches

People are becoming increasingly aware of the dangers associated with spending too much time exposed to sunlight. In the past patios used to be sited so that they were in full sun for the maximum amount of time, but now it is regarded as not only more sensible but also more comfortable to relax in the shade. Some gardens have natural shade in the form of a mature tree, but in others it is necessary to create some form of shade. This is not an insurmountable problem, and the solution need not be unsightly.

ARCHES

Whether they are made of metal or wood, are ornate or simple, arches add considerable charm to the garden. They not only provide a decorative support for a wide range of climbing plants, including traditional favourites such as clematis, roses and honeysuckle, but they can also be used as an informal division between different areas of a garden – to separate a lawn from a patio, for example. Built against a hedge, an arch can be used as an arbour, and if you build a series of arches close together you will have a pergola.

Regardless of type, a wooden arch is relatively straightforward to build, and in most cases the various wooden sections are simply held together with galvanized nails. It is a good idea to sketch out your ideas on paper first. Take photographs of the arch's position from both sides and use tracing-paper overlays to show what your ideas will be like when they are constructed and

left: Few things are more evocative of sunny summer afternoons than an arch covered with a fragrant climbing rose. *Rosa* 'Desprez à Fleurs Jaunes' has fragrant flowers all summer long.

above: A pergola with trellis attached to three of the sides and overgrown with dense climbers provides a shady room, hidden from prying eyes and sheltered from ambient noise.

in place in the garden. As a guide, an arch should give about 2.4m (8ft) of headroom and be at least 1.2m (3ft) wide. Use wood with a diameter or width of 7.5–10cm (3–4in) for the main supporting framework.

PERGOLAS

Whether they are attached to the house or boundary wall or are free-standing, pergolas are an attractive means of providing shade to a walkway or patio as well as acting as a support for climbing plants. They are invariably built of wood, although some may have

brick or block columns supporting thick wooden cross-pieces.

As with arches, pergolas can be built in many styles to suit varying types of garden, so it should not be too difficult to find something that fits in exactly with your own plot. Again, it is a good idea to take photographs of the area over which the pergola will stand and to use tracing-paper overlays to find the most appropriate style.

Constructing a free-standing pergola involves attaching individual arch frames together and setting the posts in holes in the ground with concrete collars. When the concrete has set, additional cross-pieces and rails can be added to tie the structure together. If possible, use softwood that has been pressure-treated with preservative, and the same minimum width and height used for arches should apply.

plant list:

PLANTS FOR A NATURAL ARBOUR

The following can be planted between 30cm and 1m (1–3ft) apart around a timber or metal framework. When the side branches are long enough, they can be tied together. Eventually the trunks can be tied together to form the centre of the 'roof'. After several years, an annual clip will be all the maintenance that is needed.

- *Acer campestre* (field maple)
- *Carpinus betulus* (hornbeam)
- *Cornus mas* (cornelian cherry)
- *Corylus avellana* (hazel)
- *Fagus sylvatica* (beech)
- *Ilex aquifolium* (holly)
- *Salix* spp. (willow)
- *Sorbus aria* (whitebeam)
- *Tilia x vulgaris* (lime)
- *Ulmus glabra* (wych elm)

points to remember:

MAKING A RUSTIC ARCH

Making your own arch is often cheaper than buying a ready-made one from a garden centre. The simplest style is a rustic archway, because any imprecise cutting or jointing will not be noticeable. Sweet chestnut poles are the most satisfactory type of wood, but any timber that has been treated with preservative can be used. It is important that the base of each upright is well buried, preferably in concrete, as when the arch is clothed with climbers the wind pressure is enormous, and an insecure arch will topple over. For a simple arch, four uprights are needed. Use galvanized nails to attach two or three horizontal bars between the side uprights and two horizontal cross-bars across the top between the two sides. Nail three more bars between the top cross-bars. Alternatively, use shorter cross-bars, nailed at 40° angles, to create a triangular top.

obelisks and tripods

In a small area, providing height can be a problem, especially if the amount of soil is limited. In a courtyard garden, for example, much, if not all, of the garden may be paved and planting may have to be confined to large containers and specially built raised beds. It is in such gardens especially that free-standing structures come into their own. Tripods and obelisks perform similar functions in the garden. They can be used as temporary additions to the border, supporting annual displays of nasturtiums, or as permanent supports for perennial climbers.

OBELISKS

Obelisks tend to be more ornamental than tripods. Made of wood or metal, they can be grouped in borders or used individually to give emphasis to different parts of the border. They can also be used as focal points.

It is possible to buy ready-made obelisks. Hazel structures, to about 1.6m (5ft 6in) high and 45cm (18in) across at the base, are perfect for sitting on containers to support sweet peas. Willow obelisks are ideal for standing inside large pots so that they can be used as supports for annual climbers, such as sweet peas and nasturtiums. They are available in a range of heights from about 1.8m (6ft) tall down to about 1m (3ft), and they are light enough to be moved around the garden. They should be cleaned and stored in a dry place over winter, however.

Folding willow obelisks can be bought ready-made. These are ideal for summer climbers and even for runner

above: A painted obelisk, easily made from trellis panels and square timber, is an ideal way of providing height in a small border. It can be moved, repainted or clothed in climbers as your garden evolves.

beans, and they have the added advantage that they can be taken down in winter and folded flat for storage until the next spring. The sizes range from 60cm (24in) to 1.8m (6ft) high.

In a formal garden metal obelisks might be more appropriate, and these, too, are readily available in a range of styles and finishes, which can be used to support plants or as objects in their own right to bring elegant height to a garden. Solid steel obelisks, with long

feet so that they can be inserted into a container so they will not tumble over in a strong wind, can be found in white or black. Look around for slim, upright styles or ones with twists and curves. They are mostly about 1.8m (6ft) high.

TRIPODS

There is a tendency to think of borders and beds as simply two-dimensional objects, but even the lowest arrangements have some height added by the plants themselves. Providing a free-standing tripod around which climbers can be trained is a simple way of adding the third dimension to a border, and it is a valuable way of introducing plants that could otherwise not be grown there – clematis, for example, are ideal additions to a perennial border, but they are usually not grown there because there is nowhere suitable for them to climb. Add a tripod, and you instantly have a structure around which two or even three clematis can be grown.

A simple tripod can be made from bamboo canes, and anyone who has grown runner beans will be familiar with the process of spacing bamboo canes in a circle and tying them together at the top. These days it is possible to get little plastic gadgets with six holes through which the bamboo canes can be inserted and held at an angle. These make stable wigwams for runner beans and other climbers and are stronger than string.

The same principle can be used to make larger, more eye-catching

left: An elegant wooden obelisk, painted to match the Versailles planter, creates a stylish focal point that requires no additional decoration.

structures. Rustic poles can be used to make tripods. They are generally more successful if dressed poles – that is, those from which the bark has been removed – are used, and they should be sunk in the border, preferably in holes filled with gravel or stones, because when climbers are trained around the poles they are likely to blow over in strong winds. Plain timber, sawn to angles at the top, can be nailed together to provide a simple yet elegant tripod.

above: Metal obelisks, which have long legs that are driven into the ground for stability, can be used to support fragrant sweet peas and colourful – and edible – runner beans.

ornaments

A glance through any of the numerous gardening magazines and catalogues that are available will reveal an enormous range of items that can be used in the garden. Some are stylish and attractive, others less so. If you are selecting an ornament to use as a focal point try to imagine what it will look like in your own garden and whether it really suits the style of garden you live in. Beautiful glass spheres look fabulous arranged next to a sparkling brimming pool with a few elegantly positioned grasses. However, many materials, such as metal, stone and wood, will be quickly tarnished by exposure to the elements, so consider what the ornaments will look like in two years before parting with a large amount of money.

SCULPTURE

Sculpture has found a welcome place in our gardens ever since it was first created, and manmade objects of this type fit well with those of nature. The sculpture can be of any style of period you like, although the setting will undoubtedly influence your choice – ultra-modern pieces might not fit well into a romantic or cottage-garden style garden, for example. Pieces can be especially made for the garden, either by yourself if you are skilled or by commission. The latter is likely to be expensive, however, and there are plenty of 'off-the-peg' pieces at reasonable prices available in garden centres and even large DIY stores.

The sculpture can be positioned in isolation, as a focal point – such as at

above: Mirrors and statues are increasingly seen in gardens. Position mirrors carefully so that they provide a reflection of more than just the ornament.

the end of a path or lawn – or it can be integrated into the rest of the garden, perhaps peering out between bushes or mixed with a collection of pots. It may be used in conjunction with something else – a fountain or water spout, for example – and many pieces, especially smaller items of sculpture, look better if they are lifted off the ground on a plinth of some kind to accentuate their presence in the garden.

OBJETS TROUVÉS

There is a large number of 'objects' that can make an attractive addition to the garden, taking the place of more formal (and more expensive) sculpture. Old tree stumps that have been worn into wonderful shapes by the weather make excellent points of interest. They may be posed by themselves or they can act as a base for pots or even another object. Although it is important to exercise discretion, old pieces of rusted metal can look attractive, especially if they are pieces that naturally have a place in the garden, such as old watering cans or old tools.

Architectural reclamation businesses are a useful source of all manner of objects, including pieces of carved stone, curious artwork and a host of other things. Old chimneys or pipes can make good containers for plants or they can be used as objects in their own right. A less expensive place to look is along the seashore, especially after a storm, when all kinds of floating debris can be found, from curiously shaped bits of wood to old buoys and floats.

WEATHERVANES

Although they do not really have a place in an urban garden, a weathervane can be an attractive addition to a rural garden. It is possible to buy a range of patterns – from foxes to yachts, and from frogs to golfers – in black-painted steel, and these can be attached to a shed or garage roof or some other high point. If you enjoy woodwork you can make your own design from laminated softwood board or from exterior-grade hardboard, copper piping and a ballbearing. Apply several coats of polyurethane exterior-grade varnish to the finished design. Be careful if you attach a weathervane to a white-painted wall: after a while, a grimy yellow-brown mark will appear under the fixing, and the wall will need repainting.

EASY TOPIARY

'Proper' topiary, created from small-leaved evergreen plants, is a slow process, involving the regular clipping of slow-growing hedging plants (see page 101). It is far easier and far quicker to create topiary shapes with ivy, which can be quickly trained over a metal former to make attractive evergreen objects. Hearts, spirals, birds, animals and other shapes can be produced within a season and will need only the lightest of clipping thereafter. Choose a small-leaved ivy, such as one of the cultivars of *Hedera helix*, and either buy a purpose-made former or make one for yourself out of chicken wire.

below: The increased availability of metal formers for topiary, created from a small-leaved evergreen such as *Lonicera nitida*, as here, has made it possible for the beginner to create an amusing feature in the garden.

left: In a cottage-garden style planting, an old-fashioned sundial will be a charming and appropriate ornament. Take the trouble to position it carefully.

mirrors, mosaics and painted illusions

As gardens have come to be regarded as extra living space rather than simply a convenient place to grow flowers and vegetables, the inclusion of features that might previously have seemed out of place in a natural setting has become commonplace. Materials such as ceramic, stainless steel and glass are now often found in gardens, where they are increasingly usurping the role of more traditional materials. Although it might be tempting simply to introduce these materials because they are available, care is required so that they sit comfortably with your overall scheme and have a specific, role and do not seem merely to have been incorporated into your beds and borders by accident. Unless the introduction of such items is approached with caution, your garden can easily become a jumble of odds and ends without a coherent theme. Used with discretion, these elements can add sparkle to a garden and bring a factor that is often missing from gardens – fun.

MIRRORS

As well as being used to create the illusion of greater space (see pages 52–3), mirrors can be used in a purely decorative way to reflect light. Fragments can be used in mosaics that are built into walls and other structures (see pages 90–91). Small mirrors can be suspended from trees and bushes so that they catch the light as they swing and rotate, and they can be suspended in dark corners so that they catch shafts of light to brighten the gloom. Most mirrors, however, will be erected against walls or built into free-standing

structures so that they reflect particular areas of the garden or individual features such as statues or specimen plants. They are particularly appropriate when they are used in association with water, either reflecting the surface of a smooth pool or rill or doubling the effect of the sparkling drops from a wall-

above: Wall-mounted mirrors in a small basement garden not only make the area seem larger than it is but also increase the available light by reflecting back the white-painted walls.

mounted fountain. Large mirrors must be carefully positioned so that they do not simply show the person standing in front of them or reflect an unattractive wall. Disguise the edges by training climbers around them, and hide the base of the mirror with clumps of low-growing plants to make the illusion more complete.

project: making a wall mosaic

1

2

MOSAICS

Wall mosaics are an excellent way of disguising or drawing attention to a dull wall, and if you have a narrow passage running alongside a house wall a mosaic pattern or image could be a great way of providing interest and colour in a space that may be unsuitable for plants in containers. The pattern can be abstract or figurative, but the colours should be selected to complement the overall style of the garden or your house, so that it reinforces and underlines your chosen theme.

If a wall mosaic seems rather daunting and far too permanent, smaller mosaic patterns can be used to decorate a table on a patio, especially if the colours you choose reflect the colours of the tableware you use. If the table is to stand outside, use exterior grade adhesive and grout to protect the surface from rainwater. If you do not want to buy special mosaic tiles, use small pieces of broken household crockery – the surface of your table will match your plates and cups.

PAINTED ILLUSIONS

Skilful painters may choose to use a *trompe l'oeil* to create the illusion of space (see page 53), but it is also possible to create a sense of place.

If you are skilful enough, paint an appropriate scene on a wooden panel, which can be held to a wall on battens. This has the advantage that you can work on it where you wish and take it with you if you move house.

If you prefer, work directly on a wall or fence, although to be realistic the

Large-scale mosaics can be fixed directly to a wall, but a small arrangement can be easily attached to a piece of exterior-grade hardboard or MDF (medium density fibreboard) so that it can be moved around the garden at will. Although you can use small, loose ceramic tiles or even small pieces of broken crockery or mirrors, it is also possible to buy sheets of specially made square tiles, which are available from craft shops.

MATERIALS AND EQUIPMENT

waterproof MDF, chipboard (particle board) or plywood
circular mirror
sheets of mosaic tiles
tile clippers
tile adhesive and spreader
waterproof grout

1 Cut the MDF into a circle and stick the mirror in the centre. Draw the outline of the design. Our simple pattern is made up of three shades of blue in alternate segments. Working on small sections at a time, spread tile adhesive over the area and arrange the individual tiles.

2 When you have stuck all the tiles in position, leave overnight for the adhesive to set. Mix some waterproof grout and apply a layer over the tiles, making sure that all the gaps are filled. Leave the grout to begin to go off for about 30 minutes and then wipe off the excess with a damp cloth.

surface should be smooth, so you may need to spend some time priming or even replastering the surface. Remember to use waterproof paints.

It is possible to buy ready-made *trompes l'oeil* in the form of plastic or metal silhouettes, which can be easily fitted to a wall. Some of these are quite

complex and are designed to give the impression of arches, or areas of a garden glimpsed through a partly open door or of a paved courtyard. Many ready-made *trompes l'oeil* are rather clumsy, however, and do not give the effect they are meant to portray. It is always more satisfying to paint your

own and it makes a good talking point. Any *trompes l'oeil* can be improved by being partially obscured by climbers so that they are glimpsed rather than seen in their entirety. These pieces can be screwed directly onto a wall: drill the holes in the appropriate places and insert plugs before screwing them in.

7

One of the great things about containers is that they make gardening flexible. This is partly, of course, because they can be moved around, making it possible to vary plant combinations and positions. It is also, however, because the choice of the containers themselves is so wide. There is a huge variety of pots available from garden centres and nurseries, but some gardeners prefer to look around for more exciting and unconventional containers.

There is scarcely any limit to what can be used, as long as it will hold compost. Some containers that were only recently regarded as rather outlandish have become almost everyday objects in the garden, as ideas have gained wider acceptance through being shown in magazines and books and on television. Galvanized watering cans, for example, are now quite a common sight, and they do at least have the advantage of fitting into the garden scene as, in their own ways, do buckets, water butts and old wheelbarrows. Chimney pots are also popular and suit a variety of plants.

Containers will play an important role in establishing the style of the garden. An earthy look, with terracotta used as the main material, was once considered the height of fashion. Then painted pots enjoyed a brief heyday, as did pots decorated with shells or lengths of cord. Later still, other materials came into favour, and now the spotlight has fallen on stainless steel.

There is a greater range than ever of pots and containers available in garden centres and DIY stores. They vary in style from the classic to the ethnic, and include traditional types, such as barrels, to brightly coloured and vividly patterned ceramic ones. No matter what material or style you select, however, it is vital that the pot has at least one drainage hole in the base so that excess water can drain freely away. Stagnant water will kill most plants. Placing a layer of broken crocks or small stones in the bottom of the container will also help drainage.

containers

conventional containers

There is no reason why you should not use any style or material of container that you come across as long as you are happy with the effect it has in your garden. Terracotta, for example, although it is perhaps no longer as popular as once it was, is a timeless material for the garden, and for most gardeners it will never go out of fashion, but traditional containers are also available in cement and stone substitute, ceramics and plastic.

TERRACOTTA

Terracotta pots have long been the favourite of most gardeners. It is a sympathetic material, which fits in well with both the garden and the plants it contains. Plants also grow well in it. It is porous and so it is difficult to overwater plants (a frequent cause of death), and it is cool in summer and warm in winter. Some terracotta pots are not frostproof and can shatter in winter; these should be placed under cover in very cold weather. Make sure that the pots are slightly raised from the ground so that water can drain away. In winter, even if the frozen water around their roots does not kill your plants, the ice will crack the pots.

CEMENT AND STONE SUBSTITUTE

Stone containers are still available, but they are usually expensive. Many of the reproduction ones, which are made of cement or stone substitute, are good imitations and worth buying. Choose with care, however, because the cheaper versions are poor in quality,

above: A traditional white-painted Versailles planter and a bay tree are the perfect partners. A small-leaved, variegated ivy will soften the edge, and summer colour can be provided by bright annuals.

even though they will, eventually, weather and begin to look more attractive. Containers that are made of cement will also eventually weather, although not as gracefully as stone. If you would like to make a cement container age more quickly, painting the surface with sour milk or yogurt will allow spores or lichen and algae to adhere to the surface and provide nourishment while they develop.

CERAMICS

Until recently terracotta was the only form of ceramic material widely used for garden containers, and because it was unglazed the only available colour was reddish-brown. A range of new ceramic containers has appeared on the market in recent years, and most of these are glazed in a variety of colours and carry a range of incised or slip decorative patterns. Green, blue and brown glazes are among the most popular, but other colours can also be found and the range is now so wide that it can be difficult to choose.

PLASTIC

Most plastic pots look like plastic, and they do not, on the whole, blend sympathetically in an attractive garden. The recent trend towards glass-fibre reproduction containers has, however, made available a range of pots that are so like the original that it is difficult to tell them apart without touching them. They include things like lead tanks, as well as wine jars and other ancient terracotta containers. They can be expensive, but they are so realistic that

below: As long as the plants are in good-quality compost, even a small container will happily accommodate several plants all summer long. Do not forget to feed and water regularly.

it is worth it. Plastic has one great advantage over other materials in that it is light, which makes it easier to move containers from one place to another, even when they are full of compost. One disadvantage is that the sides are not porous, and it is easy to overwater the plants.

above: Old-fashioned terracotta pots are difficult to find, but they are the ideal containers for plants of all kinds as well as being attractive objects in their own right.

left: The sides of a large Cretan vase can be softened by the trailing stems of a pretty perennial such as *Convolvulus sabatius*.

SHAPES

As with materials, there has been an explosion in the number of different shapes and sizes in which pots are available. The basic shape of the everyday flowerpot still takes a lot of beating for its simplicity, and many plants are displayed perfectly in them. A row sitting on a wall or windowsill can look stunning. Many of the other shapes are derived from classic styles, particularly the larger urns, but the new glazed ceramics are available in a whole new range of shapes.

unusual containers

Keen gardeners will be alert for out-of-the-ordinary articles that can be used to hold plants. A good source are junk and antique shops, carboot sales and the like, where a wide range of objects suitable for plants can be found.

FREE EXPRESSION

Anything that can hold some compost can be used as a container, and the object can be used as it is found or it can be fabricated. A simple example of the latter would be to crumple up a piece of sheet metal and place a plant within it. Old garden equipment, from wheelbarrows to watering cans and milk churns, can be pressed into secondary use as containers, and such objects look natural in the garden and blend in easily.

There are plenty of objects that will make amusing containers – a pair of old walking boots or wellington boots, for example, filled with compost and planted up can be witty and not look out of place in the garden. You might even consider planting up the pockets of an old raincoat hanging from a nail on a wall or using an old hat as a home for a plant. These items will not last long before rotting or falling to pieces, but you do not really want to have them hanging around for ever, or the fun will go out of them.

FITTING THE OBJECT TO THE PLANT

Some types of container will suit some types of plant better than others. Plants with long or vigorous roots will do best in deep containers – a hosta, for

above: Stylish containers from junk: an old chimney stack provides an unusual, but attractive, home for *Muscari armeniacum* (grape hyacinth) and primroses.

example, would look good and would thrive in a large cooking pot, whereas smaller sedums and sempervivums would be more at home in something shallow. The plant should also visually go with the container. Hostas will generally go better with more sober-looking containers, but brightly coloured annuals look great in a range of shapes and objects. Dwarf, bright blue cornflowers will look cheerful and festive in a tin can suspended from its still-attached lid.

Treading the line between what is appropriate and what is not is difficult when it comes to unconventional containers. One person can take a few empty tin cans and convert them into a sophisticated, eye-catching display, while someone else, given the same plants and the same cans, will produce what looks like a row of empty baked-bean tins. Be critical of what you do, and if you have any doubts about your creations, discard them.

DECORATING CONTAINERS

If the container is plain, decorate it before you fill it by either painting it or sticking objects or even a mosaic pattern on the sides. Even conventional flowerpots can be decorated to make them more interesting or more personal. Ordinary terracotta pots, for example, can be painted a different colour; you might choose a single, overall colour, or prefer to decorate it in some other way.

Clean the surface of the pot thoroughly, especially if it is greasy. Unless you want the natural colour to show through, apply a coat of white undercoat. Use masking tape to provide temporary protection for areas that you want to leave their natural colour. Paint the decorations on the undercoat, using gouache paint or, for less usual shades, tester pots of emulsion paint which are available in DIY stores. When the paint is dry, remove any masking tape and cover the decoration with a layer of matt polyurethane varnish to protect the surface.

Another way to make containers more personal is to add mosaic or three-dimensional decorations. Shells are a traditional ornamentation, but they can look rather dated unless they are applied with care. You can also use pebbles, stones or pieces of wood – almost anything, in fact. It is possible to build up the ornamentation to such an extent that the pot itself is entirely hidden, thereby creating a completely different object while retaining the original pot inside, which is ready to take the compost and plant.

ADAPTING CONTAINERS

The principles for adapting a container to hold plants are the same no matter what object is selected. For most plants the container should be deep enough to allow the roots to grow, which means a depth of at least 15cm (6in), although there are a few plants, such as sedums and sempervivums (houseleeks), that will grow in a thin layer of compost, and for these something as shallow as a dustbin lid can be sufficient.

In addition to the container, you will need something with which to make holes in the base, a few stones, potting

compost and some gravel or chippings for top-dressing. Before you do anything else, make some drainage holes in the bottom of the container. If the base is not flat, the holes should be at the lowest points. Cover the bottom with a layer of small stones to improve drainage before filling with good-quality, general-purpose compost. Add the plant or plants of your choice and top-dress with gravel.

above: Discarded kitchen utensils have been pressed into service for a collection of grasses. Stand the flowerpots on a bed of gravel so that the plants do not sit in stagnant water for too long.

points to remember:

INSULATION

One of the great advantages of terracotta or glazed ceramic containers is that they offer the roots of plants some protection from extremes of heat and cold. The thin walls of stainless-steel planters afford no such protection. Placing a sheet of plastic bubblewrap around the inside of a metal container before you fill it with compost (not across the base, of course) will help to protect the plant from baking in summer and freezing in winter.

plant list:

PERENNIALS FOR CONTAINERS

- ● *Acanthus mollis* (bear's breeches)
  A stately plant with purple and white flowers in erect spires in late summer.

- ● *Agapanthus campanulatus* (African blue lily)
  Strap-shaped, grey-green leaves are surmounted by blue or white flowers in summer.

- ● *Dianthus 'Doris'*
  Fragrant, double, pale pink flowers have a dark pink centre.

- ● *Diascia vigilis*
  A spreading plant with pink flowers in loose racemes from early summer to autumn.

- ● *Euphorbia characias* subsp. *wulfenii* (spurge)
  Bright yellow-green flowerheads are borne from spring to early summer.

- ● *Hosta* 'Gold Standard'
  Pale green-yellow, heart-shaped leaves form a dense clump surmounted by tall scapes of grey-purple flowers in summer.

- ● *Nepeta x faassenii* (catmint)
  Grey-green leaves are aromatic and topped by mauvish flowers.

- ● *Ophiopogon jaburan* 'Vittatus' (lilyturf)
  This tufted plant has grass-like leaves that are finely striped with green and creamy-white.

- ● *Phormium tenax* (New Zealand flax)
  Rigid, sword-shaped leaves form dense rosettes.

- ● *Primula vulgaris* (primrose)
  In spring lovely yellow flowers are borne above the rosettes of green leaves.

- ● *Stachys byzantina* (lamb's ears)
  Grey-green leaves form dense rosettes with spikes of purple-pink flowers in summer to early autumn.

seasonal displays

The simplest and easiest way to use containers is to plan a series of plantings, one for each season. You could use a single-colour theme, such as white and silver, or create a splash of colour using a mixture of plants. Plant breeders bring out new cultivars every season, and containers can be filled with bright summer annuals in every shade imaginable.

SUMMER AND AUTUMN

Most summer interest is created by brightly coloured annuals in a range of colours. Red, pink and purple are popular summer colours when mixed with interesting foliage plants, and the result will be lively and eye-catching. When you are composing a planting scheme, choose plants with contrasting flower shapes. Masses of tiny blooms, such as sweet alyssum and trailing lobelia, create a hazy effect, softening the edges and hiding the container. They contrast well with the larger plants that form the main focus of the container.

Many summer displays will last into autumn and can then be replaced with winter plants, but to tide the arrangement over there are several plants, such as fuchsias and sedums, that will provide autumnal interest.

WINTER AND SPRING

Foliage comes into its own in winter, along with shrubby plants that produce berries. These can be supplemented with winter-flowering bulbs in mild climates. Spring interest is mainly provided by bulbs and biennials, which burst into colour from early to late

above: The dark, chocolate flowers of *Cosmos atrosanguineus* and dark brown leaves of *Heuchera micrantha* var. *diversifolia* 'Palace Purple' are a wonderful contrast to the glass mulch.

spring, sometimes lasting into early summer. Yellow is a favourite spring colour, either on its own with some fresh foliage or combined with white, cream and, perhaps, a hint of blue. For more of an impact, add a splash of

yellow to a vibrant mixed planting of reds, blues and whites.

When you are planting containers for winter, concentrate on shape and form to create bold, striking outlines with a variety of foliage plants and fill in the gaps with bulbs. The foliage of some miniature conifers has an intriguing aromatic quality when it is bruised. *Chamaecyparis lawsoniana* 'Ellwoodii' smells of resin and parsley, *C. pisifera* 'Boulevard' has a resinous scent, and *Juniperus communis* 'Compressa' smells faintly of apples. Interplant these conifers with small bulbs, such as the honey-scented *Iris danfordiae* or the violet-scented *I. reticulata* for a wonderful winter display that both looks and smells delightful.

FOLIAGE FOR YEAR-ROUND INTEREST

Foliage plants are an important part of any planting, but particularly so in containers, which tend to have short periods of interest created by seasonal plants. Foliage, however, provides a permanent structure against which flowers can come and go.

Grey-leaved plants such as *Helichrysum petiolare* (liquorice plant) and *Senecio cineraria* play a useful part in different colour schemes. When reds and blues are combined with white, grey will 'cool' the impact of the strong hues. Its neutral tones make the visual leap to pure white less dazzling. A subdued background of grey foliage will bring out the best in pinks, mauves and misty blues and will delicately harmonize container colour schemes.

Golden foliage tones have affinities with yellow flowers and mid-green leaves. Their presence intensifies the richness of deep blues and violets. Plants with variegated foliage, such as *Hebe* x *andersonii* 'Variegata' and *H.* x *franciscana* 'Variegata' and variegated ivies, are decorative in their own right but, mixed with flowering plants, add interest and texture.

BULBS

Bulbs can be used on their own for a spectacular seasonal display or interspersed with other plants to provide interest before other plants come into their own. It is also possible to include two or three types of bulb in the same container to give a succession of colour. The dark blue, early-flowering *Iris reticulata* 'J.S. Dijit', for example, can be planted in the same container as the silver-blue *Crocus chrysanthus* 'Blue Pearl' and the cream and yellow *Narcissus* 'February Silver'. The bulbs should be planted at different depths – the narcissus bulbs lower than the smaller crocus corms – and carefully arranged so that the plants can grow straight up and provide interest for two months when there is little other colour in the garden.

Crocus vernus 'Purpureus Grandiflorus'

A bright harbinger of spring, this Dutch crocus has bright violet flowers, shading to darker purple at the base, and bright yellow anthers. Like all spring-flowering crocuses, it does best in a sunny position in well-drained soil. It is equally at home in a container or in short grass.

Galanthus nivalis (snowdrop)

One of the earliest flowers to appear in spring, the drooping white bells are a familiar sight. They do best in partial shade, especially when allowed to naturalize under deciduous trees and shrubs. New snowdrops are best planted in late spring 'in the green' (before the leaves have died back) rather than as bulbs in autumn.

plant profiles

plant list:

SPRING BULBS

- **Anemone blanda** (wood anemone)
  A small woodland bulb, with white, blue or pink daisy-like flowers.

- **Camassia cusickii 'Zwanenburg'**
  Deep blue, star-shaped flowers are borne in dense racemes on erect stems.

- **Chionodoxa luciliae** (glory-of-the-snow)
  A small bulb with blue, white-centred flowers.

- **Corydalis flexuosa**
  Blue flowers are borne above the glaucous green leaves.

- **Crocus vernus**
  White or purple-flushed flowers can be naturalized in grass.

- **Eranthis hyemalis** (winter aconite)
  A little woodland bulb with golden flowers surrounded by green ruffs.

- **Fritillaria michailovskyi**
  Unusual dark, purplish-green and bright yellow, bell-shaped flowers are borne on short stems.

- **Galanthus nivalis** (snowdrop)
  A small, early-flowering bulb with white flowers.

- **Hyacinthoides non-scripta** (bluebell)
  Delicately fragrant, misty blue flowers.

- **Leucojum vernum** (snowflake)
  Resembling large snowdrops but flowering later in the season.

- **Puschkinia scilloides**
  A short bulb with pale blue flowers.

- **Romulea bulbocodium**
  Pale to deep lilac flowers have white or pale yellow centres.

- **Scilla siberica** (Siberian squill)
  Bright blue flowers are borne on short stems.

grouping and moving containers

One of the great advantages of gardening with containers is that they can, as long as they are not too big, be moved, allowing you to create ever-changing scenes. You can move pots around to reflect your mood, you can place them in groups, or you can change them around as plants come into flower.

CONTAINERS ON THE MOVE

There are two main approaches to the mobile garden. The first is to move a set of pots around, changing their positions and regrouping them from time to time. This can be done as the mood takes you, or it can be done in a more systematic way. You may, for example, simply feel like a change or you may feel that one or two of the pots are looking better than the others and should be moved to the front for a month or two.

A second approach is to keep pots of plants in reserve, in the greenhouse if you have one or tucked away at the bottom of the garden, so that you can move them into position as you need them or as they come into flower. Bulbs, for example, can be left in their pots all year round, and moved to positions of prominence as they come into flower but be tucked away out of sight for the rest of the year. If space is very limited, the bulbs can be removed (and kept somewhere dry and frost-free) and the containers can be replanted with summer bedding plants or something similar.

Plants in containers really come into their own when you are

above: Half-hardy and tender plants that are grown permanently in containers can be moved outdoors in warm weather and will combine happily with container-grown summer annuals.

entertaining. You can move plants indoors to enhance the mood you are trying to create: brightly coloured ones for a party or a convivial evening, or softly coloured ones for a more romantic setting. If you have a terrace you can stand fragrant plants near to where you may be eating during the

evening. On a more practical level, you could place pots of herbs, especially mint, near where you are serving drinks or eating for instant garnishes.

LANDSCAPE WITH POTS

If your garden has been covered with hard landscaping, almost all of your gardening is going to be done in pots. It is surprising what can be grown in a container, even vegetables. You can have different pots representing different areas of the garden – a group of pots containing vegetables, cheerful summer bedding, herbs, a few shrubs and even flowers for cutting.

Some people, especially those living in flats and apartments, have no garden at all, but they do have a balcony or even access to a roof. Both these make admirable places for creating small potted gardens. Before you begin, however, make sure that the structure is strong enough to support the weight. Roof areas may need adapting, not only to bear the load but also so that there is an acceptable surface for walking on. Flat lead roofs, for example, look ideal for a mass of containers, but the lead can be easily punctured and will need decking above it. If you are at all unsure, seek professional advice.

plant list:

ANNUALS AND TENDER PERENNIALS FOR CONTAINERS

● **Argyranthemum frutescens**
A variable subshrub with white, daisy-like flowers in summer.

● **Begonia** Semperflorens Cultorum Group
Compact plants with rounded bronze-green leaves and small pink or red flowers.

● **Bidens ferulifolia**
Golden-yellow flowers appear from midsummer to autumn.

● **Brachyscome iberidifolia** (Swan river daisy)
A spreading plant that has white, blue-purple or violet-pink daisy-like flowers in summer.

● **Helichrysum petiolare 'Variegatum'**
A trailing shrub with cream-variegated, grey-green leaves.

● **Impatiens walleriana** (busy Lizzie)
The light green or bronze-green foliage is covered by red, pink, orange or white flowers in summer.

● **Pelargonium** cultivars
Colourful flowers are borne on erect or trailing stems throughout summer.

● **Petunia** cultivars
Showy flowers in white or shades of blue, purple, pink and red are borne from summer to autumn.

● **Verbena** cultivars
Spreading, mat-forming plants bear dense heads of purple-blue, pink, red, yellow or white flowers in summer.

● **Viola x wittrockiana** (pansy)
The familiar flowers are available in a range of colours and sizes for colour from early spring to late autumn.

VARYING THE HEIGHT

When you have a collection of pots it is a good idea to vary the level so that the plants form a cohesive group rather than looking like a random selection of containers that look as if they have just been left to fend for themselves. Place tall plants towards the back and mix the foliage and flowering plants so that they make an attractive combination and colours do not clash. Plants at the back that are obscured by the ones in the front of them can be brought into view by being raised off the ground.

above left: Metal buckets make elegant containers, but must have drainage holes drilled in the base.

Place the pots on some form of support, such as bricks or upturned pots. If you want them much higher, use a specially made table or a system of shelves, but make sure that it is properly made and sturdy.

above: *Agave americana* 'Variegata' is not reliably hardy, and should be taken indoors at the first sign of frost.

points to remember:

SAFETY FIRST

The larger pots are extremely heavy when they are filled with compost, especially when the compost is moist, and they will be too heavy to move. Use the largest containers as permanent features and put them in position before you fill and plant them up. Even small pots may be filled in situ, especially if they are awkward shapes, which are difficult to carry.

windowboxes and hanging baskets

Many people regard container gardening as little more than having a few well-positioned pots on a terrace or beside the front door. Containers can, however, be used to advantage at any height. They can be placed on the tops of walls or on windowsills or they can be suspended from the branches of trees or even from the eaves.

WINDOWBOXES

Because they are reasonably large, you can get quite a number of plants in each windowbox, and this gives greater scope for creating a series of miniature gardens, each one as colourful or as subtle as you wish. You need not keep windowboxes for windowsills, however. There is the advantage with such boxes that they can be fitted almost anywhere. Windowsills are the obvious place, of course, although they are better on houses that have inward-opening or sash windows than on those with outward-opening casements. Even if a window opens outwards, however, a box can be fitted to the wall below the window rather than on the window ledge itself.

Windowboxes can also be fixed on blank walls and can do much to cheer up what could otherwise be a rather bleak scene. There is also a large number of containers, mainly ceramic, but some plastic, that have been especially designed for fixing to walls. Many are the equivalent of half a conventional pot, and they have one flat side instead of being completely round. These are often small enough to hang on a hook or nail.

above: Foliage, in the form of the trailing stems of *Glechoma hederacea* 'Variegata' and *Helichrysum petiolare*, will provide a lasting background for summer annuals.

HANGING BASKETS

Another way of filling vertical space is to use hanging baskets. Over the years many new cultivars have been developed to have a trailing habit, from unusual foliage plants to colourful petunias and lobelias. These are ideally suited to hanging baskets, which can be suspended from any overhang or from brackets fixed to vertical walls. They can also be hung from poles placed around the garden, perhaps next to a patio or along a path. These could also support lighting of various kinds.

Because they roll about, filling a hanging basket can be awkward. Stand the basket in a large bucket to hold it steady while you work. Add a liner – there are several types to choose from, ranging from pressed cardboard to old knitwear – and partially fill the basket with good-quality compost, to which you have added some water-retaining granules and some slow-release fertilizer. Cut up to three slits around the basket, level with the surface of the compost, and poke a plant through each slit. It is usually easier to do this if you wash off the existing compost from around each plant's roots and wrap the roots in wet paper tissue. Poke this through the slit from the outside, remove the paper and spread out the roots. Add some more compost. If it is a large, deep basket, add a second row of plants, staggering their position in relation to the first row. Fill the basket to the rim and firm down the compost gently. Plant the remaining plants in the top of the basket and level off the soil, removing or adding compost so that the

left: A scaled-down version of a Versailles planter is an attractive windowbox for a traditional house. The autumn-flowering *Cyclamen hederifolium* provides both colour and scent.

below left: Half baskets can be attached beneath an outward-opening window. They should be planted up with a liner and good-quality compost.

final surface is just below the rim of the basket. Water thoroughly and hang up.

WATERING

The main problem with containers of all kinds is making sure that the compost does not dry out. In hot weather containers usually need to be watered at least once a day and sometimes more often. This is tedious enough when the containers are standing on the ground, but once they are above head height it becomes difficult to lift a watering can sufficiently high to pour out the water. One solution is to use a garden hose attached to a cane or broomstick, which can be easily raised in the air. Another method is to use one of the pump-action watering devices that are available. These have a long lance with a bend in the end, and pumping forces the water out of the reservoir and up and into the container.

points to remember:

LOOKING AFTER HANGING BASKETS

Hanging baskets can dry out very quickly, not only because they are generally in a sunny position but also because the compost is exposed to the elements more directly than it would be in a conventional, thick-sided container. Daily watering is essential, but it is important not to add so much water at once that it drains straight through the bottom of the basket, leaching out the nutrients. If you do not add slow-release fertilizer to the compost, apply a liquid feed once a week. Remove spent flowers and withered leaves regularly, not only to keep the arrangement looking tidy but also because deadheading encourages new blooms. Cut back any fast-growing or trailing plants to keep the arrangement looking tidy and to stop any one plant from taking over and dominating the scheme.

planting tips and maintenance

For robust plant and season-long flowering, make sure your containers get the very best start. Use the right compost, keep it well watered and deadhead the plants regularly. Summer-flowering plants will need regular feeding, and you should also keep the containers free of weeds.

GROWING MEDIUMS

Well-drained but moisture-retentive compost is essential for all plants in containers. The planting medium must also be fertile for summer-flowering bedding plants, which need to develop rapidly and sustain growth throughout summer. Spring bulbs, which are planted in late summer or autumn, do not need highly fertile compost.

A suitable mix consists of equal parts of a loam-based and a peat-based compost (use a peat substitute, such as coir or bark, whenever possible). The peat or peat substitute retains moisture, while the loam-based part provides nutrients, especially the minor ones. The addition of perlite or vermiculite further assists the retention of moisture while helping to maintain a free-draining, open character to the compost. If weight is a consideration – on roof gardens and in windowboxes and hanging baskets, for example – use a loam-free compost, although, unfortunately, these are mostly peat-based.

DRAINAGE

It is essential that containers have adequate drainage or the planting medium will become waterlogged and the plant roots will rot. Make sure that every container you use has at least one large central drainage hole, preferably more, in the base. Place a layer of crocks (broken pieces of clay flowerpots or household crockery) over the bottom of the container before filling it with compost. A layer of well-washed pea shingle can be used instead of crocks for more permanent displays. So that the shingle and compost does not get washed through large drainage holes, it can be a good idea to cover the holes with a piece of plastic mesh.

All containers should be raised slightly from the ground so that excess water can drain away. It is possible to buy special terracotta feet that match the containers. Make sure that the feet you use do not raise the container so far above ground that it becomes top-heavy and could be blown over. Pieces of brick and flat stones will do the same job. You could also use the metal trivets that are sold for protecting kitchen surfaces from hot pans.

PLANTING

When it comes to planting containers it is a good idea to place the plants you have chosen, still in their pots, on top of the soil so that you can experiment with different arrangements before you plant them. Once you have decided on the best composition, press each pot lightly into the soil to leave a slight indentation so that you can see where to make the hole.

The planting holes should be large enough to accommodate the roots with a little room to spare. Carefully remove the plants from their pots: place your hand flat over the surface of the pot with the stem of the plant between two fingers. Ease off the pot. If the rootball looks solid, gently tease it apart to loosen it slightly before planting. Once planted, firm the compost around the plant and water well.

above: All containers should be raised above the ground for drainage. Terracotta feet that will match your planter are available, but small stones will suffice.

left: The grass-like leaves and dainty flowers of *Sisyrinchium* 'Biscutella' are enhanced by a mulch of fine gravel, which protects the neck of the plant from winter wet.

WATERING

The relatively small volume of compost and large numbers of plants in most containers makes it essential that they are watered regularly throughout summer. The compost should also be kept just moist at other times of the year. In hot weather plants sometimes appear to wilt during the early afternoon even though the compost is moist, and this is because they cannot absorb moisture quickly enough. The plants usually recover by the evening. Water-retaining granules can be mixed with the compost before planting. They do not eliminate the need for watering in hot, dry weather, but they do mean that plants are under less stress if, for some reason, you cannot water the containers every day.

FEEDING

Summer-flowering bedding plants need feeding regularly from early to late summer at intervals of about three weeks. Spring-flowering displays, consisting of bulbs and biennials, such as wallflowers and daisies, do not need to be fed as long as fresh, fertile compost was used when they were planted. Feed winter-flowering displays in late spring and in midsummer.

A liquid fertilizer of some kind is the most convenient way of feeding plants because it is easily absorbed by the plants' roots. Sticks and pills of concentrated plant fertilizer provide nutrients over a long period. They are quick and clean to use, but the chemicals in them are not as readily available to plants as those applied in water. If you are using granular or powdered fertilizers for containers, they must be dissolved first in clean water.

DEADHEADING AND PINCHING OUT

Regularly removing dead flowers encourages the development of further buds and prolongs the display. Blooms left on plants will decay and encourage disease. If plants have long stalks, cut these back to the base. If the flowers are borne in tight clusters close to the main stem use scissors to cut them off. Pick up all the dead flowers and put them on the compost heap. Left among the plants they will encourage diseases.

Tall, lanky plants can be encouraged to put out more sideshoots if you nip out the growing points when they are young. Fuchsias, for example, benefit if the shoots are snapped sideways or the tips pinched off after three sets of leaves have formed. Try to position the break just above a leaf so that you do not leave a short stem, which will die back and decay.

CLIMBERS IN CONTAINERS

In a limited area using every possible surface to grow plants is important, and growing climbers against a wall can be a problem if the surface is paved. You might be able to lift a paving slab and grow the plant in the soil beneath. A better choice might be to grow the climber in a container, which should be as large as possible to give plenty of root space. It is essential that the container never dries out, and it is likely to need watering on most dry days.

Viola x *wittrockiana* (pansy)

Winter- and summer-flowering cultivars of the well-loved pansy are available in every imaginable colour. Although they are perennials, treat them as annuals and replace your plants regularly.

points to remember:

VINE WEEVILS

When it comes to pests, most gardeners suffer from nothing worse than aphids and slugs, but there is a pest that is becoming increasingly widespread and that is a real menace to gardeners everywhere. The adult vine weevil, which is greyish-brown with yellowish spots and about 1cm (⅓in) long, will eat U-shaped pieces out of leaves, but the real damage is done by the grubs. Each adult can lay about 1500 eggs, which develop into small, C-shaped, creamy-yellow larvae. The larvae eat their way through root systems and stems, causing plants to collapse and die. Container-grown plants are particularly vulnerable. Watering nematodes into moist, warm compost in summer is the best solution, because the nematodes destroy the grubs and are perfectly safe to use around children and do not harm soil-borne organisms.

plant profile

8

There is always plenty of choice when it comes to selecting plants to fill a particular space in a garden. You can choose plants for their decorative flowers or their fragrance, for their evergreen or variegated foliage, for their coloured stems and bark, for their fruits and berries, for their ability to climb or trail, or for their upright or spreading habit. You can choose from annuals, perennials, shrubs and trees. You can design a garden around bulbs and climbers or even around a single species if you wish. If your time is limited, there are plenty of plants that, once established, require little attention.

Some plants, of course, need a special environment. Alpines need a rock garden or scree bed, bog-garden plants need damp soil and aquatic plants need a pool, and in a small garden it may be possible to provide the conditions that are suitable for only one of these groups.

Whichever plants you choose to grow, they must be displayed well if they are to look their best. Plant association is not just a question of putting together plants that flower at the same time or in succession. Instead, look for plants that complement each other in terms of habit and size, texture and colour.

Having chosen your plants, you must look after them if they are to reward you with form, fragrance and colour. Providing the optimum growing conditions and remembering to water and feed your plants when they need it are just as important as laying a safe patio or building strong decking.

planting

plant shapes and positioning

Although colour is probably the most prominent aspect of a border and the thing we notice first, the shape and texture of plants also play an important role in the garden and can be used to create interest in their own right. The outline of every plant is different: some are tall and narrow, while others are flat and ground covering; some are squat and rounded, while others have cascading stems. These shapes should be used to create an interesting and diverse picture.

LOW-GROWING PLANTS

Prostrate plants tend to let the eye skate over them. A bed or border entirely filled with such plants will look boring and be in need of something to break the monotony, but they are perfect for providing linking passages between other, more interesting plants. Low-growing plants can also be effective when they are allowed to flow over surface features so that their own surface becomes sculptural.

Rounded and dome-shaped plants, on the other hand, have a rather self-contained feel about them. They are comfortable plants to have in a border and contrast well with spikier plants. They are also useful for providing the basic structure in a border.

UPRIGHT PLANTS

Any tall shape emphasizes the vertical elements in a border, but slender, erect shapes are especially useful. They are sometimes used as focal points, and some of these plants can be used to play a part in the overall shape of a

above: A well-planted border provides colour over a long period, but evergreens, such as a neatly clipped box and spreading blue fescue, create permanent structure.

border, especially in autumn and winter, when form in the garden is needed.

Many plants have stiff stems that list slightly away from the centre, roughly forming a fan as they spread out to find the light. These have a certain vertical emphasis and act as a good contrast to more rounded shapes. Other plants have a narrow base and leaves that curve upwards and outwards and

downwards, almost as if they were a fountain. These are dramatic plants and often catch the eye. Both types are best used in isolation rather than in groups so that their shapes can be appreciated. Yet other plants have rigid leaves that tend to splay outwards in a spiky spray or ball.

LEAF SHAPE

In addition to the shape of the whole plant, it is important that the shape of the leaf is taken into consideration. Some leaves directly influence the shape of the plant – strap-shaped leaves, for instance, form a fountain and pointed ones form a halo of spikes – but there are also the filigree leaves

of plants like ferns, which have a delicate, airy appearance that contrasts with the regular, oval leaves of plants such as hostas. A combination of leaf shapes and forms is always more interesting than a border composed of just one type.

PLANT TEXTURE

The texture of plants is not as obvious an attribute as the other characteristics, but it plays a related and important part in the overall design of a border. Texture is seen mainly in the individual parts of the plant – the leaves or sometimes the bark – but it can also be evident in the plant as a whole, as the sum of the parts comes into play.

left: The unusual flowers of *Dodecatheon puchellum* (shooting stars) are seen at their best in a scree garden in spring.

protect them from the sun, rain, insects or something else that might threaten them. The leaves usually have a furry feel to them and are often given common names that reflect this – *Stachys byzantina* is known as lamb's ears or bunny's ears. Such leaves have the double benefit of texture and colour, which is usually silver or grey. Both the texture and colour can be used for linking stronger colours and cooling them down. For example, they go well with bright magenta, a colour that is not always easy to cope with.

Other leaves have a matt or even velvety texture that absorbs light. This gives the leaves a richness and depth of colour. Although frequently interesting in their own right, they work particularly well when they are used to link more colourful plants.

FLOWER TEXTURE

The texture of flowers has much the same effect as that of foliage. Shiny petals reflect light, which lifts the colour and makes it sparkle. Velvet-textured petals, on the other hand, have a sumptuous feeling about them, especially if they are dark red, when they create a rich and luxurious effect.

Another way in which flowers are textured is that they have lines, stripes, dots or splashes on the petals, which draw you into the flower in the same way they are intended to guide a bee to the nectar. The texture of flowers is most noticeable when they occur in drifts, but it is most appreciated when the flowers are seen close to, when cut or at the border's edge.

The diversity of appearance is one of the most fascinating things about plants. One of the most obvious textures in a garden is glossy or shiny foliage. The leaves on these plants tend to reflect light and even sparkle. These are ideal plants for darker corners, where the light catching the leaves will be reflected back and lighten the gloom. Foliage with deep ribs and prominent veins always looks interesting. These features break up flat surfaces and allow light to be reflected from different angles. This will often have the effect that a plain green leaf will appear to consist of several different greens. Some leaves, like those of *Oxalis adenophylla*, are so folded that they appear to be pleated, and this is an especially appealing feature.

The leaves of many plants are densely covered in hairs, usually to

Phormium tenax 'Bronze Baby'

The arching, sword-shaped leaves are reddish-bronze and will eventually form a dense rosette about 80cm (32in) high and across. Phormiums, which are not reliably hardy, need a position in full sun and well-drained, humus-rich soil. They are ideal plants for creating focal points.

plant profile

creating structure

Structure is an important element in the garden, especially in winter, when herbaceous plants have died back below ground. It is also important in summer, however, because it will provide a sense of continuity as other plants come and go. Trees, hedges and climbers will contribute a sense of permanence to a garden, and they are the keys around which many garden features are designed. It is these plants that provide the vertical dimension that is so important in every garden and that brings the year-round structure against which other plants are viewed.

HEIGHT

The general principle with beds and borders that have a background is to plant the tallest plants at the back and the shortest ones at the front. In island beds the received wisdom is that the tallest plants should be in the middle, with the shorter ones around them. If you follow this rule to the letter, however, the bed or border will end up looking like choir stalls, with even ranks of plants graded by height. This not only becomes boring, but also tends to make the eye move towards the end of the bed without appreciating the plants in between. Bring a few of the taller plants forward so that the overall impression becomes a little more uneven.

There are some plants, such as *Verbena bonariensis* and many of the grasses, that, although they are tall, are fine and airy and allow you to see through them, with the plants beyond appearing in a haze. Plant a few of these at the front to break up the rigid

above: The bold edging of the patio could easily overpower the plants, but the strongly shaped and variegated foliage more than holds its own.

lines of the border even more. One advantage of pulling forward some of the taller plants is that they will partially obscure what lies beyond, which is not revealed until you have moved a little further down the garden, making the design more exciting.

DEPTH

The depth of a border is important, because the deeper it is the taller the plants you can grow in it. Growing tall plants in a narrow border rarely works, although, as with all principles of gardening, there are always plenty of exceptions, and one of these is when a border is backed by a high wall or hedge. In general, however, the width or depth of a border should be at least twice the height of its tallest plants.

Generously deep beds always seem more pleasing to look at than narrow ones, and, whatever the size of the garden, it will look more effective with fewer, deeper beds than with a greater number of narrow ones. Deep beds, of course, allow you to include a wider range of plants and in greater numbers, which makes arranging the plants much easier. It also allows you to set out herbaceous plants in drifts, creating a better overall effect than is possible with a single planting.

POSITIONING PLANTS

Good design in a border is as much about how you arrange the plants as it is about the plants you choose. If you have the luxury of a deep border, this task will be made much easier, because you will be able to use groups of the same plant rather than using plants singly. Using single plants can leave a bed looking spotty and rather cluttered.

When you are planting a group, always try to use an odd number of plants because it is much easier to arrange odd numbers than even ones. Once you get above nine (as with

RHYTHM

In cottage-garden style plantings and other informal borders everything can be mixed together, which is interesting in its own right, but one way to create a more formal sense of interest is by creating rhythm down the length of the border. This can be done by repeating particular plants or colours. Topiarized box bushes or bay trees will produce this effect, but there are many other more subtle ways of doing it. These include the repeated use of colour and the use of related shapes of plants, such as those with spiky or cascading foliage. Formal bedding schemes often take this technique to the extreme by repeating patterns as well as colours and shapes.

Sometimes the effect is not so much a rhythm but more of being led on. One group of colours may lead naturally to the next, for example. Dark blue flowers might merge into plants with pale blue ones, which in turn merge into white and on to creamy yellow and so on, creating a pleasing natural progression.

left: *Allium* cultivars (ornamental onions) are used to punctuate the mass of densely planted herbs. The edges of the borders are softened by the pretty leaves of *Alchemilla mollis* (lady's mantle).

bulbs) it is not so important, but three or five plants are always much easier to lay out than four or six. The best effect is achieved by creating seemingly random drifts of plants that interlock to fill the space. Vary the heights a little to make the display more interesting. Above all, be bold: use large drifts for the best effects.

SPECIMEN PLANTS

Although most plants in a border should be planted in drifts, stunning effects can be created by using some plants singly as specimen plants to add focal points to the scheme. The plants best suited to this are those with a distinctive shape or texture, which will stand out from the surrounding plants. Use these intermittently down the border to create rhythm or at the end of the border to add a definite full stop. This type of plant can also be used to highlight a feature, such as an urn or gateway, by being planted symmetrically to balance the view. When you are planting the border, leave enough space around these plants so that they really stand out. Choose spiky plants, such as cordylines and yuccas, or plants with a distinctive habit, such as grasses or columnar conifers.

Corylus avellana 'Contorta' (corkscrew hazel)

In early spring yellow catkins appear; in summer the stems are clothed with heart-shaped leaves; and in winter the unadorned but strongly twisting stems can be appreciated. Cut out any straight stems to prevent the plant from reverting, and grow in sun or semi-shade in well-drained, humus-rich soil.

plant profile

small plants for a small space

One way that a keen gardener can grow a lot of plants in a small area is simply to grow small plants. Because these types of plant can be easily grown in raised beds, they are ideal for people who cannot tend conventional ground-level beds. There are two types of small plants to grow – alpine plants and small plants – and they are not necessarily the same.

ALPINES

Growing alpines is a specialist activity. Some are easy to grow, but others, especially the so-called high alpines, are extremely difficult and need a great deal of skill and dedication. One of the secrets of growing good alpines is to use a free-draining but moisture-retentive soil or compost. The actual mixture varies according to the plants grown and the individual grower's preferences, but as with any specialist subject there are plenty of books to consult. Alpine growers tend to become addicted to their pastime, and they spend a great deal of time tending the plants and even making field trips to see how they grow in the wild. Once you are bitten with alpine bug, it can be a fascinating form of gardening, but to do it well you need both time and dedication. What you do not necessarily need, however, is space, so it is an ideal form of gardening for the owner of a small garden.

Most alpine plants are completely hardy, but many are susceptible to damp, mild winters. These plants need some protection, as much from the rain as from the cold. Enthusiasts for alpine species will want to have an alpine house, which is basically the same as a greenhouse but with much better ventilation. Even in winter the windows are left open for air to circulate unless rain or snow is likely to blow in. The staging is usually very strongly constructed because each has to contain a deep layer of sand into which the pots are sunk. This helps to keep the roots warm in winter and cool in summer, and it also helps to keep the compost just damp, because moisture can seep from the sand through the drainage holes in the bottom of the pots or, if terracotta pots are used, through the sides of the pots.

SMALL PLANTS

If you do not feel that alpines are for you there is a wealth of small plants that are not necessarily alpine but that are easy to grow and are ideal for creating a miniature garden. These plants or their seeds are readily available and can be used to make a small version of a conventional garden without anything like the amount of labour or effort involved in gardening with alpines. This makes them ideal for the elderly or infirm gardener.

Miniature gardens can be created in conventional beds, raised beds or in

above: What could have been an undistinguished mass of foliage has been given structure by the planting of carefully selected purple-flowered plants, such as *Allium hollandicum* and the wallflower *Erysimum* 'Bowles' Mauve'.

a wide range of containers. Small pieces of rock can be used to help build up the landscape, and small sunken dishes of water can be used to represent ponds. The scale can vary from reasonably sized beds, perhaps several metres (yards) across, to ones built in old sinks or troughs. You could even make a really tiny one in a dinner plate. Inverted dustbin lids and hubcaps from motorcars make good containers. Garden soil can be used in larger beds, but smaller containers should be filled with a proprietary general-purpose potting compost.

One crucial benefit about such small containers is that they can be placed on tables or raised on piers of bricks so that they are easily accessible to those who have difficulty bending or are confined to wheelchairs. People who may have had to give up conventional gardening but are as keen as ever on growing things have a great opportunity to do so without too much effort.

left: Gravel and graded cobbles will keep down weeds in a narrow border that runs along a path. The old-fashioned rope edging is ideal for cottage gardens.

plant list:

PLANTS FOR SMALL-SCALE GARDENS

In addition to the many low-growing saxifrages, sedums (stonecrops), sempervivums (houseleeks) and thymes and the smaller bulbs, such as crocuses and reticulate irises, the following are suitable for gardening in miniature.

- *Aethionema* spp. (stone cress)
- *Androsace sarmentosa* (rock jasmine)
- *Aubrieta* cultivars
- *Campanula cochleariifolia* (fairies' thimbles)
- *Cyclamen* spp.
- *Erinus alpinus* (fairy foxglove)
- *Erodium reichardii* (stork's bill)
- *Gentiana verna* (spring gentian)
- *Linaria alpina* (alpine toadflax)
- *Polygala chamaebuxus* (milkwort)

BONSAI

A popular form of miniature gardening is bonsai. As with growing alpines, there are those who become great specialists in the art and even become obsessed with it. It is, however, possible to practise it at a much more humble level and still get a great deal of pleasure and satisfaction from it. The process involves the dwarfing of shrubs and trees, mainly through the careful pruning of shoots, leaves and roots so that the plants will grow happily in small containers. It was developed by the Chinese and later adopted and perfected by the Japanese. The techniques are not complicated, but to achieve good results it is essential to follow traditional methods as described in specialist books.

It is a misconception that trees and shrubs grown as bonsai are tender. The roots, which are exposed in shallow containers, will be susceptible to winter frosts, but bonsai will usually live happily outdoors. A collection can look especially attractive arranged on shelves or an *étagère*, and such plants can be easily protected with horticultural fleece in winter.

planning a border

Planning is a vital part of the construction of any garden and of the borders within it. Even seemingly random parts of the garden, such as wildlife areas or cottage gardens, where everything may seem jumbled together, have a logic behind them, some form of underlying philosophy. It is important, therefore, to look at the elements of design that go to make up a garden before attempting to create or make changes to one.

The first step is to decide what you want to create and what will give you pleasure. Draw up a list of desirable features, such as whether you want to turn over the whole garden to borders or whether you want some lawn or patio or just paths between the beds. What type of plants do you want to grow: sun-lovers or shade-lovers, for example? What style of beds do you want to create: cottage-garden style, romantic, formal or ultra-modern?

Before you get down to the exciting task of designing these beds, you must take into account a few practical considerations. Will you have the time and energy to look after the beds or will you have to compromise and have a smaller planted area simply because you will not be able to deal with a larger one? Can you afford to create what you want or will it, again, be necessary to compromise? Are there other considerations that ought to be taken into account – do you have children or dogs; do you find it difficult to bend or work at ground level?

The position of a border within a garden is important because it will not

only determine the appearance of the garden but also what you can grow in it. The lucky gardener will have a blank canvas to work with. Often, however, gardeners are confronted with established gardens, where there may be existing beds and borders. There may be other features that have to be taken into account when you are planning the layout of the garden, such as mature trees, established shrubs, a greenhouse or a pond.

above: The dark, purplish-brown blooms of *Tulipa* 'Queen of Night' make a wonderful sight grown in a large block. These striking plants need no companion planting.

SUNNY SITES

Sunny borders are among the easiest to cope with, simply because there are so many plants that like to grow in an open, sunny position. The border can be in full sun for all of the day or perhaps lose it towards the end of the day. There is a wide range of plants that will grow in this type of position, including many with bright colours. Being in the sun and thus in the open such borders are often dried not only by the sun but also by winds. It is, therefore, important to incorporate as much well-rotted organic material as possible into the soil during the initial preparation, and subsequently to top-dress it with a mulch at least twice a year.

It is also possible to grow plants that prefer shade in a sunny border, but if they are to do well it is doubly important that you dig in plenty of well-rotted organic material to improve the moisture-retentive properties of the soil.

SHADY SITES

Shade is often considered a problem in garden design, but in fact it is an opportunity to grow an enormous range of plants: the golden rule is simply to plant species that grow in shade in the wild. If you try to grow sun-loving plants in shade they will fail, becoming etiolated and miserable and eventually dying. If, however, you choose plants that naturally grow in woodland or other shady corners, you will succeed. This may mean that you may have to forgo the more brightly coloured bedding plants, but you will discover a new world of interesting and attractive species. In fact, many gardeners create shade in their gardens just so that they can grow some of the wonderful shade-loving plants that are available.

above: Scallop shells create an unusual edging for a small border, preventing the summer plants from flopping onto the grass. Use sharp shears to cut the grass against the shells.

SHELTERED OR EXPOSED SITES

Another factor to consider when positioning a border is whether the site is sheltered or exposed to prevailing winds and frosts. An exposed site will limit the type of plants you can grow: trees and shrubs will become misshapen and softer plants, such as perennials, may simply be blown away in windy weather. This also affects the temperature: a sheltered border in a courtyard against the wall of a house will stay several degrees warmer than a border out in the garden, where it is open to the elements. Bear this in mind when planning what to grow in a border and consider creating a windbreak – a hedge or fence, for example – if the area is very exposed.

Crocosmia 'Lucifer'

From mid- to late summer the unusual heads of bright orange-red flowers are borne on long, arching stems. The mid-green leaves are upright and lance-shaped. Plant the corms in fairly rich, well-drained, moisture-retentive soil. They need a position in full sun but will grow in semi-shade.

plant profile

plant list:

RED FLOWERS

- *Dahlia* 'Bishop of Llandaff'
  A tuberous plant with red flowers in late summer and autumn.

- *Eccremocarpus scaber*
  A climber with tubular red flowers in summer.

- *Hemerocallis* 'Stafford' (daylily)
  A perennial with large, trumpet-shaped flowers in summer.

- *Kniphofia rooperi* (red-hot poker)
  A perennial with spiky foliage and flowers in erect spikes in summer and autumn.

- *Lilium* 'Black Beauty'
  A tall-growing, hardy lily, bearing dark red, turkscap flowers in summer.

- *Lychnis chalcedonica*
  A perennial with scarlet flowers in summer.

- *Mimulus cupreus* 'Whitecroft Scarlet'
  A low-growing perennial with masses of flowers in summer.

- *Monarda* 'Cambridge Scarlet' (bergamot)
  Shaggy flowers are borne in summer.

- *Paeonia officinalis* (peony)
  A perennial with huge, cup-shaped flowers in late spring and early summer.

- *Pelargonium* 'Flower of Spring'
  A zonal pelargonium, this has vivid red flowers, borne in clusters above the pretty silver-edged leaves.

- *Potentilla* 'Gibson's Scarlet'
  A perennial that will scramble among other plants and produce scarlet flowers in summer.

- *Tropaeolum speciosum* (flame creeper)
  A tall, climbing perennial with bright red flowers from summer to autumn.

- *Zinnia elegans* 'Dreamland Scarlet'
  This annual, grown from spring-sown seed, has scarlet, daisy-like flowers in summer.

above: Cabbages may not be your first choice for a colourful border, but decorative forms of *Brassica oleracea* var. *capitata* combine well with marigolds in a small kitchen garden.

URBAN JUNGLES

The small garden is the perfect size for creating an exotic, jungle garden – an exciting place surrounded by greenery and brightly coloured flowers, with spaces to sit carved out in the leafy clearing. The overall effect will be of lush green growth with occasional splashes of rich colour, which can be temporarily increased by bringing colourful houseplants outdoors on special occasions.

Tropical plants are usually too tender to grow outside in more temperate climates, but there are plenty of plants with a tropical feel to create the impression of a jungle, especially in a small, enclosed garden. The secret of success is to have plenty of large, exuberant plants so that the space becomes overcrowded and jungle-like in feel. Large-leaved plants, such as *Musa* spp. (banana), and densely growing ones, such as bamboos, are ideal.

Plants with bright reds and oranges, colours that stand out against a green background, are the types to select. Cannas, which also have excellent 'jungly' foliage, are perfect plants for this type of garden, and they can be grown in containers or, in a sheltered garden, in the ground. Many lilies will also serve the purpose – *Lilium* Bellingham Group has flowers in rich shades of pink and orange, and *L.* 'Karen North' has orange-pink blooms. The tender *Callistemon* spp. (bottlebrush) are not tropical plants, but they bring the appropriate exotic look. *Datura* and *Brugmansia* spp. (angel's trumpets) have more muted colours, but the size of the flowers makes up for this.

Not all plants need to be tender, of course. The flowers of the more brightly coloured camellias, set against the gloss of their leathery leaves, are perfect. Even humble plants, like *Impatiens* (busy Lizzie), especially the dark-leaved forms, will add to the dramatic effect.

Climbing plants will always add a vertical dimension to the garden, and they are also useful for clothing boundaries and nearby buildings. Even more appropriate in a jungle garden, however, are plants that hang down in swags, and these are especially useful for growing over pergolas and arbours. Most clematis are too bland to be used to achieve the tropical look, but jasmines can be used to clothe arches and arbours. Large-leaved ivies and the huge leaves of the vine *Vitis coignetiae* will add to the general atmosphere, and the exotic flowers and thick foliage of *Passiflora caerulea* (passionflower) make it worth growing.

HARDY EXOTICA

The backbone of a jungle garden should be formed of hardy plants so that they can stay outside all year round, but they can be supplemented by a selection of more exotic but tender species, which can be overwintered in a greenhouse or indoors if there is room. Large-leaved plants, such as *Rheum palmatum* (ornamental rhubarb), rodgersias, phormiums and hostas, work well, as do many of the larger ferns. Bamboos

left: Cottage gardens are generally thought of as being filled with pastel shades and subtle tones. The vivid red lupins and purple-leaved sage belie this.

plant list:

EXOTIC-LOOKING PLANTS

- *Abutilon megapotamicum*
- *Bougainvillea glabra*
- *Brugmansia sanguinea*
- *Canna indica* (Indian shot plant)
- *Hibiscus rosa-sinensis*
- *Impatiens walleriana* (busy Lizzie)
- *Ipomoea purpurea* (morning glory)
- *Monstera deliciosa* (Swiss cheese plant)
- *Musa basjoo* (banana)
- *Nerium oleander* (rose bay)
- *Passiflora caerulea* (passionflower)
- *Solenostemon scutellarioides* (coleus)

are ideal, because not only do they produce a thicket of growth but they also rustle in an attractive way. Other grasses, especially the tall ones such as miscanthus, are also useful.

TENDER EXOTICA

There are a large number of more exotic plants that can be grown outside in summer but need protection in winter, either indoors or in a heated greenhouse. Bananas and *Ficus elastica* (rubber plant) are two obvious examples. Hibiscus, especially the red-flowered form, are the perfect plants for the urban jungle, as are *Abutilon* spp. (flowering maple).

Many indoor plants enjoy a holiday outside in the warm days of summer, and they can be used to heighten the exotic flavour of the garden. Especially useful are those plants with colourful foliage, such as *Solenostemon* cultivars (coleus) or bromeliads with their bright red and yellow leaves. The curious flowers of *Anthurium* spp. (flamingo flower), the fiery bracts of *Guzmania* spp. (scarlet star) and the coloured foliage of *Codiaeum* cultivars (croton) will add to the impression. Such plants can be moved outdoors throughout summer or simply on special occasions. All of these plants should be moved back indoors at the first sign of the frosts of winter.

When you are using plants in pots, especially if the pots are more or less the same size, try to vary the height by standing them on plinths made of one or two loose bricks.

year-round interest

Whatever type of garden you design it is going to look different with every season. It is possible to design a garden for particular times of the year – you might, for example, want to show off a selection of plants that look good in winter – but in a small garden the aim must be to have a garden that looks interesting all year round and to blend all the seasons together in one border so that something is always happening.

SPRING

Few gardeners have enough space to devote an entire border to spring flowers, but it is surprising how many can be packed into borders that mainly flower later in the year. This is done by taking advantage of the fact that most herbaceous material does not get going until later in the year, and there is plenty of bare earth between the clumps. Bulbs in particular can make use of this space. Daffodils, bluebells, anemones, crocuses and grape hyacinths can all be planted in the gaps between plants. Spring herbaceous plants take up more space and should be given a permanent position in the garden. Some – pulmonarias and bergenias, for example – earn their place in the summer borders as foliage plants although they have long finished flowering.

If the garden is already tightly packed it is possible to introduce spring bulbs and other plants by planting them in pots, which can be arranged on the border, perhaps hidden behind emerging foliage. Alternatively, the pots can be sunk into the ground

above: An oriental-style theme is reinforced by the small plants of the variegated evergreen lilyturf, *Ophiopogon jaburan* 'Vittatus' held within a bamboo frame.

and then removed after flowering. Once the foliage has died down, the bulbs can be removed and stored somewhere dry until they are repotted the following autumn. In the meantime, the pots can be used for summer bedding.

Spring can be a busy time. Finish working through the borders, weeding, dividing plants, planting new ones and mulching. As the herbaceous plants emerge, stake those that will need it when they are about a third of their eventual height. Do not wait until they are well grown or they may fall over

and, no matter what you do, they will never look right again. Prune winter-flowering shrubs as they finish blooming and plant out annuals once all threat of frosts has passed.

EARLY SUMMER

Once summer approaches the garden palette offers a much wider range of colours. Many gardeners find it difficult to be ruthless, but if you have created a scheme that does not work dig out the offending plants. For example, if *Digitalis purpurea* (purple foxglove) appears in the middle of a hot-coloured border, remove it as soon as it shows. It may seem a waste of a plant, but it will be a waste of the border if you allow the whole effect to be spoiled. In a bed where precise colours are not important, however, self-sown plants

such as foxgloves often add a touch of spontaneity to a scheme.

Tender summer annuals should be sown in late spring and early summer. They can be treated as bedding in separate containers or as part of a mixed border. If there is space it is a good idea to grow the bedding on so that the plants are either near to flowering or just flowering as they are planted out, so that they are effective from the start.

Apart from the early-flowering perennials – hellebores and pulmonarias, for example – the transition from late spring to early summer marks the beginning of the perennial season, when the garden will be bursting with the fresh flowers and foliage of herbaceous plants. This is also the main flowering time for trees and shrubs, and deciduous trees and shrubs are now in full leaf, filling out the border and giving it a three-dimensional look. If everything has gone according to plan, the garden should be full of colour and interest by now. Keep an eye out for weeds and remove any as soon as you see them. Deadheading will help to keep your beds looking fresh, and many spring-flowering shrubs should be pruned at this time of year. In dry weather continue to water anything that was planted in spring until it is well established.

MID- TO LATE SUMMER

The colours may not be as sparklingly fresh as they were in spring, but there is still plenty of scope for a pleasing garden. At this time of year colour

above: By midsummer the mixed herbaceous border will look its best and will be rewarding you for its autumn mulch of well-rotted compost, as the hostas and primulas mass together to create dense, colourful cover.

straggly stems and cut back dying flowers so that they remain fresh. It is a good idea to keep a few spares growing in pots to slot into gaps in the border. From time to time plants will die or leave an ugly gap when they have been cut back, and a few annuals will quickly repair the damage.

themes are often at their best, and white schemes in particular usually retain their freshness and tranquillity. Blues and yellows also add a touch of freshness to the summer scheme.

Many annuals and bedding plants will continue to flower right through the summer, growing to fill the available space and often beyond. Remove

Perennials are at their best at this time of year, but those that have finished flowering should be deadheaded and flagging foliage removed so that the border does not look tatty. Cut back plants such as *Alchemilla mollis* (lady's mantle) and some geraniums to ground level to tidy the borders and stimulate new foliage. If the old leaves and stems are left they will make the borders look untidy and may encourage mildew.

Trees and shrubs will continue to create a permanent structure as everything changes around them. Most will have finished flowering and the foliage will have begun to look rather tired. One way of pepping them up is to grow late-flowering clematis, so that they grow through them. These are cut back almost to the ground in winter so they will not interfere with the appearance of the shrub in spring. Continue to weed regularly and to deadhead and remove dead and dying material. Avoid planting anything new at this time of year because it is too hot for new plants to get established.

plant profile

Malus x zumi 'Golden Hornet'

This compact form of the crab apple grows into a rounded tree about 5m (15ft) tall. White flowers open from pink buds in spring and are followed by long-lasting, golden-yellow fruits. Grow in well-drained, fairly rich soil in full sun.

Eranthis hyemalis (winter aconite)

This little bulb produces one of the earliest flowers to appear in spring. The bright yellow, buttercup-like flowers are surrounded by a green ruff. Grow in rich, moisture-retentive soil in full sun or semi-shade.

plant list:

SPRING- AND WINTER-FLOWERING TREES AND SHRUBS

- **Abeliophyllum distichum** (white forsythia)
  A deciduous shrub with pink-tinged flowers in winter to early spring.

- **Chimonanthus praecox** (wintersweet)
  A vigorous deciduous shrub with fragrant, yellow flowers in winter.

- **Daphne mezereum** (mezereon)
  A deciduous shrub with fragrant, pink flowers in late winter to early spring.

- **Erica carnea** (winter heath)
  A low-growing evergreen shrub with purple-pink flowers in late winter and early spring.

- **Hamamelis mollis** (Chinese witch hazel)
  An erect deciduous shrub with fragrant, golden-yellow flowers in mid- to late winter.

AUTUMN

The flowers of autumn have a distinct feel. In many ways they are the same colours as those we saw in spring, but now, instead of bright yellows, there are more sombre golden-yellows. The tones now have a richness about them – purples are deep, rich purples and reds are deep, brownish-reds. There is still sparkle, but it often needs the sun to bring it out. Foliage takes on a darker tone as leaves begin to age. Many eventually develop wonderful autumn tints as they prepare to drop.

Few annuals or bedding plants are specifically for the autumn. In the wild most would have to have set seed by now or their success would not be assured. In the garden, however, many

above: Grasses such as *Pennisetum villosum* are ideal for providing shape and interest in autumn, when the dried flowerheads persist on the plants.

of those that were planted out in late spring will still be flowering. They are likely to have become lax and leggy, and trimming them back will prolong their useful life by keeping them neat and tidy and promoting fresh flowers.

Many perennials – penstemons, for example – will continue to flower from summer until well into autumn. There is also a surprising number of plants that flower only in autumn, and it is worth making sure that a number of these are

included in the border – asters, such as Michaelmas daisies, and dahlias, for example. It is important to remove any flagging plants as they die back. This will not only make them border look tidier but will also allow the autumn-flowering plants to be seen clearly. There are a few autumn-flowering bulbs, such as colchicums, nerines and amaryllis, which can be planted between plants that have finished so that they fill the gaps.

While most perennials and annuals simply fade away in autumn, many trees and shrubs go out in a blaze of colour. However, these plants must be well placed so that they fit in with perennials that may still be in flower. Another aspect to remember is that many also have fruits or berries, which will add to the attraction of the border at a time when most things are rapidly fading. These are not only attractive to look at but will also provide food for birds and other animals.

As autumn passes, continue to clear up, removing all dead material as it goes over. Some gardeners like to leave some of the more attractive seedheads as winter decoration in the borders. These also provide additional food for birds in winter. Autumn is a good time to begin to prepare new borders, digging them over and leaving the soil to weather over winter.

WINTER

In theory winter is a time for both the garden and the gardener to rest, but in fact this is rarely the case. A surprising number of plants flower in winter, when there is little competition, and the gardener should be working on the garden whenever the conditions allow.

Many shrubs flower in winter, but there are also a number of perennials and bulbs that flower at this time of year. A large number of these are highly scented because there are few pollinating insects around, and the flowers must do everything possible to attract them. Those that are unscented are mainly wind-pollinated. Most seem to be resilient to the weather and need no protection: they may bow their heads in a frost but soon come up again. Winter-flowering trees and shrubs are usually grown in the general border, but because many of them can look rather drab in summer it is a good idea to plant them at the back of the border or somewhere they can be masked by herbaceous plants in summer. This arrangement will allow them to show up in winter, when everything else is below ground or, at least, out of leaf yet covered up and out of sight in summer.

There is a number of trees and shrubs that have attractive bark, which shows up to best advantage in winter, when there is little to obscure it. In a small garden it may be difficult to justify growing a tree or shrub purely on the grounds of its winter bark, but many of these plants have another feature that makes them doubly welcome – *Acer griseum* (paper-bark maple), for example, has vivid scarlet autumn leaf colour and peeling russet-coloured bark.

In winter the dead stems of many grasses and herbaceous plants can

look very attractive. If they are left standing for at least part of the winter they will create interesting shapes, especially when viewed from indoors on a cold, frosty day.

An hour spent working on a border in winter will save several hours' work later in the year. If the weather is fine and the soil not waterlogged or frozen, the more work that is done the better. Working on waterlogged ground will

left: Evergreen grasses, such as *Pennisetum* provide form throughout the year, with the added benefit of producing attractive flowerheads.

damage the soil's structure, and if you are uncertain it is better to work from a path or from planks so that you do not stand directly on the soil. Dig between plants, weed and mulch. Remove all dead material from last year's plants and any dead or damaged material from trees and shrubs.

plant list:

TREES AND SHRUBS FOR WINTER INTEREST

- *Acer davidii* (snake-bark maple)
  A conical tree with green, white-striped bark.

- *Acer griseum* (paper-bark maple)
  A broadly columnar tree with peeling, russet bark.

- *Betula utilis* var. *jacquemontii* (birch)
  An elegant tree with wonderful silver bark.

- *Cornus alba* 'Sibirica' (red dogwood)
  A vigorous shrub with scarlet stems.

- *Corylus avellana* 'Contorta' (twisted hazel)
  A tree with curved and twisting branches.

- *Euonymus alatus* (winged spindle)
  A medium-sized shrub with bright autumn colour and interesting winter bark.

- *Rubus cockburnianus*
  A medium-sized shrub forming a thicket of white stems.

- *Rubus thibetanus*
  A medium-sized shrub with white-bloomed brown stems.

- *Salix alba* subsp. *vitellina*
  A shrub with bright yellow shoots in winter.

- *Salix alba* subsp. *vitellina* 'Britzensis'
  A medium-sized shrub with bright orange-red new shoots.

Cotoneaster microphyllus

The small, dark green leaves of this compact evergreen shrub cover the slender stems. In autumn, bright red berries appear amid the leaves. This tolerant plant will grow in any type of well-drained soil, although the best berries are produced when the plants are grown in full sun.

Mahonia aquifolium (Oregon grape)

The spiny, glossy, dark green leaves of this low shrub usually turn deep reddish tones in autumn, especially when it is grown in full sun. Clusters of yellow flowers appear in early spring and are followed by blue-black berries. Grow in well-drained, humus-rich soil.

plant profile

using colour

The use of colour in the garden is not much different from its use in the house: the essence is to bring together a combination that is pleasing and something that we feel comfortable to be in. So it is with borders. In the garden the principle is to harmonize the colours so that a restful or arresting image is created, drifting from one set of colours easily into the next, perhaps accenting here or there with a brighter or contrasting colour. Not all schemes need be mixed, however: many successful borders have been created based on a single colour.

Creating a single-colour border may seem a simple solution to the problem of what to plant, but it is not as easy as it sounds. The number of variations of each colour is enormous, and they do not all necessarily combine well together. Colours often have two different sides. Yellows, for example, can have a touch of green or a touch of red in their make-up, and the two do not combine satisfactorily in the same border. The same problem with integration can also be seen in orange-reds and purple-reds.

In practice there is no such thing as a single-colour border. The flowers may be all one colour, but there is always the foliage as well. This is no bad thing, because a border of unrelenting yellow or red, for example, would be too much to take in. The foliage creates a background against which the colour stands out and also acts as a buffer between two areas of slightly different colours that would not otherwise work well together.

above: In late summer the spires of *Verbascum* 'Gainsborough' tower above the perennial border. Unlike lupins, the stout stems of verbascums rarely need staking.

Two-colour borders are an extension of the single-colour idea. Two sympathetic colours can be chosen to harmonize, or contrasting colours can be used to create a bit of excitement. Popular schemes include white and yellow, and yellow and blue. In some schemes one colour can be seen as predominant while the other is just a dash to catch the eye; In other schemes the colours can be mixed in roughly equal proportions.

As well as one- or two-colour borders it is possible to have multicoloured borders that are still selective. Soft pastel colours, for example, are popular and can be combined to make a restful picture, but a complete contrast would be a border of hot, vibrant colours, such as reds, oranges and golds.

SOFT, ROMANTIC SCHEMES

It is difficult to define exactly what people mean, when they talk about a romantic garden. It may just be the neatness: everything in its place and tidy. On the other hand, it may be the design of the garden that is meant, with bowers wreathed in swags of roses or honeysuckle. No matter what the underlying structure, one aspect tends to remain constant: the colours. A romantic garden generally consists of soft, ethereal colours, highlighted with occasional splashes of a deeper colour, usually warm red.

COOL COLOURS

Cool colours are the blues, green, greys and whites. These are gentle on the eye, especially in the paler shades of the colours. They tend to have a soothing, tranquil quality about them that makes them good for relaxing and hence for romance. They also tend to be receding colours, which appear further away from the viewer than they really are.

PASTEL COLOURS

Pastel colours are primary colours to which white has been added: pinks, peaches, primroses and lilacs. They are the soft colours that do not offend or assault the eye. They are easy to look at because the white content gives them a linking theme so that they can sit next to each other without conflicting with each other.

OLD-FASHIONED PLANTS

Many of the more old-fashioned plants have a more romantic feel about them than their modern equivalents. This is not necessarily because 'old is better' but is more to do with the shape and texture of the flowers. Old-fashioned roses, for example, tend to look soft and more textured. Modern roses have more clear-cut profiles and colours, which make them look modern. Even what would normally be a soft colour may appear quite harsh in modern cultivars. Pink, for example, is often very bright, with overtones of magenta, and the blooms lose a lot of the subtlety of old-fashioned flowers.

ROMANTIC BORDERS

Romantic borders are those that look relaxed and make the viewer seem relaxed. They tend to be created for overall effect rather than for the interest that individual plants might create. The plants are selected for their colour and general effect. As with all planting, the border will look best if the plants are arranged in clumps or drifts, with the colour effortlessly blending with their neighbours.

Unlike brighter colours, however, softer shades can be dotted around to give the impression of a haze. This is particularly true of wildflower meadows, where the misty quality is further enhanced by the grasses. Even in a more conventional border, grasses such as *Hordeum jubatum* (squirrel tail grass) can be used to create the same

plant list:

PINK FLOWERS

- *Anemone* x *hybrida* (Japanese anemone)
  A medium-sized perennial with cup-shaped flowers in late summer and autumn.

- *Deutzia* x *elegantissima* 'Rosealind'
  A deciduous shrub with cymes of flowers in late spring and early summer.

- *Dianthus* 'Doris' (pink)
  A clump-forming perennial with spiky foliage and summer flowers.

- *Diascia vigilis*
  A low-growing perennial covered with flowers in summer.

- *Geranium endressii*
  A medium-sized, summer-flowering, hardy perennial.

- *Lamium maculatum* 'Roseum' (deadnettle)
  A low-growing perennial with variegated foliage and flowers in spring and summer.

- *Monarda* 'Croftway Pink' (bergamot)
  A medium-sized perennial with shaggy flowers in summer.

Primula denticulata (drumstick primula)

From early spring to early summer, dense umbels of flowers are borne on sturdy stems. The flower colour varies from shades of pink and purple to red, but all have a yellow centre. Plants get to about 45cm (18in) high and across. These primulas need humus-rich, moisture-retentive soil and should be watered regularly in dry weather.

plant profile

effect. The receding nature of cool colours and the softness of pastels means that a long border, even one planted in blocks of colour, blurs into a haze of colour the further it gets from the viewer. The softer colours can be enhanced with an occasional flash of a bright one such as red. A few red poppies, for example, in a wildflower border help to create just the right dash of vividness.

It is important to add height to romantic borders; they should be three-dimensional. Climbing roses can be very effective, especially if they are arranged as swags growing along ropes at the back or front of the border. A seat in the middle of the border surrounded by an arbour of roses or another fragrant climber will help to create the right atmosphere.

Fragrance is also an important adjunct to romantic colour. The two go together perfectly for creating atmosphere. Again, the old-fashioned plants, as opposed to modern hybrids, are the most likely to have the strongest fragrance.

above: Keeping the planting in a roof garden towards the edges places the weight over the load-bearing walls. Dense planting helps to create its own micro-climate.

BOLD, EXOTIC SCHEMES

At the other extreme from soft, romantic colours are bold, brash, hot colours. These demand attention and draw the eye. They do not form a soothing or romantic background, but are full of excitement. Like all excitement, however, these colours can become tiring after a while, so they should be used with restraint.

HOT COLOURS

The hot colours are those that lie opposite the cool colours on the artist's colour wheel. They are the flame reds, oranges, golds and yellows. They are eye-catching colours, which create bold statements and stand out in a crowd. Such colours can be used with individual plants as focal points to draw the eye, in groups to enhance an otherwise dull border or mixed with other hot colours to create a fiery, warm border.

The hot colours are the extremes of a wider group known as the warm colours. These colours are welcoming and tend to create a warm feeling. They include soft colours, such as pinks, as well as the earthy colours of dried, stems, seedheads and foliage. These softer colours are not as powerful as the hotter ones and are of little use in hot, exotic borders.

REDS

It is the reds with a touch of yellow, reminiscent of flames and fire, that are the most exciting. They cover that part of the spectrum between pure red and orange. The reds that have a touch of

blue in them, on the other hand, are warm, but they are not hot and exciting in the same way. The two sides of red do not mix satisfactorily and are best kept apart in the garden.

YELLOWS

The hot yellows are those between pure yellow and orange and include golds. The other side of pure yellow is tinged with green, and these form the cool yellows, which have no place in a hot border because they are likely to have the reverse effect – that is, they will cool it down.

ORANGES

Orange is a mixture of yellow and red, and it is a good colour for the hot border because it retains the eye-catching quality of both parent colours. In some of its paler manifestations, such as peach, it remains warm but loses its heat and excitement.

HOT BORDERS

Hot borders are lively and exciting. They have plenty to look at and are constantly darting from one colour to another. Yet, like an exciting party, there comes a point when the eye has had enough and wants to find somewhere quieter to rest for a while. It is not a good idea, therefore, to fill the whole garden with hot borders. The best approach for a colour scheme is to combine the border with cooler tones and large areas of lawn, which will give the eye somewhere peaceful to rest.

There is little red or orange foliage to be found outside a tropical house or

left: In an informal garden the perennials and annuals will mix happily together, with one or two accent plants, such as the evergreen *Santolina chamaecyparissus* (cotton lavender), providing a point of reference all year round.

conservatory, but there is no reason these should not be used in a hot border as long as they are planted outside for the summer months only. There are, however, many variegated plants, which include warm yellow and gold in their leaf colour. Green foliage has the advantage that the hot colours stand out against it; it acts as a good backdrop, but too much will emphasize individual plants or clumps of plants and may swamp the bold overall feeling of the border.

Hot colours are good for making exotic borders that are created to imitate the tropics. The use of strong, bold foliage and bright colours, using houseplants for a boost if necessary, can create a powerful illusion, especially in a small garden where the effect is concentrated.

Liatris spicata (gayfeather)

The bright pinkish-mauve florets of this perennial are borne in dense flowerheads on robust, sturdy stems from late summer into autumn. The flowers are useful for cutting and last well in water. In the border grow in a sunny position in moisture-retentive, well-drained, fertile soil.

plant profile

plant list:

PURPLE FLOWERS

- *Aster amellus* 'King George'
  A perennial with daisy-like flowers in late summer to autumn.

- *Campanula* 'Birch Hybrid'
  This vigorous perennial boasts deep violet, upturned, summer-long, bell-shaped flowers.

- *Clematis* 'Mrs N. Thompson'
  A compact, large-flowered climber.

- *Echinacea purpurea*
  A striking perennial with large, daisy-like flowers in summer.

- *Edraianthus pumilio* (grassy bells)
  Neat little cushions of grass-like leaves are covered with deep lavender-blue flowers in early summer.

- *Erysimum* 'Bowles' Mauve' (wallflower)
  A perennial with a bushy habit and masses of flowers in summer.

- *Geranium pratense*
  A medium-sized, perennial geranium with flowers from spring to summer.

- *Liatris spicata* (gayfeather)
  A perennial with bottle-brush flower spikes in summer.

- *Lythrum salicaria* (loosestrife)
  A handsome perennial with erect racemes of flowers in summer.

- *Penstemon* 'Russian River'
  A prolific, upright perennial with flower spikes in summer and autumn.

- *Primula denticulata* (drumstick primula)
  A short, clump-forming perennial with flowerheads on erect stems in spring.

- *Verbena bonariensis*
  A tall, airy perennial, which will self-seed, producing flowers in late summer and autumn.

small-scale kitchen garden

In recent years, as gardens have got smaller, the vegetable plot has disappeared, but now increasing numbers of people are beginning to realize just what they are missing: taste. Home-grown vegetables may not look as perfect as those produced under the sanitized eye of the supermarket, but they will be fresher and taste better.

FINDING SPACE

The problem with small gardens is that there is never enough space to do all the things you want to. Features like lawns and patios are multi-purpose: they can be used for relaxation, play and other activities. A vegetable plot, on the other hand, can be used only for growing vegetables, and so they are given a low priority when it comes to the allocation of space. It is, however, possible to grow quite a lot of vegetables in a small space as long as they are tended and as long as you do not want to grow things like rows of potatoes, which take up a lot of space (for the unique taste of new potatoes, grow a few tubs). Use raised beds where the soil can be kept fertile and you can plant close together. Blocks are better space-savers than rows, and as soon as one crop is over replace it with another.

SAVING SPACE

Many vegetable plants are decorative and happily mix with flower borders. The leaves of the spinach-like red orach 'Oriental Red' are red-tinged and borne on pinkish-red stems, and the pretty leaves of mizuma are almost too pretty

above: Vegetables of many kinds can be grown in containers, including cabbages, as here, and potatoes. Even a cottage-garden style collection of plants can be given a modern look with stainless-steel containers.

to eat. The red stems of ruby chard, the frilly leaves of carrots and the colourful flowers of runner beans would all be worthy of ornamental plants, irrespective of their culinary qualities. The only problem with this type of approach is that you will get gaps in the borders when you harvest the vegetables, but the flowering plants do not last for ever either.

A surprising number of vegetables can be grown in containers of one sort or another. The most elegant type of container is the terracotta pot, but for convenience many vegetables, especially runner beans, tomatoes and peppers, are grown in growing bags – that is, plastic bags filled with a special compost mix. Other vegetables can be grown in larger containers that are 45cm (18in) or more across. The containers can be placed anywhere in the garden as long as they are not in the shade – tomatoes, for example, can be grown against a warm wall. Plants in containers need to be watered at least once a day, and in hot, dry weather they may require watering more often.

Early potatoes can also be grown on the patio in a container or barrel that has a movable sleeve around its base. You plant the tubers in the bottom of the container and earth them up as they grow. When you want to harvest a few potatoes, rather than digging up the entire plant you can raise the sleeve, which reveals the potatoes growing at the bottom of the barrel. Carefully remove the potatoes you want, then lower the sleeve so that the plant can continue to grow.

above: Useful marigolds are reputed to protect tomatoes from aphids, and it is even said that chemicals in the roots of *Tagetes minuta* (Mexican marigold) will kill bindweed and couch grass.

ALLOTMENTS

If you are keen on growing vegetables – and it has a lot to recommend it – it is usually possible to rent an allotment not too far from your home. These plots of land, usually available at inexpensive rents, were originally intended to be sufficient to feed a small family with a wide range of vegetables. Water is usually available, and many have local allotment associations, whereby everyone who has an allotment on the site clubs together to get seed and materials at a discount. There are usually a number of experienced gardeners around, and a tremendous amount can be learned from them about practical gardening.

plant list:

CULINARY HERBS

- **Allium schoenoprasum** (chives)
  A bulb; use the leaves and grow for the pink flowerheads.

- **Anethum graveolens** (dill)
  An annual or biennial: use the aniseed-flavoured leaves as a garnish and as a flavouring in sauces.

- **Artemisia dracunculus** (tarragon)
  A perennial: use the leaves.

- **Borago officinalis** (borage)
  An annual; use the leaves and the pretty blue flowers.

- **Coriandrum sativum** (coriander)
  An evergreen shrub; use the leaves.

- **Foeniculum vulgare** (fennel)
  An annual: use the pungent leaves in stews, curries and salads and the small seeds in chutneys.

- **Levisticum officinale** (lovage)
  A perennial: crystallize the stems (like angelica), use the leaves in salads and savoury dishes and add the seed to bread and biscuits.

- **Mentha spicata** (mint)
  A spreading perennial; use the leaves.

- **Ocimum basilicum** (basil)
  An annual; use the leaves.

- **Origanum vulgare** (oregano, marjoram)
  A perennial; use the leaves.

- **Petroselinum crispum** (parsley)
  An annual; use the leaves.

- **Rosmarinus officinalis** (rosemary)
  An evergreen shrub; use the leaves.

- **Salvia officinalis** (sage)
  A shrubby perennial: use the leaves to flavour cheeses, stuffings, soups and stews.

- **Thymus serpyllum** (thyme)
  A shrub; use the leaves.

Origanum vulgare (wild marjoram)

This bushy perennial has small, highly aromatic, dark green leaves. In late summer small purple and pink flowers are borne in dense clusters. Plants, which grow to about 45cm (18in) high and across, need a sunny position in well-drained, preferably alkaline soil.

Laurus nobilis (bay)

This useful shrub or small tree has aromatic, dark green, rather leathery leaves. On established plants clusters of creamy-yellow flowers appear in spring. Grow in full sun in rich, well-drained soil with protection from cold, drying winds.

plant profile

planting tips and maintenance

With any gardening, the more skilled you are at the various techniques, the easier the task will be and the better the results. The idea that only those with green fingers can be successful gardeners is a myth. Most people are capable of learning the basic techniques – indeed, these are so basic that many people pick them up without realizing.

The simplest way to acquire the skills is to get out in the garden and try it. Few things in gardening are irredeemable: ruining some cuttings or snipping off the stem of an annual instead of a dead flower is not too serious, but losing expensive plants is costly and frustrating, so it is worth buying cheap ones until you have learned how to handle them. After all, most common plants are as attractive as the rarer and more expensive ones. Most plants are reasonably forgiving, and if you have put them in the wrong place it is usually possible to move them in autumn or spring to somewhere more suitable.

Tools are a personal matter. One gardener will love a particular type of hoe and would never be without it, while another gardener will always use a certain type of spade. Most modern tools tend to be more or less the same size and weight. Try them in the store before you buy. You can sometimes find second-hand tools that are good quality and perfectly usable. Whenever possible, get the best tools you can afford. Stainless steel is easier to clean but will not keep such a keen edge as ordinary steel. Avoid gimmicks, which

rarely earn their keep, and go for a basic set of tools – spade, fork, hand fork and secateurs – that you like and would trust.

The days when most gardeners spent most of the time spraying chemicals over everything to kill it or make it grow are almost gone. Sprays are still used, but they tend to be safer and are used in a more responsible way. Many gardeners now realize, however, that it is not necessary to reach for the spray every time an insect pest or a weed appears in the garden. Learning to live with a few

imperfections, giving plants the best possible growing conditions and growing plants that suit your garden is much less stressful – for you and your plants.

SOIL STRUCTURE AND CONDITIONING

The soil is the single most important factor in any garden. It is important that it be thoroughly prepared, maintained and treated with respect. Organic material is vital, because it not only supplies a certain amount of nutrients but also holds enough moisture for the

left: Compost bins made of slats of wood will keep the compost tidy while it breaks down. Remember to keep the compost damp and turn it to make sure that all the material decomposes.

plants' roots without drowning them. One of the best sources of this organic material – and the cheapest – is garden compost. As with farmyard manure, another good source, garden compost must be well rotted down before it is added to the garden.

COMPOST

A great variety of garden and kitchen waste can be turned into good compost if it is properly mixed. The following materials can be used: animal manure and urine, annual weeds, crushed eggshells, dead flowerheads, lawn mowings (unless the grass has been treated with hormone weedkillers), pea pods, potato peelings, soft hedge clippings, tea leaves, tree and shrub leaves, vegetables leaves and stems. Woody material may be added if it has been shredded.

Do not add any vegetation that has been sprayed with herbicides or is

left: Ladybirds are among a gardener's greatest friends: both the adult insects and the larvae eat greenfly and many other insect pests, including scale insects, mealybugs and some small caterpillars.

affected by diseases and pests. One of the secrets of ensuring rapid decomposition is not to allow large quantities of one particular material to build up in the heap. Lawn clippings, for example, are best stored separately and added to the heap only when they can be mixed in with other, more open materials.

COMPOST HEAPS

A compost heap will cheaply and quickly turn garden and kitchen waste into valuable and soil-enriching material. To make good, crumbly compost the heap must be properly constructed so that the organic material can decompose rapidly and not turn into a pile of stagnant, slimy, smelly vegetation. Air, moisture and nitrogen have to be present if bacteria and fungi are to break down the raw materials efficiently. Air is allowed in through the base and sides of the heap.

points to remember:

MULCHES

Use a mulch to reduce the amount of watering that is needed and to prevent weeds from germinating. Before laying the mulch, however, remove all perennial weeds, because a mulch will not stop them from reappearing, and water thoroughly. The main mulches are:

- *Black polythene, which is cheap and efficient but unsightly.*

- *Chipped bark, which looks natural in most positions although some of the larger chips can look unattractive.*

- *Farmyard manure, an excellent soil conditioner but must not be used fresh because it will contain weed seeds.*

- *Grass clippings, which are readily available but are best used at the back of the border because they are unsightly and should never be in too deep a layer.*

- *Gravel, which is attractive and widely available but is not suitable for all borders because it gets mixed in with the soil and needs to be replaced constantly.*

- *Leafmould, which is an excellent soil conditioner but is not readily available unless home-made.*

plant list:

PLANTS TO AVOID

- ***Acer pseudoplatanus*** (sycamore)
  A fast-growing, deciduous tree, attaining a height of 30m (100ft) and spread of 25m (80ft).

- ***Arundo donax*** (giant reed)
  A huge plant, capable of growing to 5m (15ft) tall, with blue-green leaves.

- **x *Cupressocyparis leylandii***
  (Leyland cypress)
  A fast-growing conifer to 35m (120ft) tall and 5m (15ft) across.

- ***Cortaderia selloana*** (pampas grass)
  A clump-forming grass, to 3m (10ft) tall, with white plumes.

- ***Fallopia baldschuanica*** (Russian vine, mile-a-minute plant)
  A vigorous, fast-growing climber that will get to 12m (40ft) or more in no time at all.

- ***Gunnera manicata***
  A clump-forming perennial, growing to 2.5m (8ft) high and 4m (12ft) across, with individual leaves to 1.8m (6ft) long.

- ***Osmunda regalis*** (royal fern)
  A deciduous fern that forms dense clumps to 1.8m (6ft) high and 4m (12ft across.

- ***Phyllostachys aurea*** (fishpole bamboo)
  A handsome, clump-forming bamboo that will get to 10m (30ft) tall and spread indefinitely.

- ***Salix babylonica*** (weeping willow)
  Although the tree has a height and spread of only about 12m (40ft), the roots will spread far further.

- ***Semiarundinaria fastuosa*** (Narhira bamboo)
  This tall, almost tree-like, hardy bamboo forms an erect stand to 5m (15ft) tall and will spread indefinitely.

- ***Stipa gigantea*** (giant feather grass)
  A tuft-forming grass, to 2.5m (8ft) tall, with oat-like flowerheads.

The material should be layered and firmed down with the back of a rake or with a fork. Water should be applied with a can or hose if the heap shows signs of drying out, and moisture can be kept in by covering the heap with sacking, old carpet or polythene sheeting. Nitrogen has to be added to the heap in the form of grass mowings, young nettles or manure; alternatively, add a compost activator.

Position the heap in a sheltered and shady spot, but not under trees where tree roots might move into the compost. It must be protected from drying sun and wind.

COMPOST BINS

In a small garden a compost bin or a container is more likely to be used than a straggly, untidy heap of the kind that can be tucked away at the bottom of a largish garden. Make your own container from a square cage of wire-netting supported by four stout posts driven into the ground. Ideally, make the front removable so that you can easily get to the rotted compost.

Traditional bins made from slatted wood will keep the compost looking tidy. They can be easily made from second-hand wooden pallets or planks, or you can buy wood cut to length that slots neatly together. Some of the better composters are supplied with wooden tops; otherwise, remember to cover the full bin with old carpet or sacking.

Cone-shaped, black or dark green, plastic composters, which hold from 220 to 300 litres (8–10 cu ft) or more, are a tidy and convenient alternative to a heap. In a small garden the problem is often that there is insufficient waste material to allow a sufficiently large heap to build up, so the material never gets hot enough to begin to break down. You will get far better results with two smallish bins: fill one and leave it for a time while you begin to fill up the second bin. If the compost appears to be wet and slimy, mix in some torn-up paper or unglazed cardboard.

USING THE COMPOST

The compost is ready to use when it is brown and crumbly. If some material is still recognizable leave it behind to start the next heap. Digging in compost in autumn and winter when the annual dig was being undertaken is the traditional way of getting the best from compost. Now, however, it is thought that using the compost as a mulch on weed-free, moist soil in autumn is just

left: Cocoa shells will make an attractive mulch, and they have the advantage that, unlike mulching materials such as chipped bark, the shells are fairly rich in nutrients.

points to remember:

BIOLOGICAL CONTROLS

Effective control of pests in the greenhouse and garden is possible through the introduction of biological controls. The following are obtainable from organic garden suppliers:

- *Amblyseius* **spp.** (predatory mites): thrips
- *Aphidius aphidimyza* (fly larvae predators): aphids (under glass)
- *Bacillus thuringiensis* (bacterial disease): caterpillars
- *Cryptolaemus montrouzieri* (ladybirds): mealy bugs
- *Encarsia formosa* (parasitic wasp): whitefly
- *Heterorhabditis* **spp.** (nematodes): vine weevil larvae
- *Metaphysic helvolus* (parasitic wasp): soft scale insects
- *Phytoseiulus persimilis* (predatory mites): red spider mites
- *Copper tape applied around containers will stop slugs and snails from climbing into the containers, and non-dry adhesive can be used to stop vine weevils getting into containers to lay their eggs. Nematodes can also be used to control slugs and chafer grubs, and ladybird and lacewing larvae can be obtained to encourage these useful aphid-eating insects into the garden.*

as effective and much less hard work. Use only well-rotted compost as a mulch because partially decomposed material may contain weed seeds, which will quickly germinate when they are spread on the garden.

GREEN MANURE

The practice of sowing certain crops and then digging the resulting plants into the ground to enrich the soil, to provide a source of nitrogen and to improve the texture of the ground is known as green manuring. Rape, annual lupins, vetches, mustard and perennial rye grass may all be used. Broadcast the seed quite thickly over the ground in spring or early summer and then rake it in. The plants will grow quickly, and it is extremely important to dig them in before they flower and set seed.

LEAFMOULD

The leaves of deciduous trees and shrubs may be rotted down on their own to make soil-enriching leafmould. A wire bin, made from chicken wire stretched between four upright posts that have been driven into the ground, makes a suitable container. A fast, space-saving alternative is to pack the layers of leaves into black polythene sacks that have been perforated to allow in air. Filled and tied at the top, the sacks should be stood in an out-of-the-way corner until the following spring, by which time the contents, gathered the previous autumn, will have turned into good leafmould. Leaves that are kept in outdoor bins may take longer to break down.

PLANTING WALL CLIMBERS

In a small garden walls are often the only suitable support for climbers, but one of the problems is that the area next to a wall is usually in a rain shadow, so plants that are too close to the wall often do not become established. Dig the soil where the climber is to be planted and incorporate as much well-rotted organic material, such as garden compost, as you can. The planting hole should be 30–45cm (12–18in) from the base of the wall. Plant at the same depth as the plant was in the pot and use a cane or canes to train it towards the wall supports.

Most climbers, apart from those that have clinging aerial roots such as *Hedera* spp. (ivy), need some form of support. The least obtrusive method is to attach horizontal wires across the

wall. It is possible to use wooden or plastic trellis, but the wood often looks too heavy and tends to dominate the wall, and trellis should be used for small areas rather than over an entire wall. Plastic always looks like plastic, and it breaks down eventually and often gives way suddenly in the middle of a storm.

above: Foliage provides all the colour required to make this calm courtyard garden into a verdant, enticing space.

points to remember:

ERECTING WIRES FOR CLIMBERS

Drill holes in the wall at intervals of about 1.2m (4ft). Plug the holes and insert a vine eye in each. Thread galvanized wire through these and secure it at the ends. The wires should be spaced about 45cm (18in) apart over the face of the wall. Plant the plants 30–45cm (12–18in) away from the wall and water well. As the plants grow, use string or plant ties to tie them in to the wires. Spread out the young shoots at the base of the wall so that they cover as much of it as possible. Keep the plants tied in and prune as and when necessary.

9

Creating a garden in the city where there is little or no space is a task faced by a large percentage of today's gardeners. In spite of the obvious difficulties, many manage to provide a green oasis for themselves, cut off from the hurly-burly around them.

The secret is to make use of any available space. This may mean looking up to the roof or down to the basement. As a compromise, there is always the balcony, halfway up. All these spaces open up possibilities for the keen gardener to create something, but they will have to learn new techniques. Exposure to the elements, particularly the wind, poses problems for the roof gardener, while the basement gardener must think carefully about the lack of light. The balcony gardener may face both these problems as well as a chronic lack of space. However, all these difficulties are surmountable, and overcoming them is part of the fun of gardening.

The lack of space in these situations will test the gardener's ingenuity to the limit. Every plant used must be worthwhile in its own right, adding to the overall effect as well as having other functions, such as cutting down the force of the wind or creating privacy. There is no reason why plants should not also provide a little something for the kitchen: a few herbs or a plate of fresh tomatoes are always welcome and not difficult to achieve.

In many cases there will be enough room left to create a living space: an area where you can put a couple of chairs and perhaps a table. Eating several storeys up while you look out over the rooftops through the greenery of your own garden is an enormous pleasure.

city sanctuaries

roof gardens

Roof gardens can be created anywhere that there is a suitable surface that will support the weight. In some cases, even sloping roofs can be pressed into service if you are willing to pay for the expense of the construction involved. Roof gardens need not always be at rooftop level; flat roofs over one-storey extensions can be ideal, and many modern blocks of apartments and flats have purpose-built roof gardens.

INITIAL CONSIDERATIONS

Whatever the situation, before you do anything else it is essential to check that any space intended for a roof garden is strong enough and suitable for such a purpose. Boxes and other containers of moist compost weigh a lot and can easily damage an inadequately supported roof. You may need professional guidance. Something else to look into before you start is the covering of the intended area. Some surfaces are unsuitable for walking on or may be easily punctured. Wooden decking, which is widely available, is an excellent material to cover the area. Railings or a balustrade will also be needed for safety, partly to stop the gardener and visitors from falling over the edge, but also to prevent pots and other objects from being knocked or blown to the ground below. Once the garden is in use, check regularly to make sure that none of the wooden structures, especially the safety railings, have rotted.

To minimize wind flow, attach a screen to the railings around the roof garden. The cheapest form is windbreak netting, but this is rather ugly, although

above: Make up for the lack of soil by using large containers and boxes, which can simply be wooden frames surrounding growing-bags full of good-quality compost.

it can be hidden behind plants. Bamboo matting is another possibility, but a better solution is to use some form of trellis, which itself will filter some of the wind, and to grow tough climbers over it. Do not block everything in, but use it mainly on the side from which the prevailing winds blow.

GETTING STARTED

Plants can be grown in containers or boxes. Boxes have the advantage that they can be carried up to the roof as planks and assembled there. Large containers, on the other hand, are not only heavy but also bulky, which can be a problem if you have to carry them up stairs and through rooms. All containers should have drainage holes so that they do not fill with stagnant water, which would mean death to most plants. Buy good-quality potting compost, preferably a soil-based one. This is heavier to carry than a soil-less mix, but it has the advantage that the filled containers will be less likely to be blown over than those filled with a lighter compost. If weight is likely to be a concern, add vermiculite or perlite to the compost.

PLANTING

The secret of success in creating a roof garden is to remember that it must be three-dimensional. A series of small pots around your feet will not be satisfactory. Add height with shrubs, climbers and even small trees to make it feel like a proper garden. This height will help to create an enclosed feeling as well as creating a background against which the lower plants can be seen. The taller plants can also be arranged to frame the view as well as to cut out ugly sights and create privacy from neighbours.

It is important to use plants that can withstand a certain amount of battering by the wind. A good choice may be those used in seaside gardens, which are used to withstanding tough conditions. A few evergreens will create

plant list:

PLANTS FOR A ROOF GARDEN

- ***Bupleurum fruticosum*** (shrubby hare's ear)
  The evergreen leaves of this shrub are blue-green, and small, star-shaped, yellow flowers are borne from midsummer to autumn.

- ***Choisya ternata*** (Mexican orange blossom)
  A handsome evergreen shrub with glossy, dark green leaves and fragrant white flowers in spring and, sometimes, again in late summer.

- ***Geranium phaeum*** (dusky cranesbill)
  A clump-forming perennial with soft green leaves and flowers, which may be dark purple to light mauve or even white, in late spring and early summer.

- ***Griselinia littoralis*** 'Dixon's Cream' (broadleaf)
  An upright shrub, to 3m (10ft) tall, with glossy, bright green, evergreen leaves, boldly variegated with cream.

- ***Hebe pinguifolia*** 'Pagei'
  A low-growing shrub with evergreen, bluish-green foliage and masses of white flowers in late spring to early summer.

roof rules:

- *Check that the structure of the building is strong enough to support your design and consider using lighter alternatives, such as artificial grass instead of pavers, plastic containers instead of terracotta, and soil-less compost instead of a loam-based medium.*

- *Keep the central area clutter-free and clean.*

- *Use one or two strategically placed containers to draw the eye to special areas of the garden.*

- *If wind is a problem, cover the fence with netting to reduce wind flow.*

- *Make sure that all urns and windowboxes are securely attached.*

- *Put large pots on castors so that they do not mark the surface and can be easily moved.*

- *Interperse the planting with splashes of bright colour so that the overall feel does not become formal.*

- *Avoid structures that obscure views of the sky.*

above: Before you pave over a flat roof, have a proper survey carried out and make sure that rainwater will be able to drain away safely.

an all-year feel, while colour can be added by the use of bright annuals. Annuals are a good choice because they often flower for a very long period, unlike many perennials which flower for only two or three weeks a year. The best perennials to use are those that can double as foliage plants once their flowers are over.

Roof gardens, which are open to plenty of sunlight, are ideal places for growing vegetables as well as decorative plants. Tomatoes are a particularly good subject, but beans, lettuces and many other crops can be easily grown in deep boxes.

WATER SUPPLY

Because they are open to wind and sun, roof gardens tend to dry out quickly and are in need of constant watering during dry periods. If your garden is not at the very top of the building it may be possible to divert water that is shed by the higher roofs into one or more water butts to provide an on-site supply of water so that you do not have to carry it through the apartment or house. With large roof gardens a permanent supply of water will be needed, and installing an outside tap will be a great convenience.

balconies

Many town houses and blocks of flats and apartments have balconies. Old town houses frequently have balconies at first-floor level and above, while modern, purpose-built apartment blocks often have specially constructed balconies. Although the area may be tiny – sometimes no more than the size of the bay window below – it is still possible to enjoy this extra part of your living area. Balconies are usually visible from indoors, and if you fill your space with plants, you will be able to look through your window on to an area filled with greenery, far above the sight, sounds and smells of the traffic below.

PREPARING THE BALCONY

Unlike most potential roof gardens, balconies were usually designed and built to be stood and walked on, and the initial costs involved in transforming your balcony into a space for plants will be lower than they would be for turning a roof into a garden. It is, nevertheless, still worth checking that the structure is secure. A balcony in a modern block is likely to be completely safe, but some old-fashioned, wrought-iron structures might have suffered corrosion, and it would be worth getting professional advice before use.

If your balcony is exposed to the prevailing wind, the first task is to erect a windbreak of some kind. Fine netting will protect you and your plants from strong winds, but a more attractive solution would be to attach wooden trellis to the balustrade and encourage a climbing plant, such as a hardy, small-leaved ivy, to grow up it.

As with a roof garden, drainage can cause difficulties. Slatted floors, of the kind often found with wrought iron balconies, are ideal, but these bring the potential problem that you might drop items through the gaps. Covering the area with wooden decking, laid so that the planks are sufficiently spaced to allow drainage and expansion in hot weather, is an easy solution, and you could extend the decking with a raised lip to prevent items from rolling off.

CONTAINERS

Finding containers that are large enough to hold a wide range of plants but that can be comfortably and safely accommodated on the balcony can be a problem. If you have erected a wooden trellis, use a windowbox for a climber, so that it can use the extra space for its roots. Windowboxes can also be attached to the balustrade, and you may be able to secure the planter to the outside of the railings, either at your foot level or to the top of the railings. It would be worth checking that there are no local regulations or covenants preventing this. Safety is important, too, and never forget that you will be responsible for any damage caused if containers fell from your balcony, so make sure they are firmly attached.

Lots of small pots attached to the individual railings can look effective, allowing you to create a dense, colourful array of plants, but a problem is that small pots hold only a limited amount of compost, so they need watering more often than larger pots, especially as these plants will be more

above: A tiny balcony can be the ideal place for a quiet drink after work on a summer evening. Make sure that furniture will not be damaged in bad weather.

left: If the view is what makes the balcony worth sitting in, do not obscure it with plants, which can be used to hide features, such as ventilation shafts and chimneys, that are not as attractive.

pelargoniums which have a long flowering season and are tolerant if you neglect to water them from time to time. Trailing petunias are another popular and reliable choice and can be grown in mixed colours. Busy lizzies, pansies, nasturtiums and lobelias will also provide colour all summer long.

IN THE SHADE

Balconies that are on the shaded side of a building can still be used to provide a green haven. Choose plants that naturally do well in shade, including some of those suggested for basements (see page 173). Hostas and ferns generally prefer the cooler conditions and both can be grown in containers. Slugs are less likely to be a problem on a balcony than in a garden, so hostas in particular can be used to provide dense greenery.

To add colour to your green plants, use busy lizzies, which do best in semi-shade and can be found in white and shades of red, orange and pink.

exposed to the drying effects of sun and wind than pots in a more sheltered position. Larger containers can be placed on the floor of the balcony, and those towards the back can be ordinary plastic ones, so that you can use your more decorative ceramic pots near the front, where they will be visible from street level. Use the larger containers to hold upright shrubs and arrange them at one end or in a row across the front to create a short 'hedge'. If you have room you could even arrange some smaller pots in front of these to give the appearance of a border.

Always use a good-quality potting compost. Because you will probably have little storage space, buy small bags from a DIY store or garden centre as you need it, and make sure that there is plenty of drainage material, such as broken crocks, in the bottom of each

container so that excess water can drain freely away. Regular watering, which may be necessary every day in dry, sunny weather, will be essential, especially for small containers. You can get moisture-retaining granules, which are mixed into the compost at planting time, and these will help, although you must still be prepared to water frequently. Because so much water passes through containers, nutrients will be quickly washed out of the soil. Plants in large containers will benefit from top-dressing in spring – that is, carefully remove the top 5cm (2in) or so of old compost and replace it with fresh. Small containers should be completely repotted every year.

CHOOSING PLANTS

The traditional way of planting up a balcony, widely used in continental Europe, is to use colourful trailing

Pelargonium
'Highfields Appleblossom'

Zonal pelargoniums – so named because of the coloured zoning or band on the scallop-edged, almost round leaves – are bushy, usually erect, evergreen plants, which are ideal for bedding or for containers. This is a popular and reliable cultivar, bearing clusters of pale pink flowers from spring to late summer. All pelargoniums do best in full sun, although zonal pelargoniums will tolerate semi-shade, and they need rich well-drained soil. They are not hardy plants and must be overwintered in a frost-free place.

plant profile

basements

One of the most apparently inhospitable places for plants is a dark, damp basement garden, but even in such conditions it is possible to create a verdant, welcoming space. Many plants will thrive in the shelter afforded in such a position, so take advantage of what may at first appear to be insuperable obstacles.

LIGHT AND SPACE

The two usual problems confronting the gardener with a basement area are lack of light and lack of space. Painting the walls white will have an immediate beneficial effect, because white reflects light rather than absorbing it. Use a light-coloured material on the floor for the same reason. Paving stones and

left: A sheltered basement garden is the ideal place for the exotic-looking *Fatsia japonica*. Covering the ground with a light-coloured gravel is a quick way to make the most of available light.

decking are available in light shades, and the decking planks can be laid to emphasize the shorter dimension in much the same way that mowing the lawn in stripes can be used to make a garden seem longer than it really is. Cream- or silver-coloured gravel is a quick and relatively inexpensive choice, but make sure that gravel cannot get washed into the drains.

Because they are often dark and damp, basement floors often become covered with algae and moss. This can look attractive, but it can also be dangerous, especially in wet weather. Algaecides can be used, but if you prefer not to use chemicals, and have the energy, scrub the surface with hot, soapy water.

Mirrors can be used both to make the area seem larger and to reflect the available light. If you place a mirror on a wall and grow a climbing plant around it to disguise the edges, you will make the area seem twice as large. A few plants in containers, carefully arranged to one side of the mirror, will double the amount of greenery in your garden.

CONTAINERS

The only constraint on the size of container you can use in a basement is how easily you can carry it. If your access is via a narrow, twisting stairway you might prefer to build a raised bed from timber or paving slabs, stood on end and supported so that they do not fall over. Line the raised bed with heavy-duty polythene or plastic and pierce holes in the bottom for drainage before adding stones or crocks beneath the soil-based compost. A raised bed will hold a wider range of permanent plants than a group of containers. Top-dress each year, but also be prepared to change the soil completely every so often so that it does not become sour and tired. Do not build a raised bed against a house wall: you will cover the damp-proof course and you may have problems with damp seeping from the compost into the fabric of the building. Often it is only the floor of the basement that is in constant shade, so consider fixing windowboxes or containers to the wall.

All containers will need regular watering, and because a basement will be surrounded on at least two sides by walls the ground may receive less water than you think. However, because the plants will be sheltered from sun and wind, they will not usually need to be watered as copiously as, say, plants on a balcony. Feel the compost regularly to see how quickly it is drying out. Feed your permanent plants throughout the growing season, adding slow-release fertilizer to your containers of summer annuals.

plant list:

COLOURFUL BASEMENT PLANTS

- *Acanthus mollis* (bear's breeches)
  A tall, stately plant with white and purple flowers in erect spires in late summer.

- *Begonia* Semperflorens Cultorum Group
  Compact, bushy plants with flowers in white, orange, pink and red all summer long.

- *Cyclamen hederifolium*
  Prettily patterned, heart-shaped leaves appear after the pink flowers in autumn.

- *Epimedium grandiflorum* 'Crimson Beauty'
  The young leaves are splashed with copper, and the flowers are copper-flushed red.

- *Hylomecon japonica*
  This relative of the poppy is a perennial with pale green leaves and deep flowers from late spring to early summer; it needs rich, slightly acid soil.

- *Impatiens walleriana* (busy lizzie)
  Light green to bronze-green leaves are almost hidden beneath white, pink, mauve, red or orange flowers in summer.

- *Lamium maculatum* 'Beacon Silver'
  A spreading perennial, with silver-coloured leaves finely edged in green and pale pink flowers.

- *Myosotis sylvatica* (forget-me-not)
  A favourite biennial with green-grey leaves and little blue flowers in spring to early summer.

- *Primula beesiana*
  A rosette-forming, often semi-evergreen, candelabra primula with rich pink flowers in summer.

- *Pulmonaria* 'Margery Fish'
  Dark violet-blue flowers are borne on arching stems in early spring above silvered leaves.

above: The combination of decking and graded cobbles have transformed a small, unusable area into a pleasant green corner. The sheltered, shady area is ideal for hostas.

ADDING HEIGHT

One of the great advantages of a basement garden is that there are walls, which can be clothed with climbers. Even if the entire floor is covered with bricks or paving, you can grow many climbers in containers, so do not let the lack of soil stop you from experimenting with a range of interesting and colourful plants. Clematis are renowned for growing well when their roots are in moist, shady soil but the topgrowth is in sun, and a basement may the ideal situation for them. *Clematis* 'Josephine', which has double, green-tinged, mauve flowers, and 'Royalty', which has rich purplish flowers, are often recommended for containers, but there are many other cultivars, rarely growing to more than 2.5m (8ft) tall and flowering at different times of the year, that can be grown in a large pot.

Climbers will need a support of some kind if they are to be trained up a wall. Wire held in screw-eyes is quick and easy to put up, but if you prefer something that will look more attractive in winter, when deciduous plants will have lost their leaves, fix a trellis panel to the wall, attaching it with hinges along the bottom to a wooden batten and by hooks and eyes at the top so that it can be moved out of the way when you need to paint the wall.

Hanging baskets are the ideal way of introducing summer colour to a basement. Make sure the brackets are securely attached to the wall because even a fairly small basket filled with compost and plants, will be heavy, especially when watered.

10

Unless you use your garden as nothing more than a convenient place to store unwanted items, you are likely to regard it as somewhere you can relax in one way or another. Children find running about and playing games relaxing, and some adults find gardening relaxing, but for most people relaxing in the garden means nothing more than sitting in the sun or shade, reading or dozing, or, perhaps slightly more energetically, entertaining in some way.

If the garden is going to mean anything at all in your life it must surely become the focus of your times for relaxation, and if your garden is nothing but a chore or a millstone something is wrong and should be put right. Changing the layout and organizing the space so that it requires less maintenance may give you more time to put your feet up and enjoy yourself. This may mean, ultimately, going to the extreme and covering the space entirely with decking or paving slabs, but if this improves your quality of your life then it may be the ideal solution for you.

Many people, however, find that spending an hour or two weeding or deadheading or just pottering around is both therapeutic and relaxing, but if you are not among that number there is no reason to feel guilty. Your garden should reflect your lifestyle, and that goes for the ways you choose to relax. A garden should not be a status symbol nor a way of 'keeping up with the Joneses'. It is a space in which you and your family are able to enjoy yourselves and your spare time in whatever ways you prefer.

outdoor space

benches, seats and hammocks

In their gardens, people probably spend more time sitting around than doing anything else, and so it is worth designing or adapting the garden to take this into account. Areas in sun and shade can be developed so that seats and sunloungers can be used in comfort without rocking irritatingly whenever you shift your position. Other areas might be designed to be more private spaces, where you can sit in peaceful seclusion. Before you spend time and money making an elaborate seat, consider the variety of seats and benches available.

TREE SEATS

Although seating should be designed for comfort, there are a few types that are made or acquired more for their appearance than anything else. If you have an established tree in the garden, building a seat around it can make an attractive feature. You can buy custom-built ones, but they may be difficult to find and will probably be expensive. With a little ingenuity, some basic woodworking skills and photographs of different styles, it should not be too difficult to build one. Remember not to make it so tight against the trunk that the tree does not have room to grow, and, obvious though it may seem, do not build the seat in the garage and forget to leave a removable section so that it can easily be set in position around the tree.

NATURAL SEATS

An unusual seat but one that can be enjoyable both to construct and use is a turf seat. In its most basic form it can simply be a rectangular block of earth covered in turf. The sides, back and front may need supporting, and this can be provided by planks or wood, bricks or thin sticks woven between uprights to form a wattle wall around the seat. The same wattle system can be used to create a round seat, which can be positioned anywhere and will not be difficult to dismantle and build somewhere else when you tire of it in one position. A similar type of seat could be cut into a bank if you have a sloping or terraced garden.

A development of the turf seat would be to construct one with a camomile seat. This will produce a wonderful fragrance when it is sat on. As with the basic turf seat, build a box of wood or brick and fill it with soil. Plant the camomile over the top, making sure you use *Chamaemelum nobile* 'Treneague', which is a tough, compact form that does not flower.

above: Simple wooden seats always look sympathetic in a garden and can usually be left to stand outdoors all year round.

Arrange the individual plants at intervals of 15cm (6in) across the seat and water regularly until the plants are established. Trim the camomile occasionally to keep it neat. A fragrant and tough alternative is a mat-forming thyme, such as *Thymus serpyllum*, but take care that you do not sit on it when it is in flower: it is likely to be covered in bees.

HAMMOCKS

The ultimate way of relaxing in a garden is in a hammock. Some people regard hammocks as the height of luxury, even more so than sitting in a comfortable chair or on a lounger.

Hammocks are readily available and are not difficult to hang safely.

There are plenty of hammocks to choose from, both at garden centres and other shops and also by mail order. Many are made from canvas or some other hard-wearing material, although some are made from netting. When you buy you must make sure that you are getting something safe and strong enough to take the weight of the heaviest person who is going to use it. Although a hammock is best taken under cover when it is not in use, few people have such well-ordered lives and the hammock will often be left outside in rain and sun. It is important, therefore, that you choose a material that will not rot.

In a small garden you will probably not have two conveniently sited trees from which you can suspend a hammock, but it is possible to use walls and other sturdy structures. Often, however, the simplest solution is to buy a special frame, which can be sited anywhere in the garden that you wish. These work well and have the added advantage that modern ones fold up or can be taken to pieces, which overcomes the problem of storage.

right: It may look uncomfortable, but a simple metal bench provides a stylish, modern touch to a silver-themed garden and complements the light foliage and metal containers.

project: turf seat

A turf seat can be an unusual addition to a natural or cottage-style garden. Similar seats can be seen in illustrated manuscripts dating from the 15th century, although modern gardeners have a range of materials that makes the construction relatively easy. Cover the seat with a fine, close-growing grass, such as a bent or fescue or, for a fragrant alternative, use a mat-forming plant, such as *Thymus serpyllum* (thyme) or *Chamaemelum nobile* 'Treneague' (camomile). Hazel rods are sold in bundles of 12, and willow withies are sold in bundles of about 50; both are available in garden centres.

1   2   3

4   5   6

MATERIALS

12 hazel stakes, each 2.5m (8ft) long
100 willow withies, each 2.5m (8ft) long
2 sq m (2 sq yd) turf
good-quality topsoil
sand or spray paint (optional)
heavy-duty polythene (optional)

1   Use string or sand to mark the outline of the seat on the ground and hammer in hazel stakes, setting them 15–20cm (6–8in) apart and using loppers to cut them to the approximate length.

2   Using three or four withies at a time, weave the willow in and out of the stakes. The willow should start and finish on the inside so there are no sharp edges on the outside. Where the thin end runs out, start the new section with the thick end of the withies to maintain a consistent thickness.

3   Build up the sides to the desired height. Tamp down the willow as

you work. To form the back take withies up from the ground, through the woven area, and plait them as you weave them through.

4   Use loppers to cut off the tops of the hazel stakes level with the top of the woven willow. If you wish, line the seat with heavy-duty polythene so that soil cannot escape through the sides. Make sure there are plenty of drainage holes across the bottom.

5   Fill the seat with good-quality garden compost. You will need about three wheelbarrows full of soil for a seat about 2m (6ft) long. Tamp down the soil as you work.

6   Cover the surface of the seat with turves, using a knife to trim the edges. Alternatively, sow densely with grass seed or position plants of mat-forming thyme or camomile, spacing them 15cm (6in) apart. Water regularly until grass or plants are established.

tables and chairs

Alfresco eating is becoming increasingly popular, for both family meals and for entertaining guests. This may require nothing more than a simple flat area on which a table and chairs can be placed, but as people increasingly want to eat and sit in shade, away from the burning sun, pergolas, arbours and other shade-producing devices have been introduced to provide a pleasant dappled light. In the evening sophisticated dining areas, complete with soft lighting and fragrant plants, provide a romantic, relaxing setting.

Producing and supplying garden furniture is big business these days, which is good news for gardeners because there is a wide choice. First-time buyers can purchase something inexpensive, then, later, when there is more money to spend, better-made and more luxurious items can be acquired. When you go to choose chairs it is a good idea to try them out by sitting in them. There is such a wide range that it makes sense to look at as many styles as you can and to choose the most comfortable you can find. You might have to decide between comfort and appearance, which do not always go together, and if you are going to use them a lot, comfort should be your main criterion.

For casual sitting around the garden it is worth looking in second-hand and junk shops for old seats and garden furniture. Such items are becoming increasingly difficult to find because they are tending to be regarded as 'antiques' rather than as

jumble, but they do still turn up. They are often in a rather battered state, and you may think they could more usefully be deployed in the garden as eye-catchers than seating. You may, however, come across pieces that can be done up and used, especially as reserve seating for when you have a lot of visitors.

PLASTIC OR WOOD?
There was a time where all garden furniture seemed to consist of folding, tubular aluminium frames and nylon fabric. It is still possible to find such chairs, especially second-hand ones, and they are often inexpensive and take up little room when they are folded up. Extra cushions will make them more comfortable, and they are useful to have in reserve if you have to find room for extra guests. Similar are the useful 'director's' chairs, which have folding, wooden frames and hard-wearing canvas back and seats.

For general-purpose garden seats tubular aluminium has been replaced by moulded plastic, which is inexpensive and surprisingly comfortable. The chairs are tough and durable and can be left outdoors all year round, although they will last longer and keep their finish better if they are stored under cover in winter. The non-folding chairs, which are light and easy to move and can be stacked to minimize storage space, can be used at table or by themselves. They are usually white, green or brown, and although they are not particularly attractive they can even be used

indoors to help seat a large party. Cane furniture is often relatively cheap and is light for moving about. It must be stored when not in use, however, or it will quickly deteriorate. It is ideal for covered areas such as conservatories and sun rooms.

above: Make eating in the garden a comfortable experience by placing the table and chairs on flat ground and by making sure there is plenty of space behind the seats.

The choice of wooden seating has increased dramatically in recent years. Some of it is relatively inexpensive, but at the other end of the scale are some extremely costly ranges of matching chairs, tables and sunloungers. Some of the cheaper items look what they are, but price is not an infallible guide, so,

rather than buy directly from advertisements, look at what you are going to get for your money to avoid disappointment. You may be lucky and find a bargain.

Wooden chairs can be upright, which is useful if they are to be used at table or by themselves, or they can be

some style of reclining chair. Many hardwoods are tough enough to require no treatment, although some are best given an annual application of preservative or least a thorough clean with a wire brush to remove the lichen and algae that might be growing on them, especially if they are standing in shade. Never buy hardwood furniture that is not guaranteed to have come from a renewable source.

Similar conventional furniture is produced in metal. Much of it is cast and has intricate designs and patterns. The ranges made in alloy are reasonably trouble-free, but those made from iron or steel will have to be painted from time to time to stop the metal from rusting. Metal is not as comfortable as wood, and you will have

to provide some cushions if the chairs are going to be used for long periods.

LYING AROUND

In addition to conventional upright chairs, benches and reclining chairs, there are several other pieces of furniture aimed specifically at those who want to relax in their garden. Sunloungers, which are, in effect, folding beds, can be used in both the sun and shade. In the past they were mostly made of aluminium tubing, but now they are available in plastic and wood. Many are quite uncomfortable for lying on without something soft on top of them, so look out for models that have cushions or mattresses.

If you have space, really luxurious loungers can be found that hang from frames so that they swing gently when you sit or lie on them. They usually have a sunshade or canopy incorporated into the framework. Although the thought of swinging to and fro in a peaceful, sunny garden may be appealing, think about where you will keep the lounger in autumn, winter and spring before you buy.

left: A focal point more than somewhere restful to sit, this seat serves as both an eye-catcher and a convenient way of disguising an inspection cover.

points to remember:

MAINTAINING WILLOW

Willow is a delightful material for furniture (see project on page 177) or for creating a 'living' arbour. Both planting and maintenance should be done in winter. Willow needs rich soil, which must never be allowed to dry out around the young withies, and to good root development the ground must be clear for weeds, but do not use chemicals. Encourage the individual withies to fuse together to make a stronger, more stable structure by tying them together with tarred string, which can be later removed.

dining and entertainment

Although eating out often involves carrying the food that has been cooked in the house or elsewhere to a table set outdoors, the use of a barbecue to cook the food next to where it is to be eaten is increasingly popular. Sometimes all that is needed is a flat surface on which the barbecue can stand, but more and more often specially built structures, which are integral parts of the garden, are preferred.

A 'DINING ROOM'

Many people feel more comfortable eating in an enclosed space than in the open. Although they may not necessarily want to be in a room, they prefer to be within an enclosure of some sort. This could be provided by shrubs and trees in a little glade or arbour, or it could be that the skeleton of a room, created by four posts and cross-bars, is sufficient to create the illusion of the defined space. Such a framework is even better if it is covered by a climber to provide some shade. In the evening, the structure could support lights. Even sitting on a small terrace rather than on an open lawn somehow seems to create an impression of a room and make people feel more at ease.

KEEPING AN EVEN KEEL

One aspect of eating outdoors that is often overlooked but that is essential to everyone's enjoyment of the occasion is a sturdy, stable table. It is hardly conducive to a relaxing, convivial event if the table rocks every time someone reaches for the salt or picks up their

knife and fork. A level patio or an area of flat lawn is needed to make sure that everything remains flat. Tables that are used outside should be as large as possible, with plenty of space for bowls and plates and room for several people to sit around it. The chairs, too, should be stable and high enough to allow people to reach their food comfortably.

If the food is prepared indoors and brought outside, the table should be as close to the house as possible so that the cook does not have to spend the evening running to and fro. If you are having a barbecue, the table should be near the cooking area, although not so close that the diners are enveloped in a cloud of smoke and smells.

If you are planning to eat only in the evening, sun and shade are not important considerations, but during the day it will be necessary to decide where the table should be sited. More and more people are choosing to sit in shade rather than face the dangers posed by direct sun. If you or your neighbour has a large tree it will usually cast sufficient shade for most purposes. Quicker than waiting for a tree to grow is to construct an arbour

above: A quiet, fragrant corner, as far as possible from a smelly, smoking barbecue, is perfect for alfresco meals.

or pergola (see pages 56 and 118–19). All that is required is a framework of posts with cross-bars attached to the top, over which climbing plants can be trained. Alternatively, consider using a canvas awning, which can be an ideal and temporary means of providing shelter and shade (see pages 56–7).

project: barbecue

1 2 3 4 5

points to remember:

SITING A BARBECUE

Consider the position of a barbecue carefully. Although a site close to your back door might be convenient, cooking smells and smoke could be annoying for your neighbours.

● *Avoid annoying neighbours and guests with smoke and smells.*

● *Other things being equal, place it as near to the kitchen as possible.*

● *Do not site it under overhanging trees or near to fences or buildings that might be scorched.*

● *Position the barbecue on a flat, stable, hard surface.*

● *Keep the barbecue away from open windows so that smoke and smells do not get wafted indoors.*

MATERIALS AND EQUIPMENT

5 concrete blocks (breezeblocks)
small bag of sand
small bag of cement
club hammer
1.2m (4ft) of 5mm (⅛in) steel rod
3m (10ft) of 3mm (⅛in) steel rod
steel fire tray
metal grille
10 terracotta tiles, 10cm (4in) square
masonry paint

A small, purpose-built barbecue will fit on most patios, and if it is built on a base of raised concrete slabs there will be additional storage space below it. Concrete blocks are widely available, are inexpensive and are easy to use and lay. Once they have heated up they will help to cook the food evenly and keep it warm. Make sure that the barbecue is on a level, stable base.

1 Use a club hammer and bolster chisel to cut one of the blocks in half. Stand two blocks on their long sides, parallel to each other, and position a half-block across the back to make a U-shape. Check that the fire tray and metal grille will fit inside the blocks.

2 Make a stiff mortar with sand and cement and lay the first course of blocks. Use a spirit level to make sure the blocks are perfectly flat and check the size again.

3 Cut four lengths from the 5mm (⅛in) steel rod to support the fire tray. Drill two holes, 8cm (3in) apart, in the centre of one end of both the remaining whole blocks.

6

Cover the top of the first course of blocks with mortar and position the four steel rods evenly across the mortar. Add the remaining blocks so that the pre-drilled holes are facing the front.

4 Point the mortar and leave it to go off for a while. Before it is completely set, cut four lengths of 3mm (⅛in) wire, each about 70cm (27in) long. Insert one piece of wire into one of the holes and bend it towards the back and insert it into the mortar in the back corner. Repeat with the other three pieces of wire. The wire will form runners to hold the metal grille and should be about 15cm (6in) above the fire tray.

5 Cover the top edge of the barbecue with terracotta tiles, positioning them so that they overhang slightly at the back and outside of the walls.

6 When the mortar is absolutely dry, paint the outside of the barbecue with exterior-grade masonry paint.

lighting

Electricity can transform a garden in terms of both how it looks and how it is used. In addition to driving pumps for fountains, cascades and waterfalls, thereby creating movement, sound and focal points, an electricity supply will make possible outdoor lighting, which can be used to highlight views and features that go unnoticed in the day and enable alfresco summer parties to go on long after sunset.

IN THE DARK

If you entertain in the garden in the evening you are likely to require some form of lighting to illuminate not only the immediate dining area but also the paths and other parts of the garden. As much thought should be given to lighting as to other aspects of garden design, and when a garden is carefully and subtly lit it will have a magical quality that is quite different from its daytime character.

In addition to providing illumination for safety and as background for activities such as eating and drinking, lighting in the garden can be used to highlight individual features. If you have an attractive statue or container, for example, a carefully positioned uplighter or several lamps can be used to make it a focal point, just as it is in daylight, but because the area around it will be dark and shadowed the feature will be thrown into vivid relief while the garden as a whole will seem larger and more mysterious.

Although lighting should always be adequate for the task, it should be subtle and it should be localized, so

above: Subtle lighting in a dramatic garden. Carefully positioned lights will transform the appearance of your garden at night, highlighting areas that are unremarked in daylight and casting other areas into mysterious shadows.

that it illuminates what needs illuminating but nothing more. The secret of good lighting is the interplay between light and shade. A soft pool of light on a table is that only because it is surrounded by darkness. A tree or shrub with a light shining into it takes on the appearance that it does only because of the way the shadows cast

by the branches and the surrounding darkness highlight the shapes on which the light falls.

Think carefully about what you want to light, how much light you want to provide and how you are going to provide it. When you are entertaining in the garden soft lights are the best way to help create the right atmosphere. If food is being prepared, such as on a barbecue, there should be sufficient light for the cook to see what they are doing and to prevent accidents, but elsewhere the light level can be kept subtle. Floodlights have their place, especially in parking areas or as security lights, but they are generally too harsh for other purposes. If you use them, make sure that they are pointing downwards so that they do not spill light into the rest of your garden or into your neighbour's garden. It can be blinding to have to walk up a path with a halogen light glaring in your eyes. An automatic switch, which allows them to come on when someone enters an area, saves not only a lot of energy but also a lot of ill feeling and irritation. Such movement- or sound-sensitive devices are particularly useful for security lighting. Paths need adequate lighting so that people can see where they are going, but, again, the lights should not be so bright that the glare is blinding. Generally, the best types of lamp are those that direct their light downwards and towards the path.

SETTING THE MOOD

One of the main benefits of outdoor lighting is the opportunity it offers to

left: Uplighters can be used to create dramatic shapes and shadows, especially in a small pool.

provide a source of light from a completely different direction or even in a different colour. There is a wide range of lamps specifically designed for use outdoors to choose from, ranging from standard lamps and tablelamps to ones that can be suspended from trees or other supports. Using dimmer switches gives you the additional flexibility of having brighter lights while food is being prepared and then being able to reduce the brightness when dinner begins. Candles give one of the most flattering and romantic of lights.

points to remember:

USING LIGHT IN THE WATER GARDEN

The following guidelines will help you make a start in exploring the full potential of lighting a water feature.

- *Avoid large, clumsy lights with casings that are so conspicuous in the day that they spoil the daylight scene. Instead, choose small, black, non-shiny casings and hide these behind boulders or plants.*
- *If you are using underwater lights make sure that the water is clear, or the green water will be exaggerated by the light.*
- *Direct the light away from the main viewing area so that people do not look into a light.*
- *For a reflective pool, underlight a feature such as a tree or sculpture on the opposite side of a still pool from the main viewpoint. This prevents light from catching the water, which could occur from a light that is positioned on the viewing side of the water.*
- *Avoid the use of too many coloured lenses. White or amber light works well with water. The water spout of a cobble fountain can dance like a flame when it is lit with an amber spotlight.*
- *For the best mix of shadow and texture on a smooth object like an urn, light from the side and at a slight upward angle.*

Even on the stillest of nights there is some breeze, which may blow out the candle, make it burn quickly or blow hot wax everywhere. It is a good idea, therefore, to enclose candles in glass shades or lanterns of some kind. It is possible to get candles specially designed for outdoor use that contain oil of citronella, which is supposed to repel insects.

Torches and flares, which can be stuck into the lawn or the soil in a border, look best when they are blown about in a gentle breeze. The light is not steady enough to eat by, but creates perfect ambient, background lighting along a path or around a patio for entertaining on summer evenings.

Small, white fairy lights or Christmas lights create a sparkling atmosphere and can be used for background lighting along paths or around a patio or more specifically for illuminating a sitting or eating area. They look particularly pretty strung through trees or along the cross-bars of pergolas or arches. Make sure you buy lights that are guaranteed as suitable for outdoor use.

LIGHTING A WATER FEATURE

There is no garden feature so appropriate for lighting as water. If the water is moving, light brings a sparkle to the movement; if the water is still, the lighting can bring reflections to an inky surface that were never even thought to exist. The types of light best suited to water features are not the same as those sold for safety or security, which produce a wide spread of bland white light. Water lighting needs a much more subtle application and a careful choice in the type of lens, the position and the colour.

The section of many small fountain features that will be most responsive to lighting is the area of moving or pouring water, which is sometimes only a small part of the overall construction. Look carefully at the moving water and decide whether it will be most effectively illuminated from the side, from underneath or from above. Often, these features look best when they are lit from beneath, and a narrow fountain spout can be highlighted by a lens below the spout that appears to restrict the beam of light into the water with an almost uncanny effect. If you have a fountain spout the wall mask may need to be highlighted, and a slightly wider beam will be required, but still most effectively used from below.

When the light source is introduced from under the water, movement on the surface is brought into play. If the surface movement is turbulent, the ripple effect of the apparently moving light is particularly effective on flat surfaces such as walls or canopies. Falling spouts from fountains are effective in producing this turbulence over an underwater light positioned at the base of the fountain, but it can also be achieved by a light under a waterfall. This not only highlights the falling water but can also bring alive the extraordinary beauty and delicacy of a fern frond clinging to the back of the waterfall, which is normally hidden in the shade in daylight.

MAINS ELECTRICITY

There are three types of garden electrical supply – mains, low-voltage and solar. Installing a permanent outdoor electricity supply should be carried out only by a qualified electrician. However, you can save money by preparing trenches for electrical cables to run through and filling them in yourself after the electrical supply has been connected and by planning for everything you need now and may want in the future, so saving money on electricians' fees and time digging out new trenches later.

Mains electricity is the most versatile and can be used to power everything from outdoor sockets, lights and irrigation systems to complex water features. It is also the most expensive to install, requiring its own permanent circuit of cables in the garden and a separate switching unit from the consumer unit in the house, incorporating its own fuse and residual current device (RCD) with a minimum trip rating of 30 milliamps. RCDs are an essential safety device; they will automatically switch off the power supply if any change in the current is detected – before anyone operating a faulty piece of equipment receives an electric shock.

LOW-VOLTAGE LIGHTING

Low-voltage garden lights connect to the mains via a transformer that steps down the mains voltage to 12 volts before it goes out into the garden. Installation is straightforward: the transformer is plugged into a 13-amp

above: The outdoor room should be lit with as much thought as any room indoors: fairy lights, wall-mounted lights and spotlights combine to cast an eerie light in a courtyard garden.

power socket in the house, shed or garage, and low-voltage cables lead outside to garden lights or a pond pump. Cables do not need to be buried and can run along the surface of the soil. Do not position them across paths, where people could trip over them, nor over solid surfaces, where the cable will be damaged if it is stepped on.

Low-voltage lighting systems come in a wide range of styles, from bollards for illuminating paths and flights of

steps to submersible spot lamps for ponds. They are versatile, easy and cheap to install and can be used to great effect. Their one drawback is that they lose power the further they are positioned from the transformer – a maximum working distance of 30m (100ft) is average – and the greater the number of light fittings on each run of cable. For this reason, multiple transformers may be necessary to light a garden effectively.

SOLAR-POWERED LIGHTS

The availability, quality and range of solar-powered lights are increasing every year. The newer models have improved light levels and are more durable than the first versions, and some are made from aluminium. It is possible to get lights that will provide illumination for up to 12 hours, although most are in the range of 5–8 hours, with a reduced output of about 3 hours in winter.

The soft light cast by solar lighting is especially appropriate in the garden. All solar-powered lights have the advantages of being quick and easy to fit – no plugs or flexes are needed – and they can be moved around the garden as your design or needs change. They are also, of course, perfectly safe, because they are low-voltage and need no mains wiring. Most importantly, they are friendly to the environment and completely free to operate.

The range of styles has also increased in recent years, and it is now possible to get wall-mounted lights, which are suitable for illuminating entrances and doorways, ground-spike models, which can be inserted along paths or in flowerbeds and borders, and post-mounted lights for providing light at higher levels. A drawback is that, generally, once they come on, they stay on, which can be annoying and unnecessary. Solar-powered security lights with halogen floodlights are activated by passive infrared motion detectors.

left: Spike-mounted, low-voltage down-lighters are ideal for illuminating a path. Visitors can easily find their way but are not dazzled by glare.

above: Although light cast from indoors may be sufficient to light a patio, it is vital that steps and changes in level are lit separately and adequately.

points to remember:

LAYING AN ELECTRIC CABLE

Installing electricity for garden lighting and water features should be carried out by a qualified electrician. Do not attempt the work yourself unless you know exactly what you are doing, and if you have any doubts at all seek professional help. All cables used in the garden should be well protected, both from the weather and accidental damage, and they are best laid below ground.

The trench should be at least 1m (3ft) deep to make sure that the cable is not accidentally dug up or punctured during general gardening, and special armoured cable for outdoor use should be employed. Lay an alkythene pipe in the trench with the cable passing through it. Electrical piping should be coloured black. Alternatively, lay the cable along the centre of the trench and cover it with a row of roofing tiles. For added protection, lay a strip of brightly coloured tape, usually black and yellow, on top of the tiles before backfilling with earth.

children

Children – your own or other people's – may use the garden more than you do, and their needs must be taken into consideration and incorporated into any garden makeover. Any attempt to ignore them and create an immaculate lawn with perfect beds may come to naught once the children start to play.

The key to planning for children is to provide what they would like rather than what the adults would like. Children are often happy with the simplest of things, such as an open space to play on and a secret place behind some bushes, which they can adapt for all kinds of real and imaginary games. Structures such as climbing frames and sandpits should be designed with the child in mind rather than being selected for what will look attractive or fit in with the garden.

With some thinking ahead, however, the playthings that you provide for the children can be turned into something else once they have outgrown them. A sandpit, for instance, can be transformed into a pond. A wooden climbing frame can be clad with timber and become a shed or summerhouse. A playhouse might become a bicycle shed or a store of some sort. They can be originally sited and constructed with the potential conversion in mind.

PLAYHOUSES

Playhouses are fun for children. It is possible to buy a ready-made version, but it is probably more satisfying to make your own, especially if you plan into it some future use for when the children have grown out of playing with

left: A strongly built pergola built of hardwood and with the uprights securely embedded in hardcore and concrete can do double-duty as a support for a child's swing.

it. It can be to your own design or be based on one of the children's favourite stories. Safety and stability are the priorities, no matter what the design.

A more adventurous adaptation of having a playhouse is to build a tree house. This is, obviously, more appropriate for older children, but adults often get as much fun out of it as their children do. It can really be built in a tree if there is one, but it can equally well be above ground in some other way, such as being built on sturdy stilts

of lengths of redundant telegraph poles. It can be a fine work of architecture or it can be left to the children, when it is more likely to resemble a disreputable shack. Before you build a tree house, check the planning regulations in your area to make sure that you do not need planning permission.

CLIMBING FRAMES

Climbing frames can be made at home or bought for home assembly. Home-made frames will probably be made of

wood. Make absolutely certain that they are sturdy, stable and unlikely to collapse. There should be no awkward corners or holes in which fingers can become trapped, and the wood should be smooth and splinter free. Ready-made frames may be made of metal or wood. Follow the manufacturer's instructions for erection and ensure the frame is securely fixed to the ground.

Around the frame and in all areas where children climb or are likely to fall it is a good idea to cover the ground

left: Decking, is softer than concrete and an ideal surface for children. Later it can be used as an extension to the patio to site a barbecue.

with bark chippings, which are relatively soft and will help to cushion the fall. It is not the equivalent of a feather mattress, and anyone will be hurt if they fall from a height or fall awkwardly, but it will reduce the number of grazes and bruises. Rake it over occasionally and top it up so that there is a constant depth of no less than 5cm (2in).

SANDPITS

Sandpits never seem to be out of favour with children. With forethought, a sandpit can be constructed in such a way that it is turned into a garden pond once the children have grown up. If the pit is constantly supervised, it is possible to have a combined sandpit and paddling pool.

THE JUNIOR GARDENER

Sharing your enjoyment of gardening with your children is a rewarding experience. Although space is clearly at a premium in a small garden, you may be able to set aside a secluded corner or vegetable patch. Even a windowbox is enough to foster interest.

Plants for children need to be colourful and quick-growing. Sweet peas, sunflowers and nasturtiums are ideal for fast results. Even a pot of daffodil bulbs can be a pleasing and colourful display. Alternatively, herbs and vegetables, such as basil, mint, lettuce and runner beans (grown on a wigwam of the child's own making) are good choices as the young gardener will have the satisfaction of eating the plants they have grown.

Lathyrus odoratus (sweet pea)

An annual climber, sweet peas are easily grown from seed sown in mid-spring. Plants should be trained up a framework. They need a position in full sun and rich, well-drained soil. Pick flowers regularly to encourage bloom.

plant profile

plant list:

PLANTS FOR A CHILD'S GARDEN

- ● *Allium schoenoprasum* (chives)
  A bulb producing edible, grass-like leaves and spherical mauve-pink flowerheads.

- ● *Borago officinalis* (borage)
  A self-seeding annual edible, grass-like leaves and spherical mauve-pink flowerheads.

- ● *Carum carvi* (caraway)
  A self-seeding annual with bright blue, edible flowers in summer.

- ● *Dicentra cucullaria* (Dutchman's breeches)
  A hardy, clump-forming perennial with ferny, blue-green leaves and curiously shaped, white, yellow-tipped flowers.

- ● *Foeniculum vulgare 'Purpureum'* (bronze fennel)
  A tall perennial with aromatic, feathery leaves that are bronze-purple as they emerge, turning darker green as they mature.

- ● *Helianthus annuus* 'Autumn Beauty' (sunflower)
  A tall, fast growing annual with large, dark reddish-brown flowers.

- ● *Limnanthes douglasii* (poached egg plant)
  A freely self-seeding annual for a sunny position with bright yellow, white-edged flowers all summer long.

- ● *Nigella damascena* (love-in-a-mist)
  A self-seeding annual with bright blue flowers followed by striking seed heads.

- ● *Physalis alkekengi* (Chinese lantern)
  A vigorous perennial with cream flowers and nodding, papery, bright orange seedheads.

- ● *Tagetes* 'Mischief Series' (French marigolds)
  Compact annuals with flowers in bright shades of yellow, orange and brownish-red.

index

acknowledgements

Senior Editor   Trevor Davies
Picture Research   Zoë Holtermann
Senior Designer   Peter Burt
Design   Les Needham
Additional text   Richard Bird
Production controller   Ian Paton

Projects designed and photographed by Toby
Buckland and Howard Rice

Garden Design on p.17 by
Clare Louise Buzan – Tanglewood Designs

PICTURE ACKNOWLEDGEMENTS

Mark Bolton 108, /Design: Cannington College/ National Amateur Gardening Show 2000 154, /The Chef's Garden, Conran/ RHS Chelsea Flower Show1999 160, /Maurice Green, Lemington Spa, UK 15, 26, 50 /Hedens Lustgard, Gothenburg, Sweden 88, 92, 114, /National Amateur Gardening Show 2000 94, 110 /Pecorama, Devon, UK 74, /Design: Bob Purnell 132, /RHS Chelsea Flower Show 2000 81 right, 144, 159 top, /Scypen, Devon, UK 51 top, /The World Life Garden/ Nailia Gree/ RHS Chelsea Flower Show 99 112.
Corbis UK Ltd/Robert Picket 163.
Eric Crichton/Design: Ruth Chivers (Gardening Which?)/ RHS Hampton Court Flower Show 1999 93, /Design: Carol Klein/ RHS Chelsea Flower Show 1999 115, /RHS Hampton Court Flower Show 99 34 Bottom, /Design: Alan Sargent/ RHS Chelsea Flower Show 1999 65, /Design: Jane Sweetser/ RHS Hampton Court Flower Show 1999 80.
Emap Gardening Picture Library 185 top.
Elizabeth Whiting Associates 171 top, /Julia Boulton 131, /Rodney Hyett 77, /Di Lewis 130, /Dominic Whiting 30 Bottom.
Garden Picture Library/David Askham 84 left, /Lynne Brotchie 162, /Linda Burgess 127, /Jaqui Hurst 172 /JS Sira 121 right, /Janet Sorrell 57 top, /Ron Sutherland/ Design: Anthony Paul 11 top, /Ron Sutherland/ Design: Duane Paul Design Team 183.
John Glover 9, 164, /Design: Gaila Adair 179, /Design: Jonathan Baillie 29 bottom, /Design: Diarmuid Gavin 134, /Design: Terry Hill 152, /RHS Chelsea Flower Show 1993/ Moss Garden 24, /RHS Chelsea Flower Show 1994 145 left, /RHS Chelsea Flower Show 1995/ Country Living 150, /RHS Hampton Court Flower Show 1994 107, /Design: Alan Titchmarsh 10, 38, /Design: Maurice Walker 148, /Design: Claire Whitehouse 151, /Design: Allison Armour Wilson/ RHS Chelsea Flower Show 2000 52.
Octopus Publishing Group Limited 27 bottom, 31 left, 31 right, 35 left, 35 right, 37, 39 right, 41, 43 right, 51 bottom, 57 bottom, 117, 133 left, 133 right, 139 bottom, 143 top, 143 bottom, 145 right, 149 left, 149 right, 153, 153 bottom left, 155 bottom right, 155 bottom left, 157, 159 bottom, 161 bottom right, 161 bottom left, 171, 173 bottom, /Jerry Harpur 14, 23, 23 left, 25 left, 25 right, 33, 43 left, 58, 156, 187 bottom, /Jerry Harpur Bob Flowerdew 82, /Neil Holmes 21, 85, 128, 137 bottom, /Andrew Lawson 81 left, 123 left /Howard Rice 59 top right, 59 bottom right, 71, 75, 79, 83, 89, 97, 101, 109, 113, 125, 177 top, 181. /Mark Winwood 32, 69, 96, 103, 118, 122, 129 left, 129 bottom right, 138, / RHS Chelsea Flower Show 2000 19, 70, /Steve Wooster 99, 120, 135 left, 136, /Polly Wreford 147, 149 top, 180, /Mel Yates 111, 123 right, 129 top right.
Jerry Harpur 12, /Design: Michael Balston, Wiltshire 16 right, 56, /Design: Martina Barzi & Maria Casares, Buenos Aires 168, /Design: Zea Berry, London 68, /Design: Robert Broekema, Amsterdam 66, /Design: Design: Peter Causer & Roja Dove, Brighton 39 left, /Design: Sir Terence Conran, London 13, /Design: Keith Corlett, NYC 78, /Design: Stephen Crisp, London 45, 54, /Design: Simon Fraser, London 186, /Design: Edwina Von Gal, NY 40 bottom, /Design: Sonny Garcia, San Francisco 100, 182, /Design: Luciano Giubbilei, London 178, /Design: Richard Hartlage & Graeme Hardie, New Jersey 105, /Design: Keyes Brothers, London 53 bottom, 59 top left, 165, /Design: Christopher Masson, London 16 left, 46, /Keeyla Meadows, California 141, /Design: Jeff Mendoza, NYC 47, 167, /Design: Patrick Miler, California 72, /David Pearson, London 98, /Design: Judith Sharpe & Charlotta Holmes, London 91, /Design: Ron Simple, Pennsylvania 53 top, /Design: Ernie Taylor, West Midlands 42, /Design: Donald J Walsh, NYC 64, 76, 158, /Warwickshire College/ RHS Chelsea Flower Show 2000 73, /Design: Andrew Weaving, London 55, /Design: Stephen Woodham 11 bottom, /Peter Wooster, Connecticut 27 top.
Marcus Harpur/Design: Jonathan Baillie 20, 22, /Design: Jonathan Baillie 119, /Bart's Hospital/ RHS Chelsea Flower Show 2000 84 right, /RHS Hampton Court Flower Show 2000 63, /Design: David Stevens/ RHS Chelsea Flower Show 2000 67, /Design: Stephen Woodhams/ RHS Chelsea Flower Show 2000 135 right Andrew Lawson 139 top, 153 top, 155 top, /Design: Ruth Chivers/ RHS Hampton Court Flower Show 1999 177 bottom, /Design: Patrick Wynniatt-Husey & Patrick Clarke/ RHS Hampton Court Flower Show 2000 175 /Design: David Magson 121 left, /Design: Diana May & Mark Watts/ RHS Hampton Court Flower Show 2000 176, /The Mosaic Garden, Melbourne, Australia 90, /Design: Simon Shire 95, /Design: Gordon Taylor & Guy Cooper 169, /'"You" Go Organic' Garden/ RHS Hampton Court Flower Show 2000 161 top, Marianne Majerus/Design: Ruth Collier 124, /Design: Dominique Lubar 173 top, /Mark Reeder 170, /Design: Paul Thompson 30 top.
Clive Nichols Photography/Jill Billington 60, /Cartier, Chelsea 1998 61, /Design: George Carter, Christies Sculpture in the Garden/ RHS Chelsea Flower Show 1999 87, /Wynniatt-Husey Clarke 28, /Design: J. Dowle & K. Ninomiya, Honda Tea Garden/ RHS Chelsea Flower Show 1995 104, /Design: Ann Frith 36, /Cesar Manrique 102, /Trevyn McDowell & Paul Thompson 40 top, /Lisette Pleasance 146, /The Nichols Garden, Reading 142, /Design: Nina Thalinson 184.
/Welbeck 137 top.
Louis Poulsen/Tony Craddock/ tcr-uk@lpmail.com (Surrey Business Park, Weston Road, Epsom, Surrey, KT17 1JG, UK) 185 bottom right.
Photos Horticultural 116
Harry Smith Collection 34 Top, 48, 49, 187 top.